The Story Behind the Song

150 Songs that Chronicle the 20th Century

Richard D. Barnet
Bruce Nemerov
and
Mayo R. Taylor

GREENWOOD PRESS
Westport, Connecticut • London

Library of Congress Cataloging-in-Publication Data

Barnet, Richard D., 1949–
    The story behind the song: 150 songs that chronicle the 20th century /
    Richard D. Barnet, Bruce Nemerov, and Mayo R. Taylor.
        p.   cm.
    Includes bibliographical references (p.   ) and index.
    ISBN 0-313-31976-6 (alk. paper)
        1. Popular music—United States—History and criticism.   2. Music—Social
    aspects—United States—20th century.   I. Nemerov, Bruce.   II. Taylor, Mayo R.
    III. Title.
    ML3477.B36   2004
    782.42164'0973—dc22   2003064303

British Library Cataloguing in Publication Data is available.

Library of Congress Catalog Card Number: 2003064303
ISBN: 0-313-31976-6

First published in 2004

Greenwood Press, 88 Post Road West, Westport, CT 06881
An imprint of Greenwood Publishing Group, Inc.
www. greenwood.com

Printed in the United States of America

The paper used in this book complies with the
Permanent Paper Standard issued by the National
Information Standards Organization (Z39.48-1984).

10 9 8 7 6 5 4 3 2 1

Copyright Acknowledgments

The authors and the publisher gratefully acknowledge permission to quote from
the following material:

"Streets of Philadelphia" by Bruce Springsteen. Copyright © 1993 Bruce
Springsteen. All rights reserved. Reprinted by permission.

"Scarecrow" by Melissa Etheridge. Copyright © 1999 MLE Music (ASCAP).
All rights reserved. Used by permission.

Contents

Introduction

SCOPE

This reference work offers a guide to 150 historically significant songs that helped chronicle the twentieth century. It explains the story behind each song's creation and how it reflected political, economic, and social events of the time. Songs are arranged in roughly chronological order within each decade so the historic, political, and social themes embodied in these songs unfold in an understandable sequence. Additional indices, arranged alphabetically by song title, songwriter name, and subject, are also provided.

Songwriters have often used lyrics to describe current events and social moods of the day. Even compositions without lyrics, such as patriotic marches, are able to convey a sense of national pride. Therefore, an examination of our songs, and the story behind their creation, provides a glimpse of our nation's collective psyche at different points in our history.

Why reflect on history through songs? Songs can sometimes convey emotions that no other medium can. The real pain of war is revealed through lyrics that only someone touched by such a tragedy could write. The anguish of the Depression was explained in songs that were easily understood by all listeners, even those unable to read or write. Joyful songs of prosperity were universally understood when created, and remain easily accessible footnotes of history.

Songwriters would, in all likelihood, work at their craft without its potentially lucrative rewards. Some even avoid commercially viable topics for their lyrics in favor of more meaningful, thought-provoking messages. Songwriters can, therefore, be considered historians and futurists. They describe recent events and speculate on where the world is heading. Songs—lyrics and melodies—are their diaries of people, events, and emotions. Fortunately, songwriters have left these sometimes intimate diaries of the twentieth century for us to study now and in the future.

SELECTION CRITERIA

Songs selected for consideration were typically from American vernacular or "popular" music, but songs from Broadway musicals and fine arts repertoire were considered whenever they were enjoyed by large numbers of listeners. Genre and subgenre that emerged tended to reflect social movements and were, therefore, most often included when they first emerged. Music created for specific venues (dance halls) and media (radio, television, and film) were also closely examined, because they have tended to reflect historic events.

It should be noted that lists of "Top Songs of . . ." or "Best Songs of . . ." are typically based on either commercial success in the marketplace or esthetic value of the compositions listed. This reference work attempts, instead, to present a representative selection of songs from each decade that best reflect American society at the time.

Songs were considered "noteworthy" if they remained in the public's consciousness for a significant amount of time. Another criterion was the value a song had in describing historical events—social, political, and economic—of the day. Songs that described human conditions so effectively that they have been performed and recorded by numerous artists throughout the years were considered esthetically successful. And, although it was not the primary criterion, commercial success demonstrated by record sales, sheet music sales, and radio broadcasts was considered.

Songs were typically included in the decade in which they were written. Some songs were, however, included in the decade when the most influential recording, performance, or use (for example, film score) impacted on the public consciousness, even though the song had been written in a previous decade. Songs that were cast in a dramatically different genre or arrangement were also included in the most relevant decade.

It should also be noted that it is extremely difficult to identify the exact date of creation for many songs that emerged from improvisatory inspirations, such as jazz and rap. The registration of copyright and legal date of publication for a song (typically melody and lyrics) are often business decisions rather than accurate historic milestones. Therefore, the date of the first noteworthy recording (sound recording) is sometimes the indication given for the publication date. The authors of this reference work also considered copyright registration and publication and sound recording dates in order to assign a song to the appropriate decade.

ORGANIZATION AND METHODOLOGY

The Story Behind the Song is organized by decades of the twentieth century. Each chapter begins with a historical overview of how songs from the decade reflected social, political, and economic events of that era. Each chapter includes entries of fifteen selected songs that had significance for the time period. Each song entry includes a discussion of the song's history, why it was created, and how it reflected the events of the era when it was created. Each song entry includes the song title, songwriter(s), publication information, and current availability.

This reference work also provides a selected bibliography of resources and three indices. The bibliography includes Web sites and books that are helpful in researching songs, songwriters, and events of the twentieth century. Each of the three indices are arranged alphabetically and include an index arranged by Song Title, Songwriter, and Subject.

1900–1909

The Decade of Opportunity

The first decade of the twentieth century saw the beginning of technological developments that would continue throughout the millennium. Marvels of technology, such as the Wright brothers' airplane and Henry Ford's Model T Ford automobile, made Americans more mobile than ever before. As society adjusted to these technological advances, Albert Einstein began to ponder concepts that were many years ahead of their time.

Nine million immigrants, most of whom were from European homelands, stepped off ships onto the land of their dreams. A large number of the new Americans labored in assembly lines of urban factories as the nation made its transition from an agrarian to an industrial economy. The exploitation of factory workers was the subject of Upton Sinclair's "muckraking" exposé, *The Jungle* (1905).

Max Factor, a Russian immigrant, set an example for other new arrivals to emulate. He used his knowledge of theatrical makeup to find employment in Hollywood's emerging entertainment environs. As he began to develop his own cosmetics, his empire of hair and skin products evolved. The American dream was truly possible for persons of any background. The "rags-to-riches" dream found its way into the hearts of immigrants and the lyrics of songs.

Unfortunately, the land of opportunity was not as open for African Americans as it was for European immigrants during this decade. Booker T. Washington's autobiography *Up from Slavery* (1901) revealed one man's struggle against slavery. As the decade came to a close, two significant things happened: More than 1 million people attended the celebration of the one-hundredth anniversary of Abraham Lincoln's birth in New York City at which Booker T. Washington was the keynote speaker; and the National Association for the Advancement of Colored People (NAACP) was founded.

Popular culture saw the invention of animated cartoons and the first Kodak portable camera, in this decade. The first World Series was played and baseball was christened the "great American pastime." The United Press, later called United Press International or UPI, was created and the popular press made the print media accessible to citizens of all social stations. For the first time, information and popular culture became readily accessible to most citizens of the United States.

The player piano, a piano that automatically performed music using "piano rolls" (paper rolls with perforations), was introduced in this decade. The player piano and phonograph records made many different artists and genre accessible to people who could neither read music notation nor sing. Thomas Edison's Phonograph Company began releasing music recordings, to be played on his phonographs, in increasing numbers. And, although it would not become a major force in the entertainment industry for several decades, the jukebox was invented in this decade.

New York City was the center of publishing activity in the early nineteenth century and the term *Tin Pan Alley* was used to describe part of Manhattan where many music publishers had offices. The revision of our nation's copyright laws in 1909 helped ensure that songwriting could be a career as well as an avocation.

Obviously, music from previous decades did not abruptly stop just because new genre and subgenre emerged. The opening of Carnegie Hall in 1901 revealed the ongoing public interest in operas, operettas, symphony orchestra concerts, and art song recitals. Ragtime music continued to be a popular genre in this decade, but vaudeville reviews and Broadway plays were responsible for a larger number of songs during this era.

Popular instrumental works called "exhibition-room" songs were intended to be performed as incidental music while demonstration dancers helped audience members learn the dance steps of the day. Another important genre of the decade was the "political song" for campaigns and rallies.

Music composed specifically for tent-show revivals also found its way into mainstream pop culture. But the most notable genre developed during this period might be the one we wish had not been born: the "promotional song"—advertisements set to music.

President William McKinley was assassinated in 1901 by anarchist Leon Czolgosz, and Theodore Roosevelt replaced him in the Oval Office. In 1908, William Howard Taft was elected president. The peace that the nation enjoyed during this ten-year period stands in stark contrast to the bellicose decade that would follow. The Decade of Opportunity was indeed a remarkable transition from the gentility of the late nineteenth century to the worldwide warfare soon to follow.

SONGS

1. "Stars and Stripes Forever"
Words and Music by John Philip Sousa
Copyright © 1897 (instrumental version), The John Church
Company; 1898 (song version), The John Church Company;
first noteworthy recording by Sousa, 1901.

Americans felt a deep sense of patriotism during the first decade of the twentieth century for several reasons. The nation had emerged from a civil war and, in a relatively short period of time, had developed a sense of unity once again after the reconstruction period. President McKinley began his second term in 1901, but he was assassinated by anarchist Leon Czolgosz, and Theodore Roosevelt became president. In 1904, Roosevelt issued his version of the Monroe Doctrine when he stated that the United States would send military troops to foreign countries if American interests were threatened. His "big-stick" approach to diplomacy was well received by most citizens, especially those who were recent immigrants. And the number of persons immigrating to the United States was substantial: between 1901 and 1910, 8.74 million people had emigrated to America.

John Philip Sousa could easily be called the most patriotic composer or songwriter who ever lived. His music was an artistic salute to the political philosophy presented by the Roosevelt administration. Sousa was a prolific composer of marches (135) and operettas (15) during the 1890s and 1900s. In fact, he wrote so many outstanding marches that he became known as the "March King." He wrote "Stars and Stripes Forever" onboard a steamer while sailing home to America from England. He first wrote it as a traditional instrumental march for a military wind ensemble on Christmas Eve of 1896, but added lyrics to create the song version in 1898. However, the song did not become a "hit" until it was recorded by The Sousa Band on Gram-o-Phone Records in 1901.

Sousa could be described as somewhere between a popular songwriter of his day and a composer in the European tradition. In 1867, at the tender age of thirteen, young John Philip enlisted in the Marine Corps as an apprentice musician. In 1875, he requested and was granted an early discharge from the marines in order to pursue his music career in civilian life. He quickly began a busy career performing on violin and conducting theater orchestras.

In 1880, Sousa returned to the military as conductor of the U.S. Marine Band. It was during these years that he composed some of the most popular marches ever written. Although written for concert bands, his marches were often arranged for many different instrumental combinations. The Marine Band came to be an icon of Washington, D.C., society and Sousa marches were to Americans what waltzes were to the Viennese. The attraction of Sousa's music was its orderly formal structure, reminiscent of the European classical tradition, but with a uniquely American flavor.

Although John Philip Sousa was able to improve the quality of the Marine Band to the point that it had a cult following, he himself was never promoted to a military rank as one might have expected. This lack of recognition from his Marine Corps superior officers, combined with a lucrative offer to start a civilian band, led him to resign his military position in 1892. His band was first called Sousa's New Marine Band, but was quickly changed to the Sousa Band after complaints from the Marine Corps.

The Sousa Band became one of the most popular music ensembles in history. The band toured Europe in 1900, 1901, 1903, and

1905. Sousa continued to write marches for the band and make recordings of marches and arrangements of popular songs. Attendance at the Sousa Band concerts reached its peak in the latter part of the decade when sixty thousand people per week attended their concerts.

Few songs in the history of American music have been performed and recorded as many times as "Stars and Stripes Forever." Its concise form, interesting melody and countermelody, and patriotic aura made it a staple of military, high school, and college band concerts. It is hard to imagine a Fourth of July celebration without a rousing performance of "Stars and Stripes Forever" as the finale.

This song was designated the national march of the United States of America in 1987 (U.S. Code, Title 36, Chapter 10, Paragraph 188). Although Sousa composed 135 marches during his lifetime, he is best known for "Stars and Stripes Forever." The 1952 film based on his life was called *Stars and Stripes Forever* and a ballet using his music in 1958 had the same title.

This march, like most John Philip Sousa compositions, is widely distributed by sheet music publishing companies that specialize in educational music. It is unlikely that one could find a high school or college band library that does not have at least one copy of this march. There are a large number of wind ensemble and concert band recordings of this march, but the one conducted by the composer himself is recommended for its historical accuracy: *The March King: John Philip Sousa* (CD) by John Philip Sousa (LEGACYIN 462).

2. "Lift Every Voice and Sing" (Sometimes shortened to "Lift Every Voice")
Words by James Weldon Johnson and Music by J. Rosamond Johnson
Copyright © 1900, Joseph W. Stern and Company

James Weldon Johnson, an African American, originally wrote "Lift Every Voice and Sing" as a poem. In 1900, his brother J. Rosamond Johnson wrote the music because he wished to transform the poem into a song for children. The song has been called the "Black National Anthem" and the "NAACP Anthem" due to its emotional lyrics and gospel-like melody.

Both of the Johnson brothers were extremely well educated. J. Rosamond studied music under the tutelage of his mother and later attended the prestigious New England Conservatory of Music in Boston. He toured throughout the United States and Europe with vaudeville shows and directed the Hammerstein Opera House Orchestra in London. His love of children and the African American cultures led him to become a trustee of the Music School Settlement in Harlem, New York, where he also served as music director.

James Weldon Johnson was a Renaissance man. He was a newspaper journalist and editor for the *Daily American,* the first daily newspaper for African Americans. He authored several books including two about Negro spirituals. He was active in the NAACP throughout his adult life and served as secretary of the organization for fourteen years. He served as a visiting professor at Fisk University, in Nashville, home of the Fisk Jubilee Singers.

The lyrics of "Lift Every Voice and Sing" continue to stir emotions in African Americans and anyone else who has been forced to endure discrimination:

> We have come over a way that with tears has
> 　　been watered
> We have come treading our path through the
> 　　blood of the slaughtered
> Out from the gloomy past
> Till now we stand at last
> Where the white gleam of our bright star is cast.

J. Rosamond set his brother's moving poetry to music for a group of schoolchildren to sing during a celebration of Abraham Lincoln's birthday in Jacksonville, Florida. These lyrics were intended to remind African American children in the beginning of the twentieth century that their ancestors had suffered worse consequences of racial discrimination than they would ever know.

"Lift Every Voice and Sing" gradually became known as one of the most emotional tributes to those who suffered indignation and injury during the battles against racial discrimination in the United States. The lyrics present an image of African Americans, and all others, who have overcome social injustices, treading through the "blood of the slaughtered" and emerging from the "gloomy past." These words are a grim reminder that freedoms Americans enjoy today were not easily won. This song also reminds listeners that African Americans now stand in a brighter light because of those who fought for civil rights.

"Lift Every Voice and Sing" has been incorporated into many creative works—films, documentaries, plays—as a reference to the obstacles African Americans have overcome in the past two hundred years. It was included in *I Know Why the Caged Bird Sings*, a 1979 made-for-television movie by Maya Angelou (Fox Television), and *Roots: The Next Generation* (Warner Television), Alex Haley's 1979 sequel to *Roots*.

Arrangements of this song for voice and piano are readily available in collections of inspirational songs. A fairly recent recording of this song is available on *Solitary Journey* (CD) by Melba Moore (ENCOREMU 4003).

3. "I Love You Truly"
Words and Music by Carrie Jacobs-Bond
Copyright © 1901, Boston Music Company

Although Carrie Jacobs-Bond endured many hardships throughout her life, she clung to her sense of romanticism. Perhaps she dreamed of the gentility of the faded Victorian period and tried to re-create it through her poetry, music, and painting. Her delicate love song "I Love You Truly" was one of her most successful and enduring testaments to idyllic romance.

Carrie Jacobs was born in Janesville, Wisconsin, on August 11, 1862. Her father died while she was quite young, leaving Carrie and her mother without any savings on which to live. She and her mother, therefore, moved back to Janesville to live with her grandfather, a hotel operator. Her grandfather and mother encouraged her to pursue her love of music.

Carrie Jacobs married Frank J. Smith when she was eighteen, but it was not a happy union. Despite social pressure against divorce at the time, she did divorce Smith. Two years later, she married Frank Lewis Bond, a physician. Bond encouraged her to write songs and provided her with the emotional support and loving marriage she had hoped for. Regrettably, he fell on the ice and died only a few years after they were married. Because Carrie and her husband had not invested wisely, she was left to care for their son with little savings, a sad reprise to the hardship her mother experienced.

Carrie then moved to Chicago and earned a living managing a rooming house, a vocation she had learned from her grandfather. Despite her financial difficulties, she continued to write songs in hopes of locating a publisher who would exploit her talent. Although Carrie Jacobs-Bond did not have a professional singing voice, she sang publicly in order to promote her songs. Popular opera singer Jessie Bartlett Davis heard Bond's songs at one of Carrie's recitals and their long-lasting friendship began. Davis also gave Bond the financial backing she needed to publish her first collection of songs, *Seven Songs as Unpretentious as the Wild Rose* in 1901. One song contained in the collection was "I Love You Truly," one that became immediately popular. This, her first collection, sold more than 1 million copies.

Carrie Bond experienced two worlds during her lifetime. The world of reality, in which two men whom she loved, her father and her husband, gave her very little material comfort. Her world of songs, filled with romance and happy endings, replaced the passion that was missing from her real world. "I Love You Truly" remains a song that was born from the genteel world she created using music and lyrics.

In this, the pre-radio era, songs such as "I Love You Truly" were referred to as "parlor songs." A parlor song was one that was easily singable by members of the family who assembled around the piano for an evening's entertainment. This form of family entertainment was quite popular with members of the middle and upper class who could afford to own a piano. Sentimental love songs like this one were perfectly suited for these family sings.

This song is available in many different song collections, such as for weddings and romantic love songs. This song has been recorded by an extremely diverse range of recording artists and styles such as the Lawrence Welk Orchestra, Louis Prima, the Ink Spots, and a dixieland jazz band called the Firehouse Five Plus Two. An excellent version is available on *Wedding Music* (CD and Cassette) by Jesse Crawford (MSP 20777).

4. "Bill Bailey, Won't You Please Come Home"
Words and Music by Hughie Cannon
Copyright © 1902, Howlery, Haviland and Company; 1938, Jerry
Vogel Music Company, Inc.

In 1900, the United States was still struggling with a relatively new
concept: treating all citizens, including African Americans, fairly and
courteously. Although the requisite number of states ratified the
Thirteenth Amendment to the Constitution, thereby making it illegal to own slaves, social acceptance of African Americans had not
spread very far by the turn of the century.

One popular genre of the day was referred to as the "coon
song." A coon song most likely had its origins in minstrel shows, variety shows that were popular from the 1840s to the early 1900s. Minstrel shows were presented initially by white performers in
"black-face" makeup who parodied slaves and their lifestyles. Two
stylized characters from the minstrel format were Jim Crow, a character acted to resemble an ignorant country person, and Zip Coon,
an urban character who might be compared to a modern-day con
artist. Both Jim Crow and Zip Coon were, of course, fictionalized
black characters performed by white actors. Some minstrel troupes
made up of African American performers also adopted the same
format and characters of their white actor counterparts. However,
white actors typically did not act in the same shows as black actors
during the heyday of minstrel shows.

Not all recordings during the first decade of the century were of
noteworthy musical merit. Descriptions of many recordings on the
Edison label included comic, vaudeville, and coon songs. One can
conclude, therefore, that there was a good market for humorous
recordings in the first decade of the twentieth century. Like most
songwriters hoping to earn publishing income from their songs,
Hughie Cannon probably thought little about the denigrating manner in which coon songs referred to African Americans and focused
instead on whatever genres were selling in the marketplace.

"Bill Bailey, Won't You Please Come Home" was similar to
other songs of the coon song genre in that it used stylized dialect:
"Bill Bailey is you sore?" "I know I'se to blame," and "throw'd her
down." However, it deviated from the strongly polar issues of us

versus them (that is, white society and black society). Bill Bailey's story could have easily been about a rift between a white man and his wife instead of an African American man and his wife. The more universal theme and less condescending attitude toward the characters in the song seemed to indicate a step toward acceptance of African American culture by mainstream white society. This song might have signaled the decline of the coon-song genre and the beginning of songs that made more benign references to minorities in American culture.

Recordings of "Bill Bailey, Won't You Please Come Home" were quite successful beginning the year it was composed and continuing for several decades. Both Arthur Collins (Columbia 872) and Silas Leachman (Victor 1458) enjoyed strong sales from their recordings in 1902. Thirty years later, the song was recorded by numerous dixieland, pop, and big band jazz artists including Louis Armstrong, Bobby Darin, Earl Fatha Hines, and Pearl Bailey.

A large number of recordings of this song are available, and sheet music arrangements for many instrument and voice combinations continue to be distributed. Noteworthy recordings of this song include *The Essential Louis Armstrong* (two CDs) by Louis Armstrong (Vanguard 91/92). A recent search of the Internet indicated that forty-five hundred Web sites contained lyrics to this song.

5. "(The) Entertainer"
Music by Scott Joplin
Copyright ©1902, John Stark and Son

Scott Joplin was a member of the first generation of African Americans to grow to adulthood during the postreconstruction era. As a composer who developed a truly American compositional style called "ragtime," he had to fight the prejudices of music critics. Music critics of the 1890s and early 1900s tended to view western European fine art concert music as the model for American composers of instrumental music to emulate. Joplin's highly syncopated ragtime music was distinctly different from its European counterparts, but most critics of Joplin's day thought his music was more suitable for saloons than concert stages. The Eurocentrism of music critics, combined with a general condescension toward African American composers in America, caused Joplin to struggle for acceptance during his lifetime.

Joplin's style of performing and composing music represented a blend of classical and popular entertainment styles. He was born into a musical family and was classically trained in his childhood. He later studied piano with pianist Louis Chauvin. After he matured as a musician, he became an orchestra conductor and entertainer, touring with vaudeville shows. His piano rags were precisely notated and he instructed performers to "never play ragtime fast," a reflection of his passion for neoclassical precision and restraint in his music.

Most music historians credit Joplin for developing the ragtime style and writing some of its finest extant examples. One of Joplin's most famous piano rags was "(The) Entertainer." His works received modest recognition, through recordings of ragtime music, for more than fifty years. In 1974, the Oscar Award–winning film *The Sting* gave new life to "(The) Entertainer" and other music of Joplin.

It seems sadly ironic that Joplin, one of America's most significant composers of indigenous music, died of a sexually transmitted disease in a miserable and impoverished environment. He worked throughout his life to produce a "legitimate" opera that would be recognized by serious music critics, but died without any sense of accomplishment. He was forced to finance the one and only performance of his opera *Tremonisha* himself in 1911, but was unsuccessful at finding backers to produce it. Fifty years after his death, music historians began to recognize Joplin's uniqueness as a composer. Two years later, during the U.S. bicentennial, the Pulitzer Prize committee honored Joplin's contribution to American music.

Because Joplin was extremely precise in the notation of his music, it is possible to purchase original piano sheet music for "(The) Entertainer" and other piano rags he wrote. This song has also been arranged for myriad instrumental combinations such as orchestra, concert band, and dixieland band. Of the many recordings available, *Max Morath Plays the Best of Scott Joplin and Other Rag Classics* (CD) by ragtime expert Max Morath (Vanguard 39/40) is a noteworthy interpretation of Joplin's "(The) Entertainer."

6. "Toyland" (from *Babes in Toyland*)
Words by Glen MacDonough and Music by Victor Herbert
Copyright 1903, M. Witmark and Sons

Victor Herbert was born in Dublin, Ireland, in 1859 and studied music in the classical European manner at the Stuttgart Conservatory of Music in Germany. He emigrated to the United States in 1886 to become the conductor of the 22nd Army Regimental Band and became a citizen in 1902. His knowledge of and love for European-style operettas, combined with his background in military marches, helped form his unique music compositional style.

Fred R. Hamlin and Julian Mitchell produced *The Wizard of Oz* in Broadway's Majestic Theater in 1903. To capitalize on its popularity, the producers commissioned Glen MacDonough and Victor Herbert to create a sequel. The result was *Babes in Toyland*, a very entertaining and easily accessible operetta that also had a storm, a difficult and frightening journey through the forest, and the eventual arrival at a mythical city just as in *The Wizard of Oz.* The one big difference between these two works was the superior quality of music in *Babes in Toyland.*

One of the most memorable songs from *Babes in Toyland* was "Toyland," sung in the original production by Bess Wynn. The show ran 192 times and was presented on Broadway again in 1905, 1929, and 1930. Two film versions of *Babes in Toyland* were extremely popular and rekindled interest in the song "Toyland." Comedic actors Stan Laurel and Oliver Hardy starred in an amusing film version called *March of the Wooden Soldiers* in 1934. A 1961 film produced by Disney included Ed Wynn, Ray Bolger, Tommy Sands, and Ann Jillian. The most recent incarnation of this operetta was a direct-to-video production released by MGM in 1997.

Music from the musical *Babes in Toyland*, including the song "Toyland," is readily available in many arrangements for different vocal and instrumental combinations. A noteworthy recording of "Toyland" is available on *The Music of Johnny Mathis: A Personal Collection* (four CD box set) by Johnny Mathis (LGY 48932).

7. "(I Am) The Yankee Doodle Boy" (also known as "I'm a Yankee Doodle Dandy" and "Yankee Doodle Dandy")
Words and Music by George M. Cohan

George Michael Cohan was one of America's most successful songwriters, especially in the genre of Broadway musicals. It was not unusual for him to write the dialogue as well as the songs for his musicals. He also produced, directed, and appeared in his Broadway extravaganzas.

Cohan grew up in a vaudeville family and did not receive much formal education. His nomadic life provided him, instead, with an environment in which he learned the craft of writing skits and songs, as well as performing them, for the world of entertainment. As he matured as a writer and producer, he developed a uniquely American approach to musical theater.

Prior to the twentieth century, American productions created for musical theater tended to emulate European operettas, such as those by Gilbert and Sullivan. Cohan was initially considered a maverick, because his characters were unapologetically American and they spoke in everyday vernacular complete with street slang and regional dialects. A significant feature of Cohan's style was his love for upbeat patriotic songs. Later in his career, he was awarded the Congressional Medal by President Franklin D. Roosevelt for writing the song "Over There," a song that was a patriotic standard during World War I.

One of Cohan's first hit songs was "The Yankee Doodle Boy" from the musical *Little Johnny Jones*. To say that this song was a hit would be an understatement: it continues to be performed and recorded in the twenty-first century. This up-tempo song with a marchlike rhythm is most often played during patriotic celebrations or productions. It can easily be called an American patriotic anthem.

"Give My Regards to Broadway," another song from *Little Johnny Jones*, became another classic song for Cohan. Ironically, the musical itself met with only limited success even though two songs from it have become icons of American popular music.

Warner Brothers created *Yankee Doodle Dandy*, a biographical film about George M. Cohan starring James Cagney, in 1942. Cagney's performance of "The Yankee Doodle Boy" is a classic in itself. This song is also included in *George M!*, a Broadway musical about the life and music of George M. Cohan.

Arrangements of this song are often found in collections of patriotic music. A noteworthy recording of this song is available on *George M* (CD) by the original cast of the musical (TNK 3200).

8. "You're the Flower of My Heart Sweet Adeline"
(most often called "Sweet Adeline")
Words and Music by Richard H. Gerrard and Henry W. Armstrong
Copyright © 1904, M. Witmark and Sons

The song "You're the Flower of My Heart Sweet Adeline" has most often been referred to simply as "Sweet Adeline." It has, from the first recording, been a trademark song of barbershop quartets that sing in four-part harmonies. The song was immediately popular when, in 1904, it was recorded by the Hayden Quartet (Victor 2934), the most popular close-harmony barbershop quartet in the early 1900s. It was also recorded by the Columbia Male Quartet (Columbia 32584) and Albert Campbell and James F. Harrison (Edison 8677).

The songwriters first began to write this song as "Sweet Rosalie," but they found the name Rosalie too hard to rhyme with other words. They then decided to write it for Adelina Patti, an Italian American star of the Metropolitan Opera whom both songwriters admired greatly. But they found that Adelina was too difficult to rhyme as well. Thus, they changed it to Adeline in order to create a better flow for the rhyming scheme. It is ironic that, in addition to the enduring fame of "Sweet Adeline," the song's namesake Adelina Patti became the most famous opera diva of her era. In addition, her reputation as the premier female opera star in the United States endured for decades.

After "Sweet Adeline" became popular, John J. ("Honey Fitz") Fitzgerald adopted it as his campaign song for his mayoral election bid. Honey Fitz was elected mayor of Boston due in part to him cleverly associating his campaign to a romantic song that many people sang and even more listened to. He became a two-term mayor and began a political legacy that was continued by his grandchildren Joseph Jr., John, Robert, and Edward (Ted) Kennedy. His nickname "Honey Fitz" was given to him because his friends believed his voice to be as smooth as honey.

The term *barbershop quartet* evolved from groups of male singers who allegedly sang their favorite songs, with improvised harmony parts, while waiting to get shaves or haircuts at their local barbershop. The a cappella style of singing was likely a legacy of early Calvinist church psalm singing. As the four-part harmony vocal style evolved, homogeneous ensembles (all male or all female) became associated with the genre.

In 1936, the artist Norman Rockwell painted a scene that was his imagined idea of a barbershop quartet singing in a barbershop. Like many of his nostalgic Americana paintings, it appeared as a cover illustration for the *Saturday Evening Post.* This served as publicity for the barbershop quartet revival movement, and two years later, Owen Clifton Cash founded the Society for the Preservation and Encouragement of Barber Shop Quartet Singing in America (SPEBSQSA). The organization that became known by the acronym SPEBSQSA was, and remains, for male voices only. Therefore, in 1945, an analogous organization for women was created. The women's group is called the Sweet Adelines.

"Sweet Adeline" is most often available as a four-part harmony arrangement for a cappella voices. It is also readily available in arrangements for piano and solo voice, guitar and voice, and instrumental ensembles. A representative recording is available on *34 All Time Great Sing Along Selections* (cassette) by Mitch Miller (TNK 30250). It should be noted that this song is sometimes included in collections of music from the Gay Nineties era, but this is historically inaccurate.

9. "Come Take a Trip in My Airship"
Words by Ren Shields and Music by George Evans
Copyright © 1904, Charles K. Harris Music Publishing Company

Topical songs of this decade served as journalism as well as entertainment. Events of the day were, as evidenced in "Come Take a Trip in My Airship," reflected in story lines of songs. Soon after the Wright brothers made history with the first heavier-than-air "ship," Shields and Evans immortalized the event in song.

On December 19, 1903, Wilbur and Orville Wright launched their 605-pound aircraft from a sand dune clearly visible from the beaches of North Carolina's Outer Banks. By the end of that cold winter day, the Wright brother's airplane had made four successful flights, the longest of which lasted fifty-nine seconds. Their invention gave the world something other inventors had only dreamed of: the ability to travel great distances in short periods of time. It also gave the citizens of the United States bragging rights for years to come.

Shields and Evans, like other songwriters, wrote music they hoped would be included in vaudeville sketches and Broadway shows. The success of "Come Take a Trip in My Airship" was likely due to the songwriters incorporating a timely newsworthy topic, in this case manned flight, and the romantic notion of a couple sailing the skies together. It could be considered both a romantic song and a topical song.

"Come Take a Trip in My Airship" was responsible for a smash hit by Billy Murray in 1905 (Victor 2986). That same year, J. W. Myers recorded his version (Columbia 1878), which was also extremely successful.

A vocal arrangement of this song is available in the *Backpocket Old Time Songbook* (WE publishing). A recording of this song is available on the album *Closing the Distance* (CD and cassette) by Sally Rogers (FLF 0425).

10. "Meet Me in St. Louis, Louis"
Words by Andrew B. Sterling and Music by Kerry Mills
Copyright © 1904, Mills Music, Inc./Harms, Inc.

"Meet Me in St. Louis, Louis" was written as a promotional song for the 1904 Louisiana Purchase Exposition in St. Louis, and it became an instant hit with the public. In 1904, it was recorded by four different acts: Billy Murray (Edison 8722), S. H. Dudley (Victor 2807), The Arthur Pryor Band (Victor 2960), and J. W. Myers (Columbia 1848). All four recordings were, amazingly, quite successful in the marketplace.

The exposition in St. Louis was intended to commemorate the one-hundredth anniversary of the Louisiana Purchase in 1903, but it was not ready until one year later. Therefore, it is known as the 1904 Louisiana Purchase Exposition. The exposition was the vision of David R. Francis. He recruited architect Isaac S. Taylor and together they pledged to create the most grandiose exposition the world had ever seen. By most accounts, they succeeded in their mission.

The exposition included exhibits from sixty-two countries and forty-three states and covered 1,270 acres of land. Admission to the park was 25 cents (equivalent to about $9 today) and was considered inexpensive for this magnificent event. The fair ran for seven months and 20 million visitors passed through its gates. The single-day record was set on September 15, 1904, when the attendance was four hundred thousand. The exposition cost $50 million to create, but, unlike most international fairs, it actually showed a profit after seven months.

The song "Meet Me in St. Louis, Louis" continued to be popular for fifty years after the St. Louis exposition. It was the title song for the film *Meet Me in St. Louis* (MGM) starring Judy Garland in 1944.

There are many versions of this song in song folios for voice and piano. It is included in *Songs of the 1900s* and *Songs from Hollywood Musicals*, both published by Hal Leonard. Of the several recordings of this song, the one by Judy Garland is the most notable. It is found on Garland's *Meet Me in St. Louis* MGM 305123/Rhino 71958CD, 1995/1996).

11. "In My Merry Oldsmobile"
Words by Vincent Bryan and Music by Gus Edwards
Copyright © 1905, M. Witmark and Sons; 1961,
Clef Music Publishers

Two songs written by Vincent Bryan and Gus Edwards produced hit recordings in 1905: "Tammany" and "In My Merry Oldsmobile." Like other songs of the day, "In My Merry Oldsmobile" chronicled a major event. It also holds the dubious honor of being the first promotional song about an automobile.

The songwriters of "In My Merry Oldsmobile" were impressed with newspaper accounts of the first cross-country road rally. Two drivers traveled in their Oldsmobiles from Detroit to the Lewis and Clark Exposition in Portland, Oregon. The song romanticized a ride in an automobile by describing a couple's courtship in the same brand of car that crossed the country. The song, therefore, served three purposes: a commercial about Oldsmobiles, recognition of the transcontinental trip, and the musical equivalent of a romance novel.

The first recording of this song was made by Billy Murray for Victor Records (Victor 67) in 1905. It was also made popular in stage performances by vaudeville star Anna Fitzhugh. "In My Merry Oldsmobile" was revived in the 1944 movie *The Merry Malones* and then again in the 1948 film *One Sunday Afternoon.* But the greatest exposure for this song was probably its many performances on *Sing Along with Mitch,* the television show that in the 1960s flashed lyrics on the screen for viewers at home while Mitch and his choir sang hits of yesteryear.

Arrangements of this song for voice and piano are commonly available in collections of songs for children and songs from America's past. For example, it is available in *The Big Book of Nostalgia* published by Hal Leonard. There is a jazz version of this song available on *The Indispensable Bix Beiderbecke* (two CDs) by jazz great Bix Beiderbecke (RCA 66540).

12. "Budweiser's a Friend of Mine"
Words and Music by Vincent Bryan and Seymour Furth
Copyright © 1907, Anheuser-Busch Brewing Association

One form of song that some people might wish had not matured in the early 1900s was the promotional song. However, songwriters and publishers, eager to find avenues to promote their songs, enjoyed the immediate reaction a song received when its theme mentioned a popular product. One such product, Budweiser beer, helped make this song quite successful.

Beer songs combined the nostalgia for old English drinking songs—an early adjunct of male bonding—and promotion of one's favorite beverage. Earlier beer songs such as "Down Where the Wurzburger Flows" and "Under the Anheuser Bush" successfully set the stage for "Budweiser's a Friend of Mine."

These humble songs were the progeny of modern advertising songs, known as "jingles," that can be heard on radio and television. The jingles and commercials seen during professional football games are not too unlike "Budweiser's a Friend of Mine." One of the major advertisers for sporting events is Anheuser Busch, manufacturer of Budweiser beer. And, even after almost one hundred years, the image of male bonding is a major theme in beer advertising.

Neither sheet music arrangements nor recordings are available for this song. Its historic value lies in being the prototype for music in advertising that affects radio and television programming today.

13. "Will the Circle Be Unbroken?"
Words by Ada Ruth Habershon and Music by Charles Hutchison Gabriel
Copyright © 1907, Fleming H. Revell Co.

"Will the Circle Be Unbroken?" is an example of songs created during this decade that were based on melodic phrases and lyrics of existing traditional hymns. This song was most likely an adaptation of a traditional hymn that was passed from generation to generation through the oral tradition. Subsequent versions of the song by other songwriters and performers added new verses and arrangements. Some versions of the song changed the title and chorus line to "Can the Circle Be Unbroken?" and "Will the Circle Remain Unbroken?"

Songs such as this one represent the change in turn-of-the-century United States from a rural agricultural-based economy to a more urban industrial one. Hymns and folk songs that had their roots in rural dirt-floor churches made their way to tent-show revivals and, finally, to city-based songwriters who cast them into more polished commercial songs. Because many factory workers in large cities were transplants from rural communities, songs with sentimental spiritual messages and familiar gospel melodies became popular in this decade.

"Will the Circle Be Unbroken?" was first recorded by the Metropolitan Quartet on Edison Records. The Metropolitan Quartet was a barbershop-type vocal group known for their close, lush harmonies. As artists from other genre—gospel, folk, country—created and sang different arrangements, this song became one of the most often sung and recorded songs in the United States.

This song addresses the universal question of whether there will be a better life in heaven than on earth. The song lyrics ask "Will the circle be unbroken by and by? Is a better home awaiting in the sky, in the sky?" That simple lyric likely evoked a familiar emotion for African Americans who, due to historical prejudice and oppression, were struggling to earn a living. The spiritual message that many slaves had come to believe was there is something to look forward to, if not during their earthbound life, certainly in the life hereafter.

Many African Americans related to its message so strongly that it became associated with the struggle for civil rights in the South. In fact, the Peabody Award–winning National Public Radio series about civil rights was called *Will the Circle Be Unbroken? An Audio History of the Civil Rights Movement.*

The theme of this song—thinking about better conditions in the future—remains a metaphor for the civil rights movement. Early gospel songs also drew analogies between the struggles of biblical characters, such as Moses or David, and slaves in America. The song "Will the Circle Be Unbroken?" carried that comparison from the reconstruction period through the twentieth century.

"Will the Circle Be Unbroken?" has been recorded by numerous performers representing many genres of music, including gospel, country, folk, and rock. The most well-known recordings of it were made by Maybelle Carter and the Carter Family in the late 1920s and 1930s.

One of the most innovative rock bands to emerge during the 1960s, The Nitty Gritty Dirt Band, brought more attention to the song than any other act. Their 1972 recording for EMI America Records was a multiple-record set entitled *Will the Circle Remain Unbroken?* It included some of traditional country music's most notable artists such as Maybelle Carter, Doc Watson, and Roy Acuff. They reprised the recording in 1989 with *Will the Circle Remain Unbroken? Vol. 2* (CD and cassette) by The Nitty Gritty Dirt Band (USL 12500). The album won the Country Music Association's Album of the Year Award. However, the signature recording of this song can be heard on *Press On* (CD) by June Carter (RISK REC 4107).

Because the original copyright has expired, the 1907 version of this song is in the public domain. The original sheet music was published in *Alexander's Gospel Songs, No. 2* in 1910 by the Fleming H. Revell Company. It should be noted that many of the recordings of this song have new lyrics that have copyright protection. In addition to the many recordings of this song that are available, there are more than twenty-seven published sheet music arrangements for voice or instruments. For example, it is included in *150 Songs with Three Chords,* a song collection published by Warner Brothers.

14. "Get on the Raft with Taft"
Words and Music by Harry D. Kerr and Abe Holzman
Copyright © 1908, Leo Feist, Inc.

Political campaign songs became popular in the last half of the nineteenth century and continued to be a popular genre of music until the end of World War II. Songwriters and publishers were motivated every four years to produce songs for each candidate. Songwriters were probably more excited by the prospect of selling sheet music and recordings than an allegiance to any one candidate. They approached their campaign songs in one of several ways: adding lyrics to existing melodies, creating parodies of popular songs, adding lyrics to existing patriotic music, or creating original music and lyrics.

Like many writers of political campaign songs, Harry Kerr and Abe Holzman were more interested in composing a memorable song, using a simple melody and strong rhymes, than creating a masterpiece of prose and music. The song's purpose was, after all, to help William Howard Taft get elected president of the United States. In an effort to give the candidate strong name recognition, Kerr and Holzman referred to Taft throughout the song, but used his first or middle name only once. Their use of the catchy phrase "Get on the raft with Taft" was a simple way to create name recognition for Taft by offering listeners a memorable rhyme with which to associate his name.

This song is a wonderful example of political public relations copywriting. The song establishes the boat metaphor and explains that Taft will "lead our strong and mighty craft thru [*sic*] storm and sea." It goes on to assure listeners that the Taft team will save the country from "Bryan, Hearst and graft," an allusion to their opponents. The songwriters, obviously adept at the craft of rhyming lyrics, wove the words *Taft, raft,* and *graft* skillfully into the chorus of this song.

The copyright was renewed in 1912. The four-year interval indicates a second version was created for the 1912 presidential contest. The copyright was renewed by the publishing company Leo Feist, Inc. in 1940. One would assume that Feist was interested in retaining the rights to the melody of the original song. The lyrics would, obviously, not have much commercial value after Taft left politics.

The value of "Get on the Raft with Taft" is its snapshot of political practice, with the accompanying propaganda, of the 1900s. Veiled in a cheerful melody and lyrics full of simple rhymes, the public relations message of this song could be updated and used for contemporary political campaigns: Our candidate is honest and upright; the other one is not. No recordings are available.

15. "Take Me Out to the Ball Game"
Words by Jack Norworth and Music by Albert Von Tilzer
Copyright © 1908, York Music Corporation; 1936, Jerry Vogel
Music Company, Inc.

In 1903, two different baseball leagues, the well-established National League and the newly formed American League, agreed to have a best-out-of-nine postseason playoff series to determine the top team in the world. Of course, it was instantly successful with fans and became the annual World Series.

By 1908, baseball had become entrenched as the great American pastime. To capitalize on the cultlike following baseball had developed, Jack Norworth and Albert Von Tilzer wrote the lighthearted song "Take Me Out to the Ball Game." It is unlikely that either member of this songwriting team ever dreamed that their little ditty of a song would become as familiar to Americans as baseball itself, but it remains one of the most performed songs ever written, even today. Ironically, Albert Von Tilzer did not see a baseball game until twenty years after he wrote this, the baseball anthem.

The year this song was created, it was recorded by the tremendously popular Billy Murray and the Hayden Quartet (Victor 5570) and Harvey Hindemyer (Columbia 586). Over the next ninety years, numerous artists from every genre have performed and recorded this simple song. It was included in *Shine on Harvest Moon*, the 1944 biographical film about Nora Bayes and was the title song for the 1949 film *Take Me Out to the Ball Game* (MGM) that starred Gene Kelly and Frank Sinatra. But more people have heard this song sung during the seventh inning stretch at major league baseball games than all recordings combined.

This song is available in more song collections than one might expect. It is most frequently found in collections of childrens' songs because of its simple melody and easily learned lyrics. This song is included on *Greatest Sports Rock and Jams, Vol. 3* (a six-CD box set) by Ronnie Neuman (CDF 6333).

1910–1919

America Joins the Global Community

The second decade of the twentieth century was a period of dramatic change. It saw the United States emerge from a relatively isolationist posture to a position of global power after it entered, and endured, World War I. In this ten-year period, American society began to mature beyond its turn-of-the-century ethnocentrism because of mass immigration from Europe and, of course, soldiers returning home from foreign soil after the war.

Developing technology also contributed to the globalization of America. Airplanes became faster and the distances they could travel without refueling increased. On October 17, 1911, Cal Rodgers was the first person to pilot an airplane across the United States. His flight from New York to Pasadena gave birth to the concept of commercial air travel.

Coast-to-coast telephone calls became a reality in this decade. Radio and radio broadcasting evolved quickly from 1915 through the end of the decade. Both of these technological developments contributed to faster, more national communication of news.

The United States became an attractive "new land" for many European immigrants beginning at the turn of the century. By 1920, 8.7 million immigrants, mostly from Europe, moved to America in hopes of finding employment and a better lifestyle. The contributions of these millions of immigrants, particularly those of Italian,

Irish, and Jewish descent, to our culture was evident in our music, theater, and newly emerging film art forms.

The domestic economy continued to move from agrarian to industrial. As cotton plantations in the South became increasingly mechanized, laborers moved to more urban areas in search of employment. One such city, New Orleans, benefited from the influx of rural African Americans who interacted with French-speaking "Creoles" and "free blacks," many of whom were well-educated European emigres. This cultural mix provided the tinder that was ignited by a social experiment, called the "Storyville district" in New Orleans, and resulted in the development of jazz, one of the most uniquely American genres of music.

Even prior to World War I, the United States began to enter foreign conflicts. The Roosevelt Corollary, Teddy Roosevelt's modification of the Monroe Doctrine, justified our nation's entry into the wars of other nations whenever our sovereignty is threatened. He called his foreign policy the "New Nationalism." During the second decade of the twentieth century, the United States invaded Cuba, occupied Nicaragua, invaded Mexico, and sent the marines to Haiti and Santo Domingo. It was Woodrow Wilson, however, who would test the limits of this new nationalism after being elected president in 1912 and reelected in 1916. In 1917, Wilson began sending Americans overseas to fight the "war to end all wars."

The role of women in society was changed during this era. In 1914, Margaret Sanger was indicted for sending "obscene literature" through the mails. The material considered obscene was actually information about birth control directed toward women, many of whom worked outside the home. The womens' suffrage movement gained tremendous strength throughout the decade and won the fight for a woman's right to vote with the passage of the Nineteenth Amendment in 1920.

SONGS

1. "Casey Jones (the Brave Engineer)"
Words by T. (Talifero) Lawrence Siebert and Music by Eddie Newton
Copyright © 1909, Shapiro, Bernstein and Company, Inc.
In the score of the musical play *The Wife Hunters*, 1911

On the front page of the May 1, 1900, edition of the *Memphis Commercial Appeal* was the account of the "sad end of engineer Casey Jones." On the night of April 30, John Luther Jones, Illinois Central Railroad engineer, ran the New Orleans fast mail and passenger train known as the "Cannonball Express" into the back of a freight train stopped at Vaughn, Mississippi. Jones, in his haste to make up lost time, apparently ignored flagmen warnings of the blocked tracks ahead. With the collision imminent, Jones applied the airbrakes and told fireman Sim Webb to jump, thus saving Webb's life. Other crew members and some passengers were slightly injured; Jones was the only fatality.

In 1909, with the real events all but forgotten, two West Coast vaudevillians wrote a "comedy railroad song" also billed (on the sheet music cover) as "the greatest comedy hit in years." By 1911, it certainly was that with numerous hit recordings by popular stars Billy Murray, Collins and Harlan, the American Quartet, and Gene Greene. Sheet music sales, first for the composers' own Southern California Music Company and, shortly thereafter, New York's Shapiro, Bernstein and Company, Inc., were also very large. By November 1911, "Casey Jones" was part of a Broadway musical *The Wife Hunters*.

How two small-time vaudevillians, comedian T. Lawrence Siebert and ragtime pianist Eddie Newton, learned of the event of Jones's death and came to write the comedic song is puzzling. Siebert and Newton, who formed a professional partnership in Venice, California, far from the scene of the actual event, likely heard or read a folk ballad about Casey Jones. The May 1908 issue of *Railroad Man's Magazine* contained the text of a song purportedly written by a black railroad worker, most likely engine wiper Wallace Saunders, a friend of both Webb (who could have supplied the details) and Jones.

Folklorists, such as E. C. Perrow, collecting in Mississippi in 1909, had also found songs about Jones in circulation in black and white communities in the south. Most of the stanzas found in the Siebert–Newton composition are found in the oral and magazine sources, though the vaudevillians changed the railroads from eastern to western lines and set one stanza near Reno, Nevada.

However it happened, the popular recomposition of the Jones saga by Siebert and Newton lodged in America's mass culture and has been issued on commercial recordings over one hundred times during the ensuing nine decades. Country artists, blues singers, big band leaders, rockabilly, and rock 'n' roll musicians all found something of interest in the saga of "the brave engineer" who "took his farewell trip to the promised land." Indeed, the Grateful Dead, in the 1970s, recorded their recomposition portraying Casey as "driving that train high on cocaine." It is safe to say that without this song the name Casey Jones would be unknown today.

The Siebert–Newton song is available in many song folios currently in print. One of the many recorded versions is by Jo Stafford (Jazz Classics CD 6005). Recordings of the folk version of "Casey Jones" by Memphis' Furry Lewis (Fantasy CD 24703) and the Grateful Dead's Jerry Garcia (Acoustic Disc CD 21) are also in print.

2. "The Grizzly Bear"
Words by Irving Berlin and Music by George Botsford
Copyright © 1910, Ted Snyder Company, later owned by
Irving Berlin Music Company

As a new decade got underway in 1910, ragtime music moved out of the brothels and saloons, down from the vaudeville stage, and into America's dance parlors to fuel a mania for social dancing. Social dancing itself was not new, as evidenced by the waltzes, cotillions, and polkas of the nineteenth century, but the dance craze of the new century was different. America was increasingly urban, affluent, and young, and ready to have fun dancing to the syncopated rhythms of ragtime.

Thus the fad of animal dances arrived: the bunny hug, the crab, the kangaroo dip, the camel walk, the turkey trot, and the fox trot (which was actually named for performer Harry Fox). But first came the grizzly bear, which involved a swooping, swaying walk that ended with a tight bear hug. Like the ragtime songs to which they were danced, animal dances were not quite respectable, making them even more attractive to youths. Helping to propel the animal dance craze was the sensational team of Vernon and Irene Castle. Smooth, elegant, and extremely contemporary on stage, with Irene's clingy dresses and short hair, they inspired millions to learn the newest steps.

In 1910, George Botsford, a serious young composer from Iowa, wrote an instrumental rag and named it after the dance. He had already published the "Black and White Rag," which sold more than 1 million copies for the Remick Company, but for this new composition he turned to the Ted Snyder Company. Snyder realized that there was a market for instrumental rags, but there was a much larger market for rag songs (rags with lyrics), so he turned to his staff lyricist for some clever words. Israel Baline, who had recently renamed himself Irving Berlin, obliged with lines like "If they do this dance in heaven, shoot me hon, tonight at seven." Both versions were published, but the rag song far outsold the instrumental arrangement.

Introduced on stage by Fanny Brice in The Follies of 1910 (renamed the Ziegfeld Follies in 1911), the song became a trademark of the flamboyant Sophie Tucker. George Botsford enjoyed a successful career as a staff composer for Remick, but Irving Berlin went on to dominate American popular music in a career that spanned six decades. He wrote more than fifteen hundred songs in a wide variety of genres, including the notable "White Christmas" and "God Bless America."

The "Grizzly Bear" is still available in sheet music form (Hal Leonard 00005068) and in a few recorded versions, such as *The Whistler and His Dog* by the Paragon Ragtime Orchestra (Newport Classic CD 60069).

3. "When Irish Eyes Are Smiling"
Words by George Graff Jr. and Chauncey Olcott and Music by
Ernest R. Ball
Copyright © 1912 by M. Witmark and Sons

It is hard to name a song more representative of America's popular music industry in the "teens" than "When Irish Eyes Are Smiling." This still-familiar song, a St. Patrick's Day standard, was written by two of New York's most prolific professional songwriters in collaboration with a leading vaudeville performer, none of them Irish.

It was the most successful of dozens of sentimental tunes about Ireland that were performed during the decade, reflecting a new view of the Irish after nearly a century of rapid immigration. It was popularized on the vaudeville stage in the last vibrant decade of that soon-to-fade variety show format and was released by M. Witmark and Sons. Witmark anchored Tin Pan Alley, a cluster of music publishers that was adept (as one critic phrased it) at turning staff notes into banknotes. It was a top-ten hit in 1913, the first year that *Billboard* magazine charted the nation's best-selling music.

Composer Ernest R. Ball began his career as a piano player for vaudeville houses before becoming a staff composer for Witmark, where he collaborated with many lyricists including George Graff. It was probably through his vaudeville work that Ball met Chauncey Olcott, a famed "Irish tenor" who began his career as a comic singer in minstrel troupes. Olcott could claim Irish ties: his mother had been born in Ireland and he did eventually visit the old country so that he could polish his accent. He wrote the lyrics to many of his own stage songs, including the syrupy "Mother Machree" of 1910, his first collaboration with Ball.

The songwriters of Tin Pan Alley, in general, and Witmark, in particular, were known for songs that reflected common emotions of the day. One such emotion was a new sympathy for Irish immigrants. After the massive outflow of Ireland's poor had commenced with the potato famine of 1845–1850, successive waves of comic songs about "Paddy" depicted him as lazy, pugnacious, or drunk. But as the new century got underway, the Irish, through hard work and sheer numbers, became accepted into mainstream America.

In a decade marked by racial and ethnic strife, the Irish were pushed up the ladder by new waves of downtrodden from Poland, Italy, and Greece and it seemed the whole country longed for the Emerald Isle. Nostalgic ballads about shamrocks and colleens held the public's imagination until they were eclipsed by the harsh realities of World War I. At decade's end the American public, exhausted by war and epidemic, embraced another composition by Ernest Ball with its refrain "we'll build a sweet little nest, somewhere in the west, and let the rest of the world go by."

More than thirty recordings of this song are currently available, ranging from Bing Crosby to Frank Zappa. One recording that reflects the traditional arrangement is *The Irish Tenors* (John McDermott, Anthony Kearns, and Ronan Tynan) (Mastertone CD 8552). It is also still available in sheet music form: Hal Leonard Item No. 315245 is a piano/vocal arrangement.

4. "The Band Played 'Nearer My God To Thee' As the Ship Went Down"
Words by Mark Beam and Music by Harold Jones
Copyright © 1912, Joe Morris Music Company

In the late night/early morning of April 14–15, 1912, the British luxury liner *Titanic* struck an iceberg in the North Atlantic and sank. More that fifteen hundred people perished. Considered the worst maritime disaster to date, the event spawned musical compositions within days.

The first were probably broadsides, cheaply and quickly printed single sheets with lyrics only. One such song, "The Loss of the Steamship Titanic," was composed by John Friend of Bangor, Maine. In its ten stanzas, it gives a detailed, almost newspaper-like, account of the embarkation from Southampton, England, the collision with the iceberg, the rescue by the *Carpathia*, and the fate of the well-known passengers John Astor, C. M. Hayes, Isidor Straus, Major Butt, and the *Titanic*'s Captain Smith. Of particular interest is the stanza that portrays the passengers singing the hymn "Nearer My God to Thee."

It was not long before the commercial music industry followed with sheet music on the same theme. All of Tin Pan Alley's contributions to the lore of the disaster focused on the brave musicians who continued to play as the ship sank. Although the most reliable eyewitness, telegrapher Harold Bride, told the *New York Times* that the band played ragtime tunes and ended with the Episcopal hymn "Autumn," songwriters like Beam and Jones felt the better-known hymn more appropriate.

Another composition of 1912, "The Wreck of the Titanic, a Descriptive Composition for Piano Solo" by William Baltzell, quotes the eight measures of the chorus of "Nearer My God to Thee" in the instrumental section: "The band, knee deep in water, play their last prayer." Likewise, the last four measures of the Beam and Jones song quote, lyrically and musically, the hymn.

While the commercial music interests exploited the bravery of the crew and first-class passengers, songs were being composed by unknowns, which have survived better than their Tin Pan Alley cousins. These folk songs explore the themes of human arrogance (that man could build a ship God could not sink) and class privilege (steerage passengers not allowed in the lifeboats). One song even has a stanza about black heavyweight boxing champion Jack Johnson being refused passage from England because "this boat don't haul no coal."

Folk songs, with titles including "God Moves on the Water," "Wasn't it Sad When the Great Ship Went Down," and "The Titanic (Cold and Icy Sea)," were collected in both African American and white rural communities, proving the impact the disaster had on the public psyche.

In 1997, James Cameron's film *Titanic* again captured America's attention with its story of star-crossed lovers on the doomed ship. The music associated with this version of the *Titanic* story is, however, quite different from songs spawned by the original event.

While none of Tin Pan Alley's *Titanic* songs have survived in print or on record, more than a dozen of the folk songs are currently available on sound recordings. One is by Huddie Ledbetter, better known as Leadbelly, in the Smithsonian/Folkways box set *Leadbelly's Last Sessions* (FLW 40068).

5. "Jelly Roll Blues"
Words and Music by Jelly Roll Morton
Arranged in 1912; Published by Will Rossiter and copyright © registered in 1915; copyright transferred to Melrose Music Corporation, 1915; thought to have been composed circa 1905

This song is probably universally known to serious students of jazz because it is thought to be the first published jazz composition. It should be noted, however, that it is difficult to know for sure when many jazz works were first created and performed versus when they were first documented (Raeburn 2001). It is even possible that other musicians could have contributed to this and other jazz compositions, because musicians of this period often heard songs of other songwriters and improvised on them. As a song evolved through this improvisatory process, the performers often took credit for the song as well as their particular version.

Jelly Roll Morton, whose real name was Ferdinand Lamothe (but often incorrectly cited as Ferdinand Le Menthe), was somewhat representative of jazz musicians who were among the caste of char-

acters in New Orleans during this decade, a period when this genre
of music was blossoming into a commercial force. Ferd, as his friends
called him, was an extremely gifted musician who developed his skills
in the brothels and barrooms of New Orleans. His lyrics often described pimps, prostitutes, hustlers, and tough guys whom he had
known in real life. The music of Jelly Roll Morton evolved alongside
the culture of jazz.

In 1898, a conservative New Orleans alderman, with the last
name Story, drafted an ordinance establishing a district in which
prostitution would not be aggressively policed. The ordinance did
not openly state that prostitution would be legal inside the bound-
aries of the established area, but it vehemently proclaimed that
absolutely no "lewd women" would be permitted outside its bound-
aries. This area, which New Orleans residents called "Storyville," became a haven for adult entertainment including dancing, alcohol
consumption, and, most important, jazz music.

Although jazz (originally called "jass") was not created in
Storyville, the district provided an atmosphere in which this new
form of music could thrive. It should be noted that some jazz historians have incorrectly stated that Storyville was in the French
Quarter area of New Orleans. The Storyville district was northwest
of Rampart Street and, therefore, outside the French Quarter. It
was in this unusual social environment, created by the New Orleans city council, that Jelly Roll Morton's career as a songwriter
and performer began.

Most brothels in Storyville provided drinks and music for their
clientele. Although still a teenager, Jelly Roll reluctantly accepted a
job playing in a popular brothel. Piano players were referred to as
"professor," to distinguish their music from that of coin-operated mechanical player pianos, and most good performers earned a lucrative
income. Jelly Roll soon became known as one of the district's most
talented professors. Although the environment he worked in might
not have been very wholesome, it provided him an opportunity to
experiment with, and improvise on, his music.

Songwriters and composers of music that flourished prior to
jazz—classical, popular, and Broadway musicals—used standard
music notation to capture the intended melody and harmony. Jazz
musicians in Storyville often began with a melody and harmonic

progression that they had heard or learned from sheet music, but, as they played the same song numerous times, they began to take liberties with the melody and harmony. Their loose and spontaneous interpretations, called "improvisation," became the cornerstone of jazz.

Although performers in media such as vaudeville, Broadway, symphonic music, and recordings were not allowed to stray from the composed music, those working in Storyville were. After all, the "audience" of a brothel was less concerned about formalities than any other group in the nation. As pianists, or professors, developed reputations in Storyville, their style of improvisation gradually differentiated them from other performers. Hence, Storyville became the incubator for this new form of music.

World War I was, interestingly, the catalyst for Storyville's demise. Officials of the United States Navy had become concerned that sailors from a naval base in New Orleans were frequenting the brothels of the district too often. More important, they believed that these visits to brothels were a health risk for military personnel. Therefore, on November 12, 1917, eight months after the United States entered World War I, the U.S. Department of Navy ordered the city of New Orleans to close Storyville.

Many jazz musicians from New Orleans migrated to northern cities like Chicago, St. Louis, and New York where jazz was extremely popular in the second decade of the twentieth century. Morton told friends that during his journey northward he had encountered the lynching of an African American man in Biloxi, Mississippi, and another in Greenwood, Mississippi. He, and other African American musicians, felt as though New Orleans and Chicago were cities that respected African American jazz musicians, but all cities in between were not.

Morton moved to Chicago and quickly discovered that the Windy City audiences loved his style of music. As a matter of fact, "Jelly Roll Blues" was so popular in Chicago that Morton considered changing the title to "Chicago Blues." He did not, however, and, instead, recruited the assistance of friends and an arranger to notate and publish this important work. Jelly Roll Morton, like many jazz musicians of this decade, was not a trained musician and could not easily put his compositions in the form of traditional music notation.

The exact date of when he composed his songs is sometimes difficult to establish because his music often resided in his memory for many years before being notated or recorded.

Sheet music for "Jelly Roll Blues," arranged by James Dapogny and published by G. Schirmer Publishing, is currently available in folio collections. A noteworthy recording of this song is included on the Library of Congress recordings (music and interviews) created by Alan Lomax with the assistance of Morton himself.

6. "Memphis Blues"
Words and Music by W. C. Handy
Copyright © 1913, Theron C. Bennett
Copyright transferred to Joe Morris Music Company, 1916

William Christopher "W. C." Handy is a wonderful example of how poor African Americans could rise to a higher socioeconomic strata than their parents through education, hard work, and musical talent. Handy was born in Florence, Alabama, the son of impoverished parents. He attended the Teachers Agricultural and Mechanical College in nearby Huntsville where he learned to be a public school teacher.

While in college, Handy studied cornet and music theory. After graduating from college, he taught for a short time, but quickly quit to pursue music, his real love. He began touring with dance bands that traveled in the Mississippi Delta region. It was in rural areas of this region that he heard and transcribed many vocal blues songs. This blues style, with its characteristic lowered third scale tone, influenced Handy's music for the remainder of his career.

Handy moved to Memphis, an urban city in the Mississippi Delta, in 1909. He quickly found that his music was well received by people from his new hometown. His music became so popular and recognizable that E. H. Crump, a candidate for mayor in 1912, commissioned him to write a campaign song. Handy's song "Mr. Crump" incorporated the dance sounds of ragtime with the new, unique Delta blues. The result was a success: Crump won the election and Handy won the title "Father of the Blues."

Handy retitled his song "Memphis Blues" and issued printed copies for sale in a department store in Memphis. It sold out of the first thousand copies in three days. Unfortunately for Handy, a dishonest businessman told Handy that his song was a flop and offered to purchase the copyright for $50. Handy agreed, and thus began a long legal battle over the ownership of copyright and publishing rights.

"Memphis Blues" was the first blues song to be recorded. Although Handy did not record "Memphis Blues" until 1923, it was recorded in 1914 by Prince's Orchestra for Columbia Records. Since that time, this song has been recorded many times by artists representing a wide range of styles. It has also been arranged for virtually every conceivable combination from voice and ukulele to marching band. It, like "St. Louis Blues," another Handy song, continues to be performed and recorded after eighty years.

The influence blues has had on modern music cannot be overstated. Handy brought a musical personality, as well as a distinctive sound, to the music of mainstream America. Genres that evolved from this early form of blues include rhythm and blues, rock 'n' roll, and country. So important was his contribution to American music, the highest awards for this genre of music are named the W. C. Handy Blues Awards and are presented annually by the Blues Foundation in Memphis.

Sheet music for this song is available in *Songs of the 1910s* by Hal Leonard (HL 00311657).

7. "Brighten the Corner Where You Are"
Words by Ina Duley Ogdon and Music by Charles H. Gabriel
Copyright © 1913, Charles H. Gabriel, owned by Homer Rodeheaver

Imagine an echoing, wood-floored, hastily constructed tabernacle sheltering more than twenty thousand worshipers who have come to hear the emotional outpourings of a revival preacher. A choir of two thousand members stands on stage as a genial chorister steps forward to lead the massive congregation in song, warming them up for what is to come. He lifts a trombone to sound a note before skillfully guiding those many voices in the singing of "Brighten the Corner Where You Are," and the rafters ring with that simple but hopeful gospel song.

The preacher was Billy Sunday, the most vivid and successful of more than 650 revival preachers who worked small towns and big cities in the years leading to World War I, and the song leader was

Homer Rodeheaver. The gospel song was the theme song of the Billy Sunday revivals.

Unlike traditional hymns, gospel songs were not intended to be part of a weekly church service, but to be shared through an uplifting, communal singing experience. Rodeheaver believed that the masses who came to revivals needed simple, easily sung music to sing praises to God. However, many of the songs did find their way into hymnals of various Protestant denominations over time, but they were most often published by independent publishing houses. Rodeheaver owned his own publishing company and printed his small, soft-covered books in great quantities for distribution at revivals and singing schools. It is estimated that Billy Sunday alone preached to more than 300 million people during his career, while Rodeheaver once led a single gathering of 250,000 people in song.

Rodeheaver recalled that Ina Duley Ogdon, the woman who wrote the words to "Brighten the Corner Where You Are," had strong ambitions to become a writer but found herself restricted by responsibilities for a young child and invalid father. She overcame her despair when she "set herself resolutely to do all that she possibly could in the little corner of the world, where, it seemed, God chose to keep her." Inspired by a new Christian mission, she wrote out a song to send her message "singing itself around the globe" (1917, 4). Her words were set to the music of Charles H. Gabriel, who served for twenty years as a staff composer for the Rodeheaver Company and produced more than eight thousand works.

"Brighten the Corner Where You Are" is still widely available in various choral arrangements. It is also found in nearly forty recorded versions, including on *Voices of Praise* by The Cathedrals (River Song CD 08303).

8. "Solidarity Forever"
Words by Ralph Chaplin (1915) (sung to tune of "John Brown's Body")
Published by International Workers of the World, 1916

In January 1915, a fervent young labor activist, recalling violent coal strikes in the Kanawha Valley of West Virginia, scribbled out a song that would become the anthem of the labor movement in America for decades to come. Ralph Chaplin was a "Wobbly," a member of the Industrial Workers of the World (IWW).

The IWW had formed in 1905 as a socialist union opposed to the American Federation of Labor (AFL) and dedicated to creating an industrial democracy under "One Big Union." Early in the twentieth century, the AFL and its member unions were gaining strength as negotiators for workers on issues of wages and working conditions. The IWW and other radical unions believed that the capitalist system itself should be overturned and that the workers should have ownership of factories and businesses.

The memory of clashes between workers and mine bosses stayed with Chaplin after he relocated to IWW headquarters in Chicago to serve as editor, artist, poet, songwriter, and propagandist. One Sunday he felt compelled to finish the lyrics to a song he had begun in West Virginia, using as its base the tune to "John Brown's Body." No doubt the memorable melody of that song, coupled with its reference to an earlier radical, made it an attractive starting point. Chaplin composed many other songs for the IWW, but it was "Solidarity Forever" that would become a staple of union gatherings everywhere.

Chaplin and other songwriters for the IWW, including the ill-fated Joe Hill, frequently penned new lyrics to the melodies of well-known songs so that union members could easily learn the songs. The melody of "John Brown's Body" had become almost universally known in America in the nineteenth century because it was used for three distinct songs, each of which gained wide popularity. In the mid-1850s the melody carried a hymn, "Say, Brother Will You Meet Us," that was frequently sung at religious camp meetings. In 1859, abolitionist John Brown raided Harper's Ferry, West Virginia, and was subsequently hanged, which inspired the grim parody early in 1861, followed within months by Julia Ward Howe's "Battle Hymn of the Republic," the anthem of the Union forces in the Civil War.

In his autobiography, Chaplin recalled, "I wanted a song to be full of revolutionary fervor and to have a chorus that was singing and defiant" (1972, 167). Solidarity was both the rallying cry of the IWW and the name of its radical newspaper. For Chaplin, the catchy repetitive melody allowed reiteration of his message:

Solidarity forever.
Solidarity forever.
Solidarity forever.
For the union makes us strong.

The song appeared in the ninth edition (1916) of the IWW's little red songbook *Songs of the Workers*. It was included in all subsequent editions of the songbook and, ironically, in the song collection of the AFL–CIO decades later. The IWW was largely destroyed by the federal government in 1917 because of its antiwar stance, and never regained its strength, but its songs have lived on.

Solidarity Forever can be heard on Pete Seeger's collection *Carry It On: Songs of American Working People* (Flying Fish CD 0104).

9. "On the Beach at Waikiki"
Words by G. H. Stover and Music by Henry Kailimai
Copyright © 1915, Sherman, Clay and Company;
1943, Miller Music Company

On February 20, 1915, the Panama-Pacific Exposition opened in San Francisco for a seven-month run. This world's fair, which attracted over 17 million visitors, celebrated the opening of the Panama Canal and promotion of the Territory of Hawaii.

The main attraction at the Hawaii Pavilion was the troupe of musicians and hula dancers that performed several times a day. Millions received their first exposure to Hawaiian music at the exposition. This triggered a craze for Hawaiian music that lasted well into the 1930s.

"On the Beach at Waikiki" was the hit of the fair as played by the Royal Hawaiian Quartette, a group of two ukuleles, Spanish guitar, and steel guitar. The song itself was *hapa haole* (half white), a Hawaiian term for music with a mostly English lyric, and harmonic and rhythmic traits that reflect mainland popular trends. The music of "On the Beach at Waikiki" has a distinct ragtime feel and the "kiss-me-quickly" lyric is appealing in its stereotype of the Hawaiian maid.

The instrumentation, especially the steel guitar (*kika kila*), reflected the authentic Hawaiian culture. Noting the guitar strings with a metal bar produced a sliding singing-like glissando accompaniment and was so appealing to mainstream musicians that Hawaiian guitar method books were published yearly, beginning in 1916, by firms in San Francisco, Chicago, and New York, indicating national interest in the style.

The Hawaiian steel guitar technique was adopted by rural whites and would show up in following decades on the records of Jimmie Rodgers and Roy Acuff, as well as many others. In the 1930s, the steel guitar was electrified for use in western swing bands, and this evolved, by the 1950s, into the modern pedal steel guitar as heard in today's country music. African American musicians, especially blues guitarists from Mississippi and Georgia, used a related "bottleneck" technique, but for a quite different effect. This musical pathway evolved, after electrification, into the Chicago blues style of Muddy Waters and others.

Sheet music sales of "On the Beach at Waikiki" were so strong (Kailimai, in a 1918 lawsuit for back royalties, claimed sales of nearly 150,000 copies) that Tin Pan Alley produced dozens of imitation Hawaiian songs in 1916. In the same year, 146 Hawaiian records were listed in just one company's catalog. "On the Beach at Waikiki" maintained popularity through 1940 when it was used in the Shirley Temple film *The Young People*.

Hawaiian music suffered a decline in popularity after World War II and, except for the occasional Don Ho or Alfred Alpaca hit record, is not an influence on popular music today. There is no question, however, that in the period 1915–1919 there was more Hawaiian music sold on the mainland than any other popular genre.

Sheet music for this song is available in *Complete Hawaiian Music Collection* by Warner Brothers (MF 9923).

10. "Swing Low, Sweet Chariot"
Lyricist and composer unknown
In the public domain; vocal arrangement, John W. Work II, 1915

On October 6, 1871, eleven students from Nashville's Fisk University headed north to Cincinnati raising funds for their ailing institution through a series of vocal performances. Their music director, George White, expected his little troupe to be gone a few weeks at most. When they returned the following May with $20,000, they were hailed not only as financial saviors of Fisk, but as musical ambassadors of the Negro race.

Named the Fisk Jubilee Singers during this first tour, the group of six women and five men originally gave programs of classical and popular music as a demonstration of Fisk's mission: to prove the freedmen's (that is, former slaves) ability to benefit from the same educational opportunities enjoyed by whites. But it was when the singers included the "sorrow songs," or spirituals, from slavery that audience enthusiasm peaked. The Fisk group gained such a strong reputation that tours of Europe followed and the ensemble eventually raised over $75,000 for the fledgling school. Jubilee Hall, which still stands on the Nashville campus, was built with this money.

Fund-raising by the southern black colleges founded after the Civil War—Hampton, Howard, Talladaga, Spelman, Morehouse, Tuskegee, Southern, and others—followed the Fisk example: music performance using traditional African American spiritual repertoire presented in the trained-voice, European style. Concerts by such groups were popular with white audiences by the second decade of the twentieth century. These schools had no sports teams or wealthy alumni on which to rely for funding. They did, however, have a form of musical expression that found favor with mainstream America.

Among the slave spirituals, "Swing Low, Sweet Chariot" enjoys a special place in American culture. Since its first print appearance in G. D. Pike's *The Jubilee Singers, and Their Campaign for Twenty Thousand Dollars* (1873), this song of hope (with a subtext of escape from slavery) has become a standard in Protestant denominational hymnals, social songbooks, and choral repertoire. This popularity is due, in large part, to its graceful melody and lyric sentiment common to all people.

The song entered into white America's homes with the recording by the Fisk University Male Quartette in 1915. The original Jubilee Singers had become a quartet for economic reasons at the turn of the century and were not strictly students. The musical director and first tenor, John Wesley Work II, was a professor of Latin and history. The Fisk quartet recorded the song three times during the decade for the Victor, Edison, and Columbia recording companies, but the Columbia issue of 1915 was the most popular. Another interesting recording of "Swing Low, Sweet Chariot" (for the French company, Pathé) is from 1919 by Lt. Jim Europe's Four Harmony Kings, an African American vocal group extracted from James Reese Europe's 369th Infantry Band, which was noted for its musicianship in World War I.

Over the years, "Swing Low, Sweet Chariot" has been recorded hundreds of times in every imaginable style. Currently, over sixty versions are available by pop vocalists, big bands, modern jazz artists, chorales and bluegrass bands. Blues and rock artist Eric Clapton has an innovative version on *Timepieces, Vol. 1* (Polydor CD 800 014). Print versions of "Swing Low, Sweet Chariot" number well over one hundred arrangements for voices or instruments.

11. "I Didn't Raise My Boy to Be a Soldier"
Words by Alfred Bryan and Music by Al Piantadosi
Published by Leo Feist, Inc., 1915

This song was, in all likelihood, the first antiwar song to became a tremendous success in the marketplace. It was created to capture the sentiments of many mothers who feared that their sons would soon be drafted for service in World War I. The dedication on the original sheet music was unequivocal: "Respectfully Dedicated to Every Mother—Everywhere." Bryan and Piantadosi were not just protesting America's entry into World War I, they were opposed to any son going to war. The subtitle of the song was "A Mother's Plea for Peace."

An antiwar movement, led by anti-interventionists, developed after Europe erupted in war. This group, often called "isolationists," quickly adopted "I Didn't Raise My Son to Be a Soldier" as their anthem. The anti-interventionists were not alone—the ballad was considered the top song in the nation for eight weeks and continued to be popular for twenty-six weeks.

Not everyone admired this song or the message behind it. One song was written specifically as an answer to it: "My Mother Raised Her Boy to Be a Soldier," written in 1915 by Jack Crawford. The goal of "I Didn't Raise My Boy to Be a Soldier," to prevent our government from entering the war in Europe, was controversial. But, obviously, it was not successful.

On May 7, 1915, a German U-boat torpedoed and sank the *Lusitania,* a luxury liner. This event began the rapid disintegration of German–U.S. relations and on April 16, 1917, the United States entered World War I. U.S. armed forces had grown from a pre–World War I total of 370,000 to 4.8 million by the end of the war. Over 130,000 U.S. soldiers did not return from this war on foreign soil. Many mothers asked, "What victory can cheer a mother's heart when she looks at her blighted home," the same question that Bryan and Piantadosi posed in their song.

Although the sheet music for this song is not sold in music stores, copies can often be found in music research centers (see Bibliography). New verses have been added to the lyrics of this song as it continues to be passed from singer to singer in the folk tradition.

12. "Over There"
Words and Music by George M. Cohan
Copyright © 1917; currently in the public domain

World War I was not the first time the United States sent troops to fight in foreign lands. American soldiers fought battles in Cuba, Nicaragua, Mexico, Haiti, and Santo Domingo during this same decade. Those wars were not, however, waged against the large European nations that had already entered World War I, the "war to end all wars." More important, those smaller and shorter wars did not require extremely large numbers of GIs to leave home for an extended war overseas.

After entering the war on April 16, 1917, our nation's cultural climate quickly shifted from one of a peacetime nation to one of an emerging world power at war. Patriotism flourished as most Americans accepted their new role of policing the world for democracy. In this national climate, George M. Cohan, a songwriter who had already established himself as a "flag-waving" patriot, wrote "Over There" as a tribute to the American soldier going to war.

George M. Cohan's earliest ode to American nationalistic pride, "The Yankee Doodle Boy," written in 1904, began his love affair with patriotic songs. He continued to be attracted to this type of nationalistic music for almost forty years. Another song in this genre was "You're a Grand Old Flag," a staple in the Fourth of July repertoire. The last song he wrote, "We Must Be Ready," a warning about military preparedness, was an eerie prophecy written six months before the attack on Pearl Harbor.

"Over There" is a short song (two verses with a chorus/refrain) that captured the sentiments of most Americans at the beginning of the war. The first verse tells young "Johnnie," like every son of liberty, to get his gun and hurry away. Cohan instructs Johnnie to tell his father to be happy for his son and his sweetheart not to pine, but to be proud of him. In reality, many fathers, mothers, and wives watched sons and husbands leave home with the real fear that they would never return home. These emotions were something new to most Americans because we had never fought a war of this magnitude in another land.

The type of warfare our soldiers experienced was something they were not prepared for. The use of poison gases and relatively sophisticated tanks caused many of our "boys" to suffer and die in the trenches of France. Yet, at the same time, the economy at home was stimulated by the demand for wartime products and services. The shortage of labor forced wages up and life was quite good at home. Because the United States entered the war later than most other world powers, its duration seemed shorter. At 11 P.M. on November 11, 1918—the eleventh hour of the eleventh day of the eleventh month—Germany ceased fighting. Although the war for which Cohan originally wrote this song had ended, it would, regrettably, be sung many more times for different wars.

Cohan's song not only won the hearts of the public during World War I, it has remained a staple of wartime patriotism ever since it was first recorded. Cohan won a belated Congressional Medal of Honor in 1941 for "Over There."

This song is available in *The Greatest American Songbook* by Hal Leonard (HL 00243009).

13. "Darktown Strutters' Ball"
Words and Music by Shelton Brooks
Copyright © 1917, Will Rossiter

"Darktown Strutters' Ball" became a popular dance song as jazz began to influence the music of the decade. As a danceable piece of music, the work was instantly popular with ballroom dancers from all social strata. But, like other excellent songs written by African American songwriters, this song was first recorded by an all-white band, The Original Dixieland Jass Band (later Jass was changed to Jazz).

Shelton Brooks was somewhat representative of commercial songwriters of the second decade of the twentieth century. He learned his craft as a ragtime pianist performing in clubs and theaters and on the vaudeville touring circuits. Those experiences put him in contact with a wide range of genre and allowed him to hear other successful performers of his day.

His first big break as a songwriter came in 1910 when he met vaudeville star Sophie Tucker. Tucker fell in love with Brooks's song "Some of These Days," and it became her signature song and a tremendously successful recording for both of them.

As ragtime, blues, and jazz styles moved northward from New Orleans and other southern cities, New York and Chicago competed for the title of the best place to hear music. In 1915, Shelton Brooks became leader of a "syncopated band" in Chicago. Brooks's song captured the mood of dance clubs that, although quite respectable, were known for whiskey and parties that lasted through the night. His earlier song, "All Night Long," obviously described this type of atmosphere. "Darktown Strutters' Ball" also chronicled the world in which Brooks performed.

The ball that Brooks memorialized in his song was an annual event in Chicago during the second decade of the twentieth century. It was a formal dance and party for prostitutes, their "managers," and the best musicians that the event's producers could hire. According to descendants of Brooks, city police would not bother anyone during the event as long as there was no trouble.

The song begins with the good news that the singer received an invitation to the Darktown Ball. Brooks's lyrics refer to "high browns" and "high-toned neighbors," in reference to light-skinned African Americans. This reference might be a legacy of the inner-racial dissonance between well-educated "free blacks"—light-skinned, well-educated émigrés from Europe—and slaves freed after the Emancipation Proclamation. It should be noted that Brooks was born in Canada of Native American and African American parents and he grew up in Detroit.

It is noteworthy that "Darktown Strutters' Ball" was one of the first two songs recorded by The Original Dixieland Jass Band. Sheet music for this song sold over 3 million copies. Many versions of the song have been recorded since the first recording by The Original Dixieland Jass Band. The song is available on *Hallelujah: Ella Fitzgerald* (Camden Records 7256128). Sheet music is widely available, most often for piano and voice.

14. "Livery Stable Blues"
Words by Marvin Lee and Music by Dominick "Nick" James LaRocca
Published by Roger Graham, 1917

The "Livery Stable Blues" holds two distinctions: it is the first jazz recording known to be commercially distributed, and it holds the dubious honor of having more controversy over its true composer than any other jazz composition. Although there was a great deal of controversy and litigation surrounding this song, its impact on the musical heritage of America is beyond question. According to Bruce Boyd Raeburn, curator of the Hogan Jazz Archive at Tulane University, "It created the model for other [jazz] musicians to follow" (2001). It also helped initiate a jazz craze that lasted for decades.

Nick LaRocca began his jazz career by performing on cornet in New Orleans. His climb to celebrity status began when he joined the Reliance Band, an ensemble led by drummer Johnny Stein. In May 1916, LaRocca and three other members of the Reliance Band quit to form a new band. They called their new ensemble The Original Dixieland Jass Band (ODJB).

Dixieland, a term that had gradually become a moniker for the South, revealed LaRocca's continued ties to New Orleans, even though he relocated to Chicago and later to New York. The Citizens' State Bank building was on the corner of Iberville Street and Royal Street in the French Quarter of New Orleans from 1835 until 1924. For a short time, the bank issued its own ten-dollar banknotes. Each banknote had the word *Dix,* French for ten, printed on its face. New Orleans was soon referred to as the "Land of Dix." Soon it evolved into "Land of Dixie" and eventually "Dixieland," a term that is now synonymous with the South and early New Orleans jazz.

In addition to using Dixieland in reference to a genre of music, the ODJB helped bring the term *jazz* into the public consciousness.

The New Orleans style of music that LaRocca recorded for the first time was referred to as "Jas," "Jass," and "Jaz" before musicians and record labels settled on jazz.

The ODJB first recorded a song called "Barnyard Blues" for Columbia Records as an audition recording. Columbia did not release it, and a month later the band recorded the same song for Victor Talking Machine Company. As a result of confusion over the correct title (an older working title for the song was "Livery Stable Blues"), the correct song title, "Barnyard Blues," was not used on the recording. Victor gave it the title "Livery Stable Blues" instead. As a result, LaRocca had registered the copyright for the sheet music under the name "Barnyard Blues" yet the recording was released as "Livery Stable Blues."

If the confusion over the correct song title were not confusing enough, former ODJB members Alcide "Yellow" Nunez and Ray Lopez registered the copyright for the same song with lyrics written by Marvin Lee under the title "Livery Stable Blues." The disagreement over who owned the copyright to this song was decided in Federal District Court in Chicago and the judge's decision shocked both LaRocca and Nunez. Judge George A. Carpenter decided, after hearing an expert witness speculate that the melody was actually an old "Negro Melody," that "neither the plaintiff nor the defendant is entitled to copyright" (Abbott and Seroff, 2001, p. 13).

Sheet music for "Barnyard Blues" was published by Leo Feist, Inc. Sheet music for "Livery Stable Blues," with lyrics by Marvin Lee, was published by Roger Graham. The original recording by the ODJB was released by Victor (Vic 18255, Bm 1110). Due to the historical significance of this song and its first recording, archival copies of the record and the sheet music are generally available through music research centers (see Bibliography).

15. "It's Nobody's Business but My Own"
Words and Music by Will E. Skidmore and Marshall Walker
Copyright © 1919, Skidmore Music Company; 1932, Marks
Music Corporation

In 1919, producer Florenz Ziegfeld was at the peak of his Broadway career. Having successfully staged his *Follies* in New York each year of the decade, he opened the new show at the New Amsterdam Theater on June 16 to standing-room-only crowds. Audiences craved Zeigfeld's mix of comedy, songs (many by Irving Berlin), and beautiful chorus girls in elaborate costumes. World War I had ended in November and postwar entertainment was a thriving business.

The stars of the *Ziegfeld Follies of 1919* were Eddie Cantor, Marilyn Miller, and Bert Williams. Williams, a mulatto born in the Bahamas and raised in California, performed a "black-face" duet with Cantor, who was white, Jewish, and from New York. Both had to learn the "darky" dialect used in the act. In addition to the theatrical show, Ziegfield presented a *Midnight Frolic* on the roof garden, where food and drink were served to patrons while *Follies'* cast members, augmented by "special performances" by W. C. Fields, Fanny Brice, and Chic Sale, entertained in a more intimate setting.

Williams had made a name for himself performing in vaudeville with a partner, George Walker. One of Williams's vaudeville monologs, "Nobody," was so popular that he recorded it twice for the Columbia Company in 1906 and again in 1910 when Williams began his association with Ziegfeld's shows. Williams and Walker were the only African American entertainers booked with white acts on the Keith Vaudeville circuit. Williams became the first African American to play on Broadway in an otherwise all-white cast in 1910. Many times white cast members, showing the prejudice of the era, refused to perform in scenes with Williams, causing Williams to use solo bits of his old vaudeville repertoire. Williams refused to tour the South during his career, which ended in 1922 when he collapsed while on tour in Detroit.

"It's Nobody's Business but My Own" is the refrain of the black "hard-shell" Baptist preacher portrayed by Williams and given in reply to the deacons who questioned him about his activities with the "sisters" after the church service. "It's Nobody's Business but My Own" was number 6 in the "Deacon series" of songs written by white Arkansian Will Skidmore. A piano player and songwriter, Skidmore started his publishing activity in Kansas City, Missouri, and, in 1918, made a successful move to New York after his "Deacon" and "coon" songs were successful with entertainers like Sophie Tucker, Patricola, and Neil O'Brien's Minstrels. It is ironic that Williams, who felt so strongly about racial equality, gained his enormous popularity by portraying racial and social stereotypes.

"It's Nobody's Business but My Own" is not in print in sheet music, but a CD reissue of Williams's performance from the original Columbia 78 rpm sound recording can be found on the Document label: *Bert Williams, the Remaining Titles, 1915–1921* (DOCD 5661).

1920–1929

Gin, Jazz, and Women's Rights

The decade of the 1920s was one of prosperity until the stock market crash of 1929. It was also a period of tremendous social change brought on by women winning the right to vote and a failed social experiment called "Prohibition." Ironically, the federal government held firmly to a policy of maintaining the status quo throughout this period in which the social fabric of the country changed dramatically.

After many years of working toward equal rights, the Nineteenth Amendment was ratified in 1920, giving women the right to vote. This new sense of power and liberation gave rise to a sexual revolution and a fashion revolution for women. Many women who had left their homes to work in factories during World War I challenged social stereotypes in the 1920s. Young women began to attend college in larger numbers, opening up opportunities they did not previously have. Women, both those who attended college and those who did not, began to experience premarital sex in greater numbers than previous generations.

Women began to see new images of themselves portrayed in Hollywood films, Broadway revues, and advertising. The flapper look, with higher hemlines, fueled a youthful rebelliousness. Women began to smoke cigarettes in public, just like their male counterparts. However, male-dominated state legislatures continued their attempts to regulate morals: sale of condoms or diaphragms for birth control was illegal in most states. In 1914, Margaret Sanger was indicted for distributing literature about contraception through the mail. The materials she distributed were determined to be obscene and a potential threat to the family unit.

As if to balance the gains liberals won on the suffrage front, conservatives lobbied for and won their battle to ban alcohol. In 1919, the Eighteenth Amendment, known as "Prohibition," was adopted and the sale of alcohol in the United States became illegal beginning January 16, 1920. The proponents of Prohibition believed that consumption of alcohol was responsible for the deterioration of the moral structure in the United States. Furthermore, they felt that drinking was destroying too many families. Although the goals of Prohibition may have been laudatory, the Eighteenth Amendment created many more social problems than it fixed.

Organized crime flourished during Prohibition, because gangsters quickly seized the opportunity to earn huge profits by smuggling whiskey from Canada and illegal distilleries. Clubs that sold alcohol illegally were referred to as "speakeasies." Owners of the clubs often paid police to look the other way while their clientele consumed smuggled whiskey or a homemade brew called "bathtub gin." It was during Prohibition that major crime families became entrenched in the economies and politics of major cities such as New York and Chicago. Ironically, there were twice as many speakeasies in New York during Prohibition as there were legal bars before Prohibition. Although Prohibition became increasingly difficult to enforce, it remained the law of the land until it was repealed in 1933.

An enormous wave of immigrants flooded the United States after World War I. Immigration increased from 110,000 in 1919 to 430,000 in 1920. By 1921, the number had increased to 805,000. Fears that the number of immigrants would continue to increase and strain the U.S. economy led the federal government to enact the Emergency Quota Act in 1921 to limit immigration. Another reaction was a resurgence of the Ku Klux Klan, and African Americans were not the only targets of the Klan. Jews, Catholics, union organizers (often branded "socialists"), and Latinos were also enemies of the "new Klan" during the 1920s.

New technologies affected entertainment and communication during this decade. On November 2, 1920, KDKA in Pittsburgh was the first radio station to make a commercial broadcast. Radios quickly became a new center of entertainment in the American home, replacing parlor singing and the player piano as forms of entertainment. By 1929, more than 12 million American families had radios.

In 1927, the first talking movie, *The Jazz Singer*, was released. It was not coincidental that the film's producers chose music, an important part of life in the 1920s, as the theme of this seminal work. The first animated cartoon, *Steamboat Willie*, was released by Walt Disney, offering Mickey Mouse, Hollywood's longest living star, his debut. The first demonstration of a television broadcast also took place in 1927.

The robust economy of the 1920s encouraged many people to invest in the stock market. Many of them bought stock on margins, meaning they only paid a portion of the stock value at the time of purchase. In October 1929, the stock market declined dramatically. Some stockholders panicked because they had taken out bank loans to buy their stock. When they sold their worthless stock and could not repay their bank loans, most lost their homes and any savings they might have had. The domino effect had begun: banks closed, farmers could not sell their crops, and retailers had no customers. Thus, the Great Depression began and the exciting decade of prosperity ended.

SONGS

1. "Crazy Blues"
Words and Music by Perry Bradford
Copyright © 1920, MCA, Inc.

John Henry Perry Bradford was born in Montgomery, Alabama, in 1895. He grew up in Atlanta where he attended a private elementary school and, because there was no higher public education available to African Americans, three years of secondary school at Atlanta University.

Bradford's mother cooked meals for prisoners of the Fulton Street jail, and Bradford heard the inmates singing as he accompanied his mother at her job. Bradford taught himself piano, and by 1907 was touring with the New Orleans Minstrels as a pianist.

Fred Hager, an Anglo American born in rural Pennsylvania, was twenty-one years Bradford's senior. A trained violinist, Hager made the first commercial recording on that instrument. He was the musical conductor on the first disc record made by Columbia Phonograph Company. In 1898, Hager made a series of solo violin cylinders for Edison. By the time Hager and Bradford crossed paths in 1920, Hager was the music director for Okeh Records, a new, independent label trying to compete with giants Columbia and Victor.

With an introduction from songwriter Bill Tracy, Bradford met with Hager in the Okeh offices. Bradford pitched two of his newest compositions, "That Thing Called Love" and "You Can't Keep a Good Man Down." Hager liked the songs and wanted Sophie Tucker, the white interpreter of "hot jazz," to sing them, but Tucker was under contract to Vocalion Records, so Bradford made the suggestion that 14 million Negroes would buy records if the song was recorded by one of their own.

With little more discussion, Hager approved a recording session for February 14, 1920. Hager's studio band accompanied Mamie Smith, a twenty-seven-year-old singer and dancer who had appeared in Bradford's 1918 theatrical production *Made in Harlem*. The two above-mentioned songs were issued on Okeh (4113) as being sung by Mamie Smith, contralto, with Rega Orchestra.

Despite the record label's descriptive disguise, blacks recognized "one of their own." The record sold well enough that Hager called Smith and Bradford back to the studio in August and they recorded "Crazy Blues." The backing on this session was by black jazz players billed on the label as the Jazz Hounds and Ms. Smith's vocal range was not mentioned; only the descriptive "popular blues vocal."

The record (Okeh 4169) was a sensation, selling one hundred thousand copies in the first several weeks. Smith recorded more blues the following month and twice again in November. By 1921, the "race" market was the hottest part of the record business. Victor and Columbia were scrambling to sign black female singers in order to compete with Okeh. The discovery of this market would profoundly influence the course of American popular music in the decades to follow. Without the courage of the white violinist from the North and the inspiration of the black pianist from the South, this discovery might have taken much longer.

"Crazy Blues" is available in numerous folios of "most popular" jazz or blues songs. A reissue of the original recording can be found on *Bluesmasters, vol. 11: Classic Blues Women* (Rhino CD 71134).

2. "I'm Just Wild about Harry"
Words and Music by Noble Sissle and Eubie Blake
Copyright © 1921, M. Witmark and Sons

In 1920, at the opening of a new decade, America's popular entertainment included a peculiar mix of burlesque, vaudeville, operettas, musical revues, and variety shows. Most of those forms would soon decline while musical theater and its variant, musical comedy, were ascending. In the midst of that transformation, the musical duo of Sissle and Blake teamed up with the comedy duo of Miller and Lyles to create a "musical mélange" entitled *Shuffle Along*. The musical, and its signature tune, marked the first great commercial success of an all-black theatrical production on Broadway.

Noble Sissle, Eubie Blake, Flournoy Miller, and Aubrey Lyles were all experienced African American performers who pooled their talents and meager finances to write, produce, stage, and perform in a musical comedy about a farcical election in a small town. The entire production staff and cast were black, but that in itself was not groundbreaking. What set *Shuffle Along* apart from its predecessors was its wild success. The show opened in New York, with secondhand costumes and sets, on May 23, 1921, at the modest 63rd Street Theater, where it ran for 504 shows before taking three touring companies on the road.

Sissle and Blake would later recall that the show appealed most to white audiences. By the time it closed in 1923, the show had grossed more than $8 million, demonstrating that Broadway and America would support African American artists. At its outset, Sissle and Blake could not afford the train fare to take the show to Trenton, New Jersey. At its closing, they were wealthy men and would remain so through their long lives, in part because of the royalties from one hit song.

Sissle and Blake met in 1915 and were fortunate to come under the tutelage of James Reese Europe while playing in his popular society orchestras. Europe was a greatly respected conductor who had toured overseas with his 369th Infantry Band during World War I, only to be knifed to death by one of his musicians in 1919. After his death, Sissle and Blake toured the Keith Vaudeville circuit as the Dixie Duo. Composer Eubie Blake had begun his musical career at the age of fifteen by sneaking out of his house in Baltimore to play ragtime piano for prostitutes and their customers, then later for a touring medicine show. Lyricist Noble Sissle, by contrast, arrived at his career through college choral societies and tours with Hann's Jubilee Singers. Though an unlikely pair, together they composed all of the music for *Shuffle Along*, including its most durable hit "I'm Just Wild about Harry."

Blake originally wrote "Harry" as a waltz, but his leading actress, Lottie Gee, persuaded him to make it a catchy one-step. Broadway musicals are still judged by whether the audience members take home a song or two that cannot be forgotten, and "Harry" was just such a song. It quickly developed a life of its own apart from *Shuffle Along*, becoming a hit record for Ray Miller and His Orchestra in 1922. It was later featured in a series of motion pictures, beginning with *Rose of Washington Square* (starring Alice Faye), and *Babes in Arms* (starring Judy Garland), before becoming the theme song for the 1948 presidential campaign of Harry Truman. It was revived on stage in 1975 by Tammy Grimes in her *Musical Jubilee*, and in an archival recreation of *Shuffle Along* released on New World Records in 1976.

"I'm Just Wild about Harry" is still readily available in sheet music form and on several recordings. An instrumental version on *Memories of You* (Biograph CD 112) features Eubie Blake at the piano. For a vocal rendition, try *Always Chasing Rainbows: The Young Judy Garland* (ASV CD 5093).

3. "Second Hand Rose"
Words by Grant Clarke and Music by James F. Hanley
Copyright © 1921, Shapiro, Bernstein and Company, Inc.

In 1910, Fanny Borach reached the apex of the New York entertainment world when she was hired by Florenze Ziegfeld for his fourth edition of the *Ziegfeld Follies*. Ziegfeld had noticed the tall, gangly young woman when she sang "Sadie Salome" in the heavy Yiddish accent recommended by its composer, Irving Berlin, and hired her even though she did not match his preferred showgirl profile of beautiful, buxom, and graceful. Fanny was too tall, too slim, and could not dance, but her voice could penetrate every corner of the theater and her unique face complemented a comic genius. At the age of nineteen, she was already a veteran of the burlesque circuit and had changed her last name to Brice, reportedly because it would look better on a theater marquee.

Like many popular entertainers of the first half of the twentieth century, Fanny Brice was the child of impoverished Jewish immigrants who left homes in Europe for a new life in America. Between 1880 and 1920, more than 1 million east European Jews arrived in the United States, increasing New York's Jewish community to 1.5 million before World War I and forming what is still the largest Jewish population of any city in the world. Many went no farther from Ellis Island than the lower east side of Manhattan, where a vibrant multilingual Jewish culture developed.

The new transplants brought with them both a rich musical heritage and a Yiddish theater tradition that rooted along Second Avenue near Houston Street, where it nurtured many outstanding talents. Fanny grew up in a tenement near Second Avenue and began performing in talent shows there at the age of thirteen, but would ultimately make her name uptown in the mainstream theaters of Broadway. She would come to epitomize the talented Jew who rose from poor beginnings to master the world of American entertainment in theater, radio, and film. She was never shy about recalling her childhood, which lent poignancy to one of her signature tunes.

"Second Hand Rose" was yet another product of Tin Pan Alley, written by two Midwesterners with little grasp of the Jewish American experience but an innate feel for what was popular. Lyricist Grant Clarke was equally comfortable writing "Rose of the Rio Grande" or "Yokohama Lullaby." He teamed with composer James F. Hanley to produce "Second Hand Rose" for the *Ziegfeld Follies of 1921*. Beginning in 1907, each *Follies* presented an opulent hodgepodge of pageantry, comedy, and music. The production of 1921, which some critics considered the "last hurrah for the spectacular revue" (Bordman 1992, 363), was particularly overblown with a staging cost exceeding $250,000.

Eleven years after her *Follies* debut garnered twelve encores, Fanny Brice had top billing as both comedienne and torch singer. Only two songs became hits from the 1921 Follies, and both were sung by Brice. "Second Hand Rose" of Second Avenue lamented the fate of a poor girl of the Jewish quarter who could "never get a thing that ain't been used." The song was also a hit record for Ted Lewis and his Band, and was performed by Brice in the film *My Man* in 1929. It was later revived by Barbra Streisand in her depiction of Brice in the musical and film *Funny Girl.*

"Second Hand Rose" is readily available in sheet music form. No recordings by Brice are available, but it can be found on a number of recordings by Barbra Streisand, including her *Greatest Hits* (TNK–Columbia CD 9968).

4. "When the Moon Shines on the Moonshine"
Words by Francis DeWitt and Music by Robert Hood Bowers
Copyright © 1922, Shapiro, Bernstein and Company, Inc.

By the time Prohibition was enforced by federal law, thirty-three states had already passed laws to force abstinence, so it was not surprising that the Eighteenth Amendment was ratified. More surprising was the firm resistance of the American public and the vigor of the criminal elements that helped it circumvent the law. When Prohibition was repealed in 1933 by the Twenty-first Amendment, a convincing argument was that it had caused otherwise respectful citizens to become scofflaws, and had stimulated the rise of a dangerous criminal network. That network, the Mafia, would soon branch out into narcotics, gambling, prostitution, and extortion. It is estimated that in New York City alone fifteen thousand taxpaying pubs were replaced by thirty-two thousand illicit speakeasies. In Chicago, Al Capone developed a crime organization that netted profits exceeding $60 million per year and contributed to more than five hundred gangland murders in the city. Capone remarked that he "regarded it as a public benefaction if people were given decent liquor and square games" (Parrish 1992, 107).

Individual Americans and the criminals they supported proved resourceful in obtaining illegal alcoholic beverages. Alcohol was diverted from medical and industrial supplies; liquor was smuggled from Canada, Mexico, and the Caribbean; beer and wine were concocted in family basements; and both large and small criminals distilled hard spirits, usually known as "moonshine," including the notorious bathtub gin.

The full implication of Prohibition was not yet known when a musical revue entitled *The Broadway Brevities of 1920* was pieced together by its producers, but the scarcity of liquor was clearly on the mind of the public. Bert Williams headlined the show in what would, tragically, be his last important performance before an untimely death. His role included both the comic skit "I Make Mine Myself" and the popular song "When the Moon Shines on the Moonshine." The song lamented the loss of the lawful distillery but extolled how "the moon shines on the moonshine so merrily." The show flopped but its hit song, which was also featured in a Ziegfeld production, was a harbinger of the willful lawlessness that would develop over the decade.

Little is known about the men who wrote the song. Composer Robert Hood Bowers, who also used the pen name Robin Hood Bowers, was a schooled musician who wrote music for several early Broadway shows before concentrating on conducting. "Moonshine" was one of his most popular numbers. Lyricist Francis DeWitt had contributed to New York stage shows as early as 1910 and later became the playwright for both *90 Horsepower* (1926) and *The Absent Father* (1932).

"The Moon Shines on the Moonshine" was featured in the 1997 television documentary *The Music of Prohibition* and can be found on the soundtrack recording of the same name (Sony/Columbia CD 65326). The song is no longer available in sheet music.

5. "He May Be Your Man, but He Comes to See Me Sometimes"
Words and Music by Lemuel "Lem" Fowler
Copyright © 1922, Ted Browne Music Company/Jerry Vogel Music Company, Inc.

Two things led to a new image for women in the 1920s: many worked outside of their homes, for the first time, during World War I; and the Nineteenth Amendment was ratified, giving women the right to vote for the first time. The types of jobs women had in the 1920s tended to be different from those women were forced to accept in previous decades. In 1870, only 40 percent of the jobs women held were outside domestic service. By 1920, 80 percent of the jobs in which women worked were considered nondomestic.

Women attended college in greater numbers in the 1920s and being away from home gave young women an added feeling of liberation. Women began to feel less inhibited about smoking and drinking in public. Fashions were more revealing, reflecting the "new woman" of the Roaring Twenties. Advertising executives began to view females differently and designed advertising that reflected the changing image of women. Advertising took on a more important role during this decade and the psyche of females (major consumers) was studied from a psychological standpoint. Advertisements also affected the behavior of women: looking like models in magazine ads became extremely important.

But to many people, these beginning steps of women's liberation were the cause of social degradation. The divorce rate more than doubled in the United States between 1880 and 1916. Many critics blamed it on the Suffragists who, they believed, were dismantling family values. The Catholic Church asked members of their congregations to sign a "pledge of decency." Censorship and anti–birth control laws were state lawmakers' attempts to legislate morality during this time of changing gender roles.

One song that reflects the conflict in values surrounding the role and image of women in society more than any other is "He May Be Your Man, but He Comes to See Me Sometimes." The song was written by Lemuel "Lem" Fowler and was recorded by Lucille Hegamin. It is about a woman who simply, but bluntly, explains to another woman that she is having a relationship with the woman's man. Prior to the 1920s, songs about infidelity were, most often, sung from the perspective of a woman whose husband cheated on her. Although it always takes two people to have an extramarital affair, this is probably the first commercially successful song in which the "other woman" describes her own behavior.

Although the song was written by a male, it reflected the unapologetic and liberated woman of the 1920s. In addition to being controversial, it was also popular in the marketplace. Two other song-writers, Gus Kahn and Isham Jones, saw an opportunity to emulate the song, and wrote an answer song called "The One I Love (Belongs to Someone Else)" in 1924.

"He May Be Your Man, but He Comes to See Me Sometimes" is available on *Lucille Hegamin: Complete Recorded Works, Vol. 1* (Document Records [CD] 5419).

6. "The Little Old Log Cabin in the Lane"
Words and Music by Will S. Hays
Recorded by "Fiddlin'" John Carson, 1923
Copyright © 1871, J. L. Peters

William Shakespeare Hays (born 1837, Louisville, Kentucky) was a Louisville newspaperman with a penchant for poetry and song lyrics. He wrote more than three hundred songs in a variety of styles. His melodic sense, as evidenced in his spirituals and minstrel songs, was likely influenced by African Americans Hays heard while working on riverboats in his youth.

"The Little Old Log Cabin in the Lane" is Hays's most endur-ing minstrel piece. It tells of decay in postbellum southern planta-tion life after "Ole massa an' ole miss's am dead." The narrator, who is "old and feeble now" and accompanied by "dis good ole dog ob mine," only hopes that "de angels watches over me when I lay down to sleep."

Sentimental stereotypes were a popular element of minstrelsy in the 1870s. The cover page of the sheet music bears the legend: as sung by Manning's Minstrels. Billy Manning was a popular bones player (percussionist) and end man (comedian) with a number of minstrel troupes. From 1868, until his death in 1876, Manning led his own company through the Midwest and South from his home in Chicago. Manning's troupes and others popularized the song among rural and small-town audiences. Sheet music editions were available as late as 1913, indicating popularity in cities where musical literacy was more common.

In 1922, Atlanta radio station WSB was broadcasting programs by local singer and fiddler John Carson. "Fiddlin' John" had won most of the annual fiddle contests in the city and was a well-known performer on the streets, at political rallies, and on the new medium of radio.

In 1922, Polk Brockman was managing the record department of his father's furniture store. Brockman was selling Okeh "race" records to Atlanta's blacks in sufficient quantity to make the store the leading retailer of Okeh discs in the region. On a trip to New York, Brockman met with Okeh's Ralph Peer, who had been an assistant to Fred Hager when the race market was created (see entry: "Crazy Blues"), and asked Peer to consider recording "Fiddling" John Carson.

In June 1923, in a makeshift studio in Atlanta, John Carson sang and fiddled two of his most popular pieces, one of which was "The Little Old Log Cabin in the Lane." Peer had brought recording equipment and engineers from New York for the first commercial location recording session. Though Peer later declared the music "pluperfect awful," the speed with which Brockman sold out the initial pressing, and the quantity of the reorders, convinced Peer that a market for "old-time tunes" existed.

Later called "hillbilly," this new market soared in sales with a momentum not seen since the beginning of the race market in 1920. Unlike the race market, whose initial artist was a musically literate, seasoned professional, this new genre started with a performer and a performance that could at best be called authentic and untrained.

Carson dropped the slave dialect from "The Little Old Log Cabin in the Lane" and replaced it with his rural Georgia accent, but the sentimental portrait of a lonely old man and his dog resonated as well in 1923 as it had when it was written in 1871. This recording, made in 1923, is considered by many music historians to be the seed that grew into a genre called "country music."

"Little Log Cabin in the Lane" [*sic*] is in print in the *Backpocket Old Time Songbook* (WE Publishing). John Carson's seminal recording of the song is on *Country: The American Tradition* (Sony 65816; 2 CD set).

7. "Charleston"
Words and Music by Cecil Mack and James P. "Jimmy" Johnson
Copyright © 1923, Harms Music

The Roaring Twenties—the Jazz Age—was an era of excess in which millions of Americans became lawbreakers under the brief reign of

Prohibition. While bootleggers and speakeasies flourished, Americans danced the Charleston. This frenzied dance of the decade expressed the independence of young women who could now vote, smoke, drink, work a job, and dance as they wished. The Charleston could not be done in the modest, flowing dresses of their mothers, but demanded the scandalous short skirts of the flapper, who would be seen "flicking her knees open and closed with peekaboo insouciance" (McDonagh 1979, 44). The song to which they kicked and jiggled was a ripping stride piano composition by James P. Johnson.

"Charleston" was written in 1923 for a musical comedy entitled *Runnin' Wild*, which opened on the coattails of Sissle and Blake's *Shufflin' Along*. Though less noteworthy and successful than its predecessor, *Runnin' Wild* saw its dance hit sweep the nation. Both shows were written by the comedy team of Miller and Lyles, with music for the latter of the two provided by Johnson and lyricist Richard C. McPherson. McPherson, who used the pen name of Cecil Mack, was a well-educated man who later went to medical school but kept music as his avocation. His lyrics to the indelible melody of "Charleston" have been largely forgotten.

There is disagreement about where the name of the dance originated. Flournoy Miller credited himself with discovering a group of young street dancers, including one with the nickname Charleston, who were the model for the stage choreography. James P. Johnson believed that the dance was a standard cotillion step modified to fit a syncopated beat. Other sources link the steps to a dancer named Russell Brown who hailed from the Sea Islands near Charleston, South Carolina, where remnants of African culture still persist.

The Charleston, combined dance and tune, is a fine example of how jazz dance and jazz music evolved together as the stiff-spined European dances of the nineteenth century gave way to dances that derived from the stomping feet and swaying hips of African dance. Other dances of the period, including the Shimmy, Snake Hips, and the provocative Black Bottom, can also be traced to African sources. But what propelled the Charleston fad was the music of James P. Johnson. Many other songs were written expressly for the dance, but none are remembered like "Charleston."

Johnson was a trained pianist who began his professional career at fifteen and under the guidance of the great ragtime player Eubie

Blake. His technical skill was exceptional, making him the acknowledged master at Harlem "cutting contests" between piano players. "He made the near impossible seem easy" (Jasen and Jones 2000, 73). Over time he would influence the playing of Fats Waller, Duke Ellington, and Art Tatum, among others. It is reported that Jelly Roll Morton learned Johnson's "Carolina Shout" by slowing down the piano roll. Johnson also composed ambitious symphonic works in addition to popular songs, but his most significant contribution was the development of the stride piano style. The stride style derived from ragtime but required even greater dexterity and allowed a rhythmic freedom that moved jazz from the measured pace of ragtime toward the swing patterns that would mark jazz of the 1930s and beyond.

Several recorded versions of "Charleston" are available, including on *Carolina Shout* (Biograph CD 105) which compiles fourteen of Johnson's original recordings. It is also available in a large number of sheet music anthologies.

8. "Nobody Knows You When You're Down and Out"
Words and Music by Jimmie Cox
Copyright © 1923, MCA, Inc.

The year 1929 started out with promise. America had enjoyed a decade of postwar prosperity and the stock market was riding high. In the entertainment world, records and radio had become commonplace, making music available without leaving home. America's Negro artists had bright new opportunities with the widespread distribution of race records. The public continued to frequent all forms of stage entertainment, including the vaudeville stage. But by the end of 1929 the stock market had crashed, America was on the road to a deep depression, and musicians soon hit hard times as record sales dropped and the "talkies," motion pictures with sound, displaced live performers in theaters across the country.

Blues great Bessie Smith had been riding high as well, but her signature tune "Nobody Knows You When You're Down and Out" prophetically declared the end of good times. On May 15, 1929, she recorded the song in New York for Columbia Records, one of more than 150 recordings she made for that label. She had debuted on Columbia in 1923, became an immediate star, and earned the title of

Empress of the Blues, helping to keep the young label afloat in the process. Her accompanists included the finest musicians of the day, such as Louis Armstrong, James P. Johnson, and Eddie Lang. She toured nationwide in concert halls and vaudeville palaces, and became a wealthy woman for her day. Some critics still consider her the greatest female blues vocalist of the twentieth century, recognizing both her rich and versatile voice and the emotional nuance that she brought to any song.

She was just thirty-five when she approached the microphone that day, but she was already world weary after nearly two decades of hard touring, a failed marriage, and chronic alcoholism. The blues themselves were in decline as jazz bands and big bands vied for attention. These factors combined to color her rendition of "Nobody Knows You When You're Down and Out," a cynical lament about friends who drop away when hard times come. She had learned the song from its composer, Jimmie Cox, a vaudevillian she worked with in her early years. It is likely that Cox had performed it on stage. Its opening line, "Once I lived the life of a millionaire," would become ironic when the song was finally released in September 1929, just weeks before the stock market crash that bankrupted many millionaires and pushed the nation toward depression.

The 1930s were as cruel to Bessie Smith as the 1920s were kind. She was dropped by Columbia in 1931, made her last recording in 1933, and was struggling to support herself by the time she died in 1937, following a car accident in Clarksdale, Mississippi. (She did not die after being refused treatment at a whites-only hospital, as was widely rumored.) Fortunately, her recordings have been preserved and are available on CD, for instance, *Bessie Smith: The Collection* (Columbia/Legacy CD 044441). It is also available in print form in *The Bessie Smith Songbook* (Hal Leonard 00308232).

9. "Rhapsody in Blue" (for jazz band and piano)
Music by George Gershwin and Orchestrated by Ferde Grofe
Copyright 1924, New World Music Corporation

George Gershwin's father, Morris Gershovitz, like thousands of eastern European Jews in the 1920s, emigrated to the United States in search of employment. He was also in search of Rose Burskin, the woman he had fallen in love with in St. Petersburg, Russia. Rose had moved to Brooklyn with her family and Morris was determined to marry her. Much like a story line from a musical his sons Ira and George would create years later, Gershovitz located Rose's home in New York and proposed to her on her doorstep.

The Gershovitz's first child, Ira, became one of the world's most successful Broadway writers and lyricists. After Ira was born, Morris changed his name to Gershvin in order to sound more American. When Jacob George Gershvin was born, the physician misspelled his name on the birth certificate. Therefore, Jacob George Gershwine became his legal name. After he became an adult, George (he never used Jacob) shortened his name to Gershwin. Apparently, his family was not displeased with the name Gershwin, because they all subsequently changed to it.

As George Gershwin began to think about a vocation, he was drawn to music. He was fascinated by ragtime piano and jazz. He spent many hours in bars and clubs that had jazz performers. It is likely that Gershwin, like many eastern European Jews who emigrated to this country, related to African Americans and their music more than the established population. Russian Jews were subjected to the worst forms of discrimination in St. Petersburg. Gershwin understood the discrimination that African Americans were subjected to in this country and felt a sense of understanding through his own heritage.

George Gershwin's mother tried to persuade her son to pursue a profession other than music. After realizing his intense desire to become a musician, however, she stopped trying to change his mind. George began his quest to find a piano teacher who would teach him not only the standard classical repertoire, but also the popular and jazz music of the day. To his dismay, he found that the world of classical music did not accept jazz or popular music. Gershwin never forgot the partisan attitude that trained musicians had regarding jazz vis-à-vis classical music. During much of his life, George spent a large amount of his creative energy trying to prove to critics that jazz and popular music could be more than three-minute songs. His goal was to establish the legitimacy of jazz and popular songs.

Gershwin's first full-time job in music was with Jerome Remick and Company, one of the many publishers in New York's Tin Pan

Alley. Tin Pan Alley was an area centered around 28th Street, from 6th Avenue to Broadway. Music publishers had pianists, called "song pluggers," on the payroll to perform songs for potential sheet music customers. The experience Gershwin gained from being a song plugger gave him several things that would help him in his career as a composer and songwriter. He became quite proficient at performing on piano and often had to improvise in order to "sell" a weak song. He also learned the characteristics of songs that were most successful. And, most important, he learned about the business side of songwriting.

Gershwin found almost immediate success as a songwriter for revues and stage shows. His first true pop hit was "Swanee," written in 1919. Although the first performance of Swanee in the *Capitol Review* was not well received, it became a smash hit when Al Jolson included it in his Winter Garden Review called *Sinbad*. Jolson also recorded "Swanee" and it sold more than 2 million copies in twelve months.

Even with his tremendous success in the marketplace, Gershwin still wanted to establish himself as a serious composer and, at the same time, demonstrate the legitimacy of jazz and popular music. He received his first chance to present his songs to a traditional concert audience in 1923. Eva Gauthier, a world-renowned mezzo-soprano who was trained in Europe, invited Gershwin to perform with her at the prestigious Aeolian Hall. Gauthier sang several Gershwin songs while he accompanied her on piano. This was an extremely important event for Gershwin and other pop songwriters, because the other songs she sang were by master composers for the western European fine-art repertoire. Critics and audience members loved the performance.

Gershwin's return to Aeolian Hall was at the invitation of Paul Whiteman, leader of a successful jazz band. Whiteman, never averse to publicity stunts, arranged an event that he called *An Experiment in Modern Music*. He invited many of the leading New York music critics and some of the most famous classical composers living in the United States. He intended to have a panel of experts answer the question "What is American music?"

Although Whiteman did not give Gershwin much time to write a work for the concert, Gershwin reluctantly agreed to compose something. The original title of the work was "American Rhapsody," but

Gershwin renamed it "Rhapsody in Blue" prior to the concert. Due to the short amount of time in which he had to write the work—about three weeks—Gershwin created an abbreviated version of the score and had Whiteman's arranger, Ferde Grofe, create the full orchestration.

On February 12, 1924, the Paul Whiteman Orchestra performed "Rhapsody in Blue" in Aeolian Hall with George Gershwin performing the solo piano part. The audience brought Gershwin and Whiteman back for five curtain calls. However, most music critics were mixed or qualified in their reviews. Although he was not totally successful in winning the respect of music critics, Gershwin succeeded in bridging the chasm separating classical music and popular or jazz music. The recognition that was bestowed upon "Rhapsody in Blue" also represented a nod toward jazz and pop music as art forms. Gershwin's fusion of jazz, pop, and classical genre helped create an American school of composition that stood up against the western European masters.

Ferde Grofe created two additional arrangements of this work in 1926 and 1942. The most commonly heard is the arrangement for full orchestra and solo piano. The sheet music is readily available and there are many different recordings available. The original recording of Gershwin and the Whiteman Orchestra is available on Past Perfect records (PPCD 78106). Other recordings include those by Leonard Bernstein, Michael Tilson Thomas, Oscar Levant, and Earl Wild.

10. "The Prisoner's Song"
Words and Music by Guy Massey
Copyright © 1924, Shapiro, Bernstein and Company, Inc.

After the Okeh Record Company accidentally discovered the rural market (see entry: "The Little Old Log Cabin in the Lane"), it did not take the other record manufacturers long to seek out songs and performers they could market as hillbilly. Victor Records, one of the strongest record companies of the decade, had waited during the initial boom of the race market, and found the best African American talent contracted to their competitors: Okeh, Columbia, Vocalion, Brunswick, and Paramount.

Victor's hopes initially rested on fiddler A. C. "Eck" Robertson, who had recorded several instrumentals for Victor in 1922. On the heels of Okeh's 1923 success with John Carson, Victor issued Robert-son's discs to only modest sales. With Okeh's next success in early 1924—a railroad ballad, "The Wreck on the Southern Old 97"—Victor noted the public's preference for vocal music. When Texas-born, conservatory-trained tenor Vernon Dalhart asked Victor executives to permit him to "cover" the song, a July 13, 1924, session was arranged.

Marion Try Slaughter was born in 1883 near Jefferson, Texas. In 1910, after working in a Dallas music store and attending the Dallas Conservatory of Music, Slaughter, his wife, and his daughter moved to the Bronx. Taking the professional name Vernon Dalhart from two small Texas towns near which Slaughter worked summers as a child, he began singing light opera in various New York companies.

Using the pseudonym Vernon Dalhart, he began recording for Edison in 1916, and over the following eight years his popular and light opera selections were modestly successful. Victor's willingness to accommodate Dalhart's desire to enter the country market would change that market profoundly.

As Dalhart finished recording "The Wreck of the Old 97" on that July afternoon in 1924, Victor recording supervisor Eddie King asked for another song for the B side of the disc. Dalhart claimed to have provided "The Prisoner's Song" which he and Guy Massey, a visiting cousin from Texas, wrote in Massey's hotel room that day. Carson Robison, the guitarist at the session, claimed Massey sang the song continually while he was visiting Dalhart in New York. The Massey family, back in Texas, said that Guy's brother Bob actually wrote the song and Guy only brought it to New York. To further muddle the story, Victor staff arranger Nat Shilkret claimed that Dalhart had only written a few lines of text and Shilkret wrote more verses and the simple tune.

These competing stories only attained importance once the record was issued and the "throwaway" B side became the biggest selling vocal recording up to that time. More than 1 million copies were sold within the year; a decade later Victor was still selling the disc, then at almost 8 million copies. Thanks to an opera-singing Texan and a song with a clouded birth, commercial country music was a worldwide commodity.

"The Prisoner's Song" (also now known as "If I Had the Wings of an Angel") is still in print in a piano/vocal arrangement from either Hal Leonard Music or Plymouth Music Company. Available recorded versions number more than thirty. Vernon Dalhart's original is on *Nipper's Greatest Hits: The 20s* (RCA CD 2258).

11. "Black and Tan Fantasy"
Music by Bert Miley and Edward Kennedy "Duke" Ellington
Copyright © 1927, Mills Music, Inc.

"Black and Tan Fantasy" is difficult to categorize because it represents jazz and popular music of the 1920s combined with elements of traditional fine-art music of western Europe. It is also difficult to determine exactly what each of the two composers contributed to this work. One thing that is clear, though, is the significance of this composition in the evolution of music in the United States, especially that of African American composers, performers, and bandleaders.

Edward Ellington spent the first twenty-four years of his life in Washington, D.C. Washington was significant not only because it was the seat of the federal government, but it was also one of the few cities in which African Americans represented a large percentage of the population. During the time Ellington was growing up in Washington, the city was approximately one-third African American.

Because Washington, like other U.S. cities, was racially segregated, a separate African American social system evolved within the city. Ellington regretted the social strata of Washington's African American community, because it created an order that often dictated with whom he was supposed to socialize. The topmost layer of the social order consisted of a small number of families, many of whom were descendants of antebellum free blacks. The middle class was made up of professionals, government workers, and business owners. Ellington's parents were probably considered to be middle class. The lowest rung on the social ladder was the largest and poorest. They were primarily uneducated, unskilled agricultural workers from the South who migrated north in search of employment.

Social class of Washingtonian African Americans typically correlated with skin tone. Recent émigrés from the southern United States or foreign countries were often darker in hue than African Americans from the northern states of the United States. The most aristocratic members of the social order were more likely to have lighter skin tones than middle- or lower-class members of African

American society during this decade. African Americans who had extremely light skin tones were referred to as "High Yellow" or "High Yaller," a New Orleans colloquialism for persons of mixed French and African American heritage. Hence the terms *black*, *tan*, and *High Yaller* were adopted to mean dark, lighter, and lightest.

In 1923, Ellington moved to New York to become a part of the Harlem Renaissance, an explosion of indigenous African American talent in the relatively small area north of Central Park. By the 1920s, Edward Ellington had adopted the first name "Duke," a moniker bestowed on him because of his debonair style of dress and gracious manners. By 1927, Duke had established himself as a performer, composer, and bandleader. It was that year in which he wrote "Black and Tan Fantasy" with band mate and trumpet player, Bert Miley.

The Duke Ellington Band became a part of the Cotton Club cast in 1927. The Cotton Club, dubbed "the aristocrat of Harlem," did more than provide entertainment for New Yorkers; it provided a valuable learning environment as well. The Cotton Club hired only African American waiters and entertainers, but admitted only whites as customers. The productions included attractive female dancers, lavish sets, and, most important, Duke Ellington and his band. For whites who rarely socialized with African Americans during this era, the Cotton Club offered a close view of attractive, talented, and sophisticated persons of the "other race" in New York.

The owners of the Cotton Club only used extremely light-skinned African American females in the chorus lines. Advertisements for the Cotton Club often referred to beautiful "Creole women," meaning light-skinned blacks. The club's preoccupation with black and tan skin tones was no doubt a motivation for the song "Black and Tan Fantasy," written by Ellington and trumpet player Bert Miley.

As Ellington's popularity grew through radio broadcasts, recordings, and tours, his music and persona began to cross racial lines. In 1929, he made a motion picture (a nineteen-minute short) called *Black and Tan*. It was the second talking film, following *The Jazz Singer* starring Al Jolson, and Ellington acted in it as well as performed his music. Film studios, worried about alienating southern audiences, were careful to use either all African American performers or all white performers. Both Duke Ellington and the film *Black and Tan* were well received by audiences all across the nation.

Around the time of his film debut, Ellington toured the South. He was so charming that a journalist for the *Dallas News*, a southern newspaper, noted that Ellington and his band had "erased the color line." The song "Black and Tan Fantasy" remains one of his most important works. It also helped blend jazz, classical, and popular styles into a sophisticated big band style that would blossom in the 1930s.

Because Ellington was more conscientious about recording sessions than other bandleaders of his time, his early recordings are still gems that have been reissued in CD configuration. Many other artists, including Louis Armstrong, have recorded this work.

Sheet music is available in *Music of Duke Ellington: Easy Piano Composer Collection* published by Hal Leonard (HL 110035).

12. "Blue Skies"
Words and Music by Irving Berlin
Copyright © 1927, Irving Berlin Music Corporation

Irving Berlin, born Israel Baline, came to America from Siberia with his parents in 1892. Young Israel's family of eight struggled for existence after they arrived in what they hoped would be their promised land. After only four years in America, Israel's father died. Each child began to earn money any way they could and Israel was no exception. Israel, called Issy by his family and friends, began selling newspapers on the street for pennies. He then moved to selling songs, something he would continue to do the remainder of his life.

Issy stood in front of restaurants and sang songs in hopes that someone walking by would be entertained and drop a coin into his hat. He soon found a job as a singing waiter in a restaurant in New York's Lower East Side. Israel, in love with songs and singing, began to pursue any opportunity to sing in public.

Harry von Tilzer, an established songwriter and publisher, noticed Israel's ability to "sell" a song to an audience. Mr. von Tilzer hired Issy and paid him $5 per week to sit in the balcony of any hall in which a von Tilzer song was being sung during a show. It was young Israel's job to stand up in the balcony after hearing one chorus of the song and sing along. Harry von Tilzer believed that this type of song plugging would convince audience members that it was a great song and worthy of purchase.

Although Israel lacked any formal education in music (he never learned to read or write music notation), he learned enough as a song plugger to write his first song. The song, "Marie from Sunny Italy," was not a particular success. The sheet music did, however, change the career of Issy: the printer identified the songwriter as "I. Berlin" by mistake. When negotiating a publishing deal later, Issy decided to keep his new last name and, like many Jewish immigrants, created a more American sounding first name. Israel Baline, the poor Jewish immigrant from Siberia, was now Irving Berlin.

Influenced by the ragtime music of the South, Irving Berlin wrote "Alexander's Ragtime Band" in 1911. This song sold millions of copies of sheet music and even more records. It also established Berlin as one of the top professional songwriters in the nation. By 1926, he had become quite wealthy and had achieved celebrity status.

In 1926, Berlin married Ellin Mackay, daughter of successful businessman Clarence Mackay. Clarence, a Catholic, did not approve of his daughter's marriage to Irving Berlin. Like many wealthy socialites in the 1920s, Clarence believed that Jews were inferior to non-Jews. He threatened to write his daughter out of his will, thereby denying her any potential inheritance. Despite her father's antagonism, Ellin married Irving without her father even knowing of the wedding.

Later in 1926, the Berlin's first daughter, Ellin, was born. Irving Berlin was, understandably, elated with his life at that moment in time. He had risen from poverty to prosperity, he married the woman he loved, and he had a beautiful baby girl. Expressing his joy the best way he knew how, he wrote a song. On the original sheet music for "Blue Skies," Berlin dedicated the song to his daughter, Ellin, and dated it "Christmas day, 1926."

On December 27, Belle Baker, an old friend of Issy, called to ask him a favor. Baker, a singer with a powerful voice, was preparing to open a new Ziegfeld show called *Betsy* the next day. She told Berlin that the show was written by Rogers and Hart, but there was no song in it that would showcase her vocal style. Irving told her he could not write a song in one day and offered, instead, to play her a song he had "in the trunk." She loved the song, but it was not complete. Berlin, therefore, spent the entire evening completing and polishing the song.

Persons who tried to drown their sorrows through intoxication were often the people who could least afford bootleg liquor. Prohibition, something meant to help society by keeping people from drinking, did little toward that end. The frank, earthy style of vocal blues was well suited to stating the plight of heavy drinkers during this decade.

In response to public pressure, President Herbert Hoover created a commission to study law enforcement in 1929. The commission, headed by Attorney General George Wickersham, collected information that indicated the difficulties of enforcing Prohibition. Although the Wickersham Commission gathered a great deal of information, it was criticized for not making any specific recommendations. It did, however, indicate to many politicians that the Eighteenth Amendment was not well supported by voters. By 1932, both political parties supported repeal of Prohibition. And, in 1933, the Twenty-first Amendment was ratified, thereby repealing Prohibition.

Sheet music for "Whiskey Blues" is available in the *Paramount Book of Blues* and the *Complete Guitar Player Blues Songbook* (AM84484).

14. "See That My Grave's Kept Clean"
Words and Music by Blind Lemon Jefferson
Copyright © 1928, Northern Music Corporation

Beginning in 1921 (see entry: "Crazy Blues"), the record industry exploited the race market by signing African American female vocalists from the world of vaudeville and musical theater. By 1925, sales of the genre were dwindling. Paramount Records of Grafton, Wisconsin, found the "next big thing" in the race market; it was a happy accident that inadvertently documented a rich vein of black folk expression.

Lemon Jefferson was born to sharecropper parents in 1893 near Wortham, Texas, and like many blind people at that time, he took up music as a vocation. By 1910, he was a recognized figure on the street corners of small Texas towns south of Dallas where he sang and played the guitar for tips. In the early 1920s, Jefferson was successful on Elm Street, Dallas' African American business district. R. L. Ashford owned a record shop which sold race records to blacks. Seeing the crowds Jefferson attracted on the streets with his country-style songs and accompaniment, Ashford contacted Paramount Records and arranged a trip to Chicago for Jefferson. From his first session in December 1925, until his death in December 1929, Jefferson recorded nearly one hundred titles for the Paramount and Okeh labels.

His most enduring composition, "See That My Grave's Kept Clean" (also known as "One Kind Favor"), was recorded twice for Paramount. First, in October 1927, it was paired with a gospel song and released on Paramount (12585) under the pseudonym Deacon L. J. Bates. Four months later Jefferson recut "See That My Grave Is Kept Clean" for secular release (paired with "'Lectric Chair Blues"; Paramount 12608) under the Blind Lemon Jefferson moniker.

The song's refrain and title might have been a common saying in Texas among African Americans. However, a well-known variety artist of the 1870–1890 period, Gus Williams, wrote "See That My Grave Is Kept Green" in 1877. Williams toured nationally with Tony Pastor's variety troupe. Might Williams have sung his refrain "one little wish I ask of you, see that my grave is kept green" for a Dallas vaudeville audience in the 1880s? Whatever the source for Jefferson's inspired composition, the song resonated within the black community for decades.

Lemon Jefferson was found dead on a Chicago street in December 1929. It is thought he suffered a heart attack and froze. His body was sent to Texas by train and he was buried in Wortham. In 1997, his grave was cleaned and a granite headstone placed on it. The inscription reads: "Please See That My Grave Is Kept Clean."

There are many recorded versions of this classic song, but one that deserves mention is from Bob Dylan's Columbia recording, available on CD (Columbia CD 08579). His recording during the folk revival was responsible for introducing a young white audience to country blues. The commercially successful folk group Peter, Paul, and Mary recorded the song under the title "One Kind Favor." Their version is available in print in *Songbook of Peter, Paul, and Mary* from Warner Brothers music publishers.

15. "Ain't Misbehavin' "
Words by Andy Razaf and Music by Thomas Waller and Harry Brooks
Copyright © 1929, Mills Music, Inc.

By the end of the 1920s, Harlem's nightclubs were the most popular late-night entertainment venues in New York. Earlier, with the onset of Prohibition, hole-in-the-wall speakeasies were established to serve local patrons. Musicians working elsewhere came by for drinks and an after-hours jam session. As word of this high quality music spread, whites from downtown started coming to Harlem for the late shows.

One of the most popular attractions was the "cutting contest" between New York's best pianists. Word of a confrontation between James P. Johnson and Willie "the Lion" Smith would ensure a packed bar at any Harlem "speak." Thomas "Fats" Waller was a teenage student of Johnson's as the decade began and New York went dry.

As time passed and the music became commercialized, bars became nightclubs, with local owners squeezed out by white gangster liquor suppliers. One of the most popular was Connie's Inn, nominally owned by Connie Immerman and his brother, but actually owned by mobster Dutch Schultz.

Facing increasing competition for white entertainment dollars from other Harlem nightspots, stage shows at Connie's Inn became more lavish, and by 1929, a two-hour revue with a chorus of "50 tanskins" (a term that referred to African Americans with light skin tone) and a half dozen feature performers was the norm. Music for this type of show was typically written by the hottest songwriting teams, Andy Razaf and Fats Waller among them.

Andreamentania Paul Razafkeriefo was born in Washington, D.C., to Malagasy political refugees in 1895. A dreamy, artistic child, he grew to manhood in New York, a poet, lyricist, and singer. In 1913, while working as an elevator boy in a Tin Pan Alley building, he sold his first song. Ten years later, as Andy Razaf, he had some success as the lyricist for the nineteen-year-old piano prodigy Fats Waller.

Waller's gift for memorable melodies surpassed any of the time. His easygoing demeanor and willingness to play the clown contrasted with Razaf's overt interest in social and racial matters. Yet, as a temporarily penniless team, they could write a marketable song in a taxi, hit the publishers' offices on Broadway for a quick sale, jump back in the taxi, and head for an expensive restaurant. After lunch they could repeat the process.

When the Immerman brothers wanted new songs for their 1929 revue *Hot Chocolates*, the Razaf/Waller team (with arrangements and incidental music by pianist Harry Brooks) was the first choice. As rehearsals progressed, the Immermans decided to try the novel idea of bringing Harlem downtown to larger numbers of white New Yorkers than could be accommodated uptown at Connie's Inn. On June 20, 1929, the show opened at Broadway's Hudson Theater. The hit song of the evening was "Ain't Misbehavin'." The song was performed three times during the show, once from the orchestra pit by a young trumpeter, most recently from Chicago, named Louis Armstrong. A few weeks into the show's run of 228 performances, Armstrong was moved onstage in a trio (with Waller and the hefty Edith Wilson) billed as One Thousand Pounds of Rhythm.

Three weeks into the show's run, and desperate for cash to pay back alimony, Waller sold "Ain't Misbehavin'" and nineteen other songs to publisher Irving Mills for $500, surely the worst deal in music history. Waller would continue to work in film and onstage and in recordings until his death in 1943, but Razaf suffered a professional decline and, without the royalties from his share of "Ain't Misbehavin'," endured economic hardship during the Depression.

In 1978, a collection of Waller and Razaf songs provided the frame for a successful Broadway musical revival entitled *Ain't Misbehavin'*. At least sixty-eight print and well over one hundred recorded versions of this classic are currently available. Waller's own recording is on Bluebird (CD 6288).

1930–1939

A New Way of Dealing with the Depression

The optimism and prosperity of the 1920s came to an end on October 24, 1929, a day that was dubbed "Black Thursday." The New York Stock Exchange had begun business as usual that Thursday, but by 11 A.M. brokers noticed many more orders to sell stock than to buy. Many brokers began to panic and, instinctively, sold the stock of their clients before prices declined further. Before the end of the trading day, a group of bankers pooled their resources and bought cheap stocks. The market appeared to have stabilized and a record 13 million shares changed hands that day.

After the scare of Black Thursday, President Hoover asked citizens, especially those who still held stocks, to remain calm. He assured the nation that the economy was still sound. The truth was, however, that most economic indicators—construction, manufacturing, sales of big-ticket items such as automobiles—had been signaling an economic slowdown for several months. Despite the president's reassurance, investors continued to sell off their stock holdings. On Tuesday, October 29, the stock market tumbled once again. This time, 16 million shares were sold and many investors who had bought low the previous Thursday had to sell even lower. The stock market had indeed crashed.

The Depression lasted more than a decade and forced the federal government to take a more active role in economic and social

programs. Most farmers were as devastated as their industrial counterparts during the depression. Prices of farm goods dropped 60 percent during the first few years of the Depression. Sadly, tons of grain
lay unsold, rotting in bins and silos. Many farmers were unable to
make mortgage payments and lost their farms to foreclosure. To
make matters worse, droughts and dust storms turned the Plains
states from Canada to Texas into the Dust Bowl. In his award-winning
novel *The Grapes of Wrath,* John Steinbeck illustrates the plight of the
"Okies," many of whom migrated westward in search of work in California. As a result of high unemployment, labor unions developed
more quickly and women entered the workforce in greater numbers
than previous decades in an effort to feed their families.

Eager for new leadership, voters elected Franklin Delano Roosevelt president in 1932. The Democratic party also held a majority in
both the Senate and the House of Representatives after the election.
Roosevelt carried through on his promise of a "New Deal" for the
country. The New Deal included the creation of the Federal Deposit
Insurance Corporation to protect banks; the Federal Emergency Relief Administration for aid to the unemployed; the Agricultural Ad-
justment Administration to provide crop subsidies; and the Works
Progress Administration that provided $11 billion to create public
projects that employed 8.5 million skilled workers. The country was
happy with the New Deal and reelected Roosevelt in 1936.

Not all businesses suffered during the 1930s. Each week, the
burgeoning film industry gave 85 million fans a chance to escape
from reality for a few hours. Films such as *Gone with the Wind, The Wizard of Oz,* and Walt Disney's animated feature *Snow White and the Seven
Dwarfs* were the type of entertainment one needed in order to forget
about the Depression and rumors of America going to war again.

This decade is considered the golden age of radio as well as the
golden age of Broadway musicals. As more consumers listened to
radio, however, fewer of them bought records. The recording industry
sold only 6 million records in 1932, an industry that sold 140 million
discs five years earlier. When Prohibition was repealed in 1933, many
new venues began to offer live music. The increase in post-Prohibition
live entertainment, combined with a new phenomenon called the
"jukebox," helped promote recordings and sales began to increase.

As the decade began, consumer demand for jazz gave way to more
romantic popular music. But as the nation began to emerge from the

bleak economy, there was a renewed interest in jazz or jazz-influenced music. Much like their counterparts in the 1920s, youths were eager to hear up-tempo dance music. By mid-decade, bands that combined elements of jazz and pop music evolved to meet consumer demand.

Benny Goodman and his band performed a show at the Los Angeles Palomar ballroom in 1935. His style of popular dance–oriented music was influenced by jazz, but it had notated parts for different instrumental sections. This type of music came to be called "big band swing." Swing bands had sections of trombones, saxophones, and trumpets plus a piano, bass, and drum set. And each big band was expected to have a vocalist, or "crooner," to sing escapist lyrics to exhausted dancers. By the end of the decade, swing had made popular music more sophisticated, in terms of music technique and notation, than ever before.

Roosevelt tried to maintain an isolationist policy during the 1930s. He felt, as did the overwhelming majority of Americans, that the federal government should stay out of foreign wars and concentrate on reinvigorating the domestic economy. When Italy invaded Ethiopia in 1936, Roosevelt did little more than communicate his displeasure for their action. Later, when the Nazi regime invaded Czechoslovakia and Austria in 1938, Roosevelt again did nothing more than express his concern. On September 1, 1939, Germany invaded Poland. Because they had both signed a pact pledging to come to Poland's aid, France and Britain declared war on Germany. As the decade came to a close, World War II had begun in Europe. Although the U.S. government maintained its isolationist posture, most citizens feared that we would soon be in the second global war in twenty years.

SONGS

1. "Brother Can You Spare a Dime?"
Words by E. Y. Harburg and Music by Jay Gorney
Copyright © 1932, Harms, Inc.

In 1932, America's economy reached its lowest level. The economic collapse that began in 1929 put 25 percent of the workforce out of a job. From New York to California once-proud men, accountants and shipbuilders alike, were reduced to standing in line for soup and bread and to panhandling on the streets. Herbert Hoover was president, and the tent cities of America's economic refugees became known as "Hoovervilles."

The entertainment industry, like most others, was also enduring hard times. But the music industry produced upbeat, frivolous fare, as if the grim realities could be wished away. One lyricist, however, broke with that tradition and used his skills to confront the truth. The result became emblematic of the depression, "Brother Can You Spare a Dime?"

E. Y. "Yip" Harburg had lost a successful appliance business in 1929, but did not regret being compelled to try his real love, songwriting. To get started, he turned to his friend George Gershwin, who put him in touch with Jay Gorney, a Russian-born composer who had already seen some success. Their first collaborations were forgettable, but then they were asked to work on a modest musical titled *Americana*. Harburg would later remember walking past breadlines near Broadway and thinking about the constant plea "Can you spare a dime?" He wanted to work it into a song, and persuaded Gorney to use the melody of a torch song that they were already in the process of writing. That melody was a dark chant in a minor key, reminiscent of a sad Jewish lullaby from Gorney's childhood. Harburg's lyrics were powerful, asking how the men who had built America's steel mills and fought her wars had been reduced to panhandling for dimes. The mood of the song was so somber that it was almost cut by the show's producers, but when *Americana* opened, the impact was immediate. Critics dismissed the musical but praised the song. Recording artists, notably Bing Crosby and Al Jolson, rushed to record it, and radio play was so extensive that some political interests sought to have it banned.

That controversy foretold the future. In 1950 the left-leaning Harburg was among the creative artists blacklisted by studios and producers in the McCarthy era, largely because of his support for organizations that included communists among their leadership. He weathered the period better than many others because of a steady flow of royalties from his songs, including another masterwork "Somewhere Over the Rainbow."

"Brother Can You Spare a Dime?" is available in many recorded versions, including Bing Crosby's rendition on *Pop Music: The Early*

Years, 1890-1950 (Sony 65788), which is part of the series *Soundtrack for a Century.* It can also be found in print in *80 Years of Popular Music* (Warner Brothers MF 9824).

2. "Happy Days Are Here Again"
Words by Jack Yellen and Music by Milton Ager
Copyright © 1929, Advanced Music Corporation

In November 1932, at the lowest point of the Depression, Franklin Roosevelt became the Democratic Party nominee for president of the United States. He was chosen to oppose incumbent Herbert Hoover with a margin of just one vote on the fourth ballot of the night. Breaking with tradition, he was on hand to accept the nomination from the assembled crowd at the massive new Chicago Stadium. As he maneuvered his polio-weakened frame to the podium, the strains of his campaign song, "Happy Days Are Here Again," roared from the legendary 3,675-pipe Barton organ with the force of a 2,500-member military band. It would be a long time before happy days would return to the United States, but Roosevelt stood before the crowd and promised a "New Deal" for the American people. He would be elected three more times, though he would not live to finish his final term, and his theme song would become the de facto theme of the Democratic Party, no doubt disappointing lyricist Yellen, a loyal Republican.

"Happy Days Are Here Again" began life in an unremarkable Hollywood musical, *Chasing Rainbows.* Milton Ager and Jack Yellen, accomplished songwriters who were among the first Tin Pan Alley writers to be lured by work in motion pictures, had been collaborating for nearly ten years when the assignment at Metro-Goldwyn-Mayer (MGM) came along. They had written three songs for the movie early in production, and then were asked for one more in the final days.

"Happy Days Are Here Again" was the hurried result of Ager and Yellen's last-minute songwriting efforts. However, the studio was so disappointed in the movie that the film was shelved. Meanwhile, Ager and Yellen published the song with Advanced Music, and it was picked up by bandleader George Olsen. Olsen performed the song at the Roosevelt Hotel in Los Angeles. Reportedly, MGM executive

Irving Thalberg heard a performance and told his staff to get the song for a movie, only to be told that it had already been used. *Chasing Rainbows* was then revived, with the scene that included "Happy Days" enhanced. The movie was a flop, but the song became a great hit. Bandleaders Benny Meroff, Ben Selvin, and Leo Reisman all recorded chart toppers in 1930. Americans had been singing it in their misery for two years before FDR's campaign.

The great popularity of this song can only be attributed to its historical context, for it was not exceptional musically. The public responded to its unyielding (and perhaps satirical) optimism. Also, while the song's principal reference was to economic recovery, some assigned its meaning to the repeal of Prohibition that was supported by Roosevelt. Its most interesting appearance in the latter half of the century was its revival by Barbra Streisand, for whom it was an early hit. Her version turned the lyrics into a sardonic lament, with tone and inflections that denied the words.

For an authentic period recording of this song, try the performance by Ben Selvin and His Orchestra on *Pop Music: The Early Years, 1890-1950* (Sony 65788). Or, one can find it on a variety of Barbra Streisand compilations. It is also easily found in printed anthologies, or in a single sheet (Warner Brothers VS0263).

3. "Of Thee I Sing" (sometimes listed as "Of Thee I Sing [Baby]")
Words by Ira Gershwin and Music by George Gershwin
Copyright © 1931, New World Music Corporation

"Of Thee I Sing" is the title song from the Broadway musical of the same name. The musical play was written by George S. Kaufman and Morrie Ryskind. The songs were written by George Gershwin and his brother Ira. The literary merit of this musical was acknowledged when it became the first musical to win a Pulitzer Prize. Regrettably, the Pulitzer committee left George Gershwin's name off the award because of a technicality: they felt that he did not contribute to writing the story, only the music.

The creators of the musical *Of Thee I Sing* changed the status quo of Broadway musicals and the songs they contained. The musical was pure political satire, not typical subject matter for Broadway prior to 1931, and it alluded to contemporary issues. Although

Prohibition was still in effect, alcohol was consumed by politicians. The position of the vice president was treated as meaningless, and other politicians were totally dishonest. This was likely a reflection of public cynicism brought on by political gaffes such as the Teapot Dome Scandal and the ineffective report of the Wickersham Commission. It was also a commentary on the conservatism of Coolidge and Hoover.

In addition to domestic politics, the musical also made reference to somber issues such as growing fascism abroad. George and Ira Gershwin could, no doubt, relate to political instability of Russia, Italy, and Germany because their family had immigrated to the United States from St. Petersburg, Russia. They knew of the discrimination against Jews in both Europe and the United States. Although the overall tone of the musical was light and comedic, its creators presented some important and serious references.

The use of songs in this musical departed from the typical Broadway musical. The songs were an integral part of the story development, unlike other Broadway shows that spliced songs into the production indiscriminately. The clever lyrics of Ira Gershwin's songs were not merely inspired by the story line of the play, they were interwoven into the story and action.

The play *Of Thee I Sing* was published by the Samuel French Company and it was also made into a hardbound book. The song "Of Thee I Sing (Baby)" can be heard on the album *Of Thee I Sing/Let Em Eat Cake* by Tilson Thomas and the Orchestra of St. Lukes (Sony M2K42522).

4. "Star Dust"
Words by Mitchell Parish and Music by Hoagy Carmichael
Composed, 1927; copyright © 1929, Mills Music; first recorded, 1930, EMI Music Publishing

Hoagy Carmichael's "Star Dust" first became a nationwide hit in 1930, and went on to become (by most measures) the most recorded song of the twentieth century. It treated no topic of social significance, broke no new ground musically, was not "catchy," and was not even associated with anyone particularly famous. It was simply a haunting melody enhanced by evocative lyrics that held universal appeal. More than five hundred recordings have been made by a list of performers that reads like a who's who of leading vocalists (for example, Ella Fitzgerald, Bing Crosby, Frank Sinatra, Dinah Washington, Willie Nelson), big bands (for example, Benny Goodman, Artie Shaw, Glenn Miller, Tommy Dorsey), and jazz instrumentalists (for example, Duke Ellington, Dizzy Gillespie, Louis Armstrong, Bunny Berigan, Django Reinhardt), and yet no single recording ever dominated the charts. Its success can perhaps be attributed to the great craftsmanship of Hoagy Carmichael, who melded the two styles with which he was most familiar—popular songs played by his mother on the home piano and jazz that made its way north—to create a durable standard.

Hoagy Carmichael composed the melody at a time when he was struggling to resolve the pull of music with his desire for a stable occupation. He had grown up under hard circumstances in his native Indiana, had quit school to work, but later was able to finish high school and study law at Indiana University in Bloomington. Throughout his college years, he performed with his own band and others, and counted famed cornetist Bix Beiderbecke among his friends. Not long after graduation, he abandoned law entirely to pursue his career as composer, pianist, vocalist, and, eventually, actor.

He was on the university campus one spring night in 1927 when the melody of "Star Dust" formed in his mind. He knew he had something of value and rushed to a local hangout to find a piano. He originally conceived the song as a ragtime piece, and it was performed as one by Don Redman and His Orchestra, "but it took three years of trouping for 'Stardust' [*sic*] to make the grade. It went from Don to Jean Goldkette and then Isham Jones. . . . It was the hard way in those days. Overnight hits on radio came later" (Carmichael 1965, 186). It was Isham Jones who first played the song as a ballad, slowing down the pace and giving the melody room to enchant. In 1929, music publisher Irving Mills asked his prolific staff lyricist, Mitchell Parish, to produce words for the song. The result was memorable, leading to the song's adoption by popular vocalists as well as jazz ensembles. At least one version of the song was on the charts almost continuously from 1930 to 1944, and it is still being recorded today.

"Star Dust" (which is now usually listed as "Stardust") is available in sixty different song anthologies as well as sheet music.

Recordings are available from more than 160 different performers in almost every conceivable style. One vocal treatment is Carmen McRae's on her *Some of the Best* (Laserlight CD 12635).

5. "Take My Hand Precious Lord"
Words and Music by Thomas A. Dorsey
Copyright © 1932, Thomas A. Dorsey Publishing

Thomas Andrew Dorsey was born to an African American revivalist preacher in Villa Rica, Georgia, in 1899. The family moved to Atlanta in 1910, where Dorsey first heard blues pianists in addition to the familiar church pianists.

Moving to Chicago in 1916, Dorsey attended the Chicago College of Composition and arranging. His piano skills earned him a job as a composer and arranger for Paramount Record Company executive Mayo Williams. At Williams's direction, Dorsey put together a band, the Wildcats Jazz Band, and toured with vaudeville blues singer Gertrude (Ma) Rainey. During the four years with Rainey (1923–1927), Dorsey made his reputation as a blues composer and arranger and was given the nickname "Georgia Tom."

In 1928, Dorsey teamed with slide guitarist Tampa Red (Hudson Whittaker) to record a series of double-entendre blues, the best selling of which was "It's Tight Like That." The song spawned numerous imitations as well as a taste for piano/guitar duets in the race market.

Dorsey's conflicts between his religious upbringing and professional life increased after he had a conversion experience in the late 1920s, though he continued writing both blues and religious songs. He called the latter "gospel songs," and was trying to imbue them with the personal immediacy of the blues while retaining the evangelical spirit of his earliest, hymnlike religious songs.

In August 1932, having had some success with his first few self-published gospel songs, Dorsey set forth in his car for a religious program in St. Louis where he hoped to sell sheet music to the ministers and choir members assembled there. He left his pregnant wife, Nettie, home alone. The next night Dorsey received a telegram: his wife was dead, but the baby boy was born alive. Rushing back to Chicago, Dorsey was able to hold Thomas Dorsey Jr. in his arms before the child joined his mother in death. A devastated Dorsey buried them in the same coffin.

His faith shaken, Dorsey considered returning to the world of jazz and blues, but on the Saturday following the funeral, as he sat idly fingering the piano keyboard, he heard a comforting melody coming from under his fingers. The words to "Take My Hand Precious Lord" came tumbling into his head and he quickly wrote down what became a standard of gospel music.

In the 1930s, the sheet music sold slowly; Dorsey made personal calls on music ministers and demonstrated the song at choir conventions. In 1939, gospel quartets recorded the song for the major companies Bluebird (RCA) and Decca and religious songbook publishers Stamps-Baxter (Dallas) and R. E. Winsett (Dayton, Tennessee) brought the song to white churches. Since then the song has shown universal appeal, having been translated into thirty-two languages. "Take My Hand Precious Lord" is in print in dozens of sheet music and folio arrangements as well as in two dozen sound recordings. A noteworthy recording is an a cappella version by South Africa's Ladysmith Black Mambazo (Shanachie CD 64098).

6. "Goodnight Irene"
Words and Music by Huddie Ledbetter and John Lomax
Copyright © 1950, Ludlow Music, Inc.

On a July day in 1933, John and Alan Lomax, a father and son representing the Library of Congress, walked through the gates of Louisiana's Angola State Prison farm. They were traveling the southern states with a portable disc recorder collecting folk songs for the Library's archive. When college professor and former Texas banker John Lomax asked Warden L. A. Jones to provide black prisoners who possessed suitable musical talent, Jones recommended Huddie Ledbetter who was serving a six-to-ten-year sentence for attempted murder. Ledbetter was better known by his nickname Leadbelly.

Leadbelly was a "songster," a musician who could perform many types of songs, depending on audience requirements. Sizing up the Lomaxes, Leadbelly gave them some bad man ballads, a cowboy song, some dance and ragtime tunes, one topical blues, and a waltz that was to become his most famous song, "Goodnight Irene."

The protoversion of the song recorded that day had only two verses and the chorus, but when the Lomaxes returned to Angola the next summer, Leadbelly gave them a version with four verses. Upon his release in the fall of 1934, Leadbelly went to work for John Lomax as his driver. They worked their way back to New York, stopping at prisons in Arkansas, Alabama, and Georgia to make more recordings. When they reached New York City, Lomax lost no time in publicizing his find: the "Sweet Singer of the Swamplands." Newspaper articles touted the "Negro minstrel . . . here to do a few tunes between homicides." Lomax even had Leadbelly perform in his prison garb before members of the Modern Language Association and other gatherings of scholars.

By February 1935, "Irene" had grown to six verses and spoken contextual interludes. Leadbelly may have been a twice-convicted felon and relatively unschooled, but he knew what his audiences wanted. Had Lomax wanted a bluesman, Leadbelly was more than capable, for he had lived in Dallas and played with Blind Lemon ten years before the blues craze hit; but a folksinger was wanted, and Leadbelly delivered.

Macmillan published John and Alan's book *Negro Folk Songs as Sung by Lead Belly* in 1936. It contained a transcription of "Irene" by Dr. George Herzog of Columbia University with the note, "The melody is certainly not a Negro folk melody . . . a sweet, sentimental song from the nineteenth century."

Leadbelly claimed to have written the song as a lullaby for Irene Campbell, a niece, but other family members are certain Leadbelly's uncle Terrell Ledbetter brought the song back home to Louisiana from Texas around the turn of the century. In either case, "Irene," as of 1936, was published as by Huddie Ledbetter *and* John Lomax.

Leadbelly used the song as a theme for radio performances during the 1940s and he recorded it commercially at least four times. In 1950, a year after Leadbelly's death, the song became a million seller when recorded for Decca by the Weavers, a white New York folk group who had been friends with Ledbetter. This version, known as "Goodnight Irene," is credited with starting the folk music revival of the 1950s and making the lullaby of the "longtime Dixie convict" a standard American folk song.

Print arrangements run to more than a dozen, including those for guitar, banjo, organ, country vocal, dance band, and singalong. The folio "Weavers Sing" by Plymouth Publishing is one source. Sound recordings currently available number well over fifty, with versions by rockers Jerry Lee Lewis and Little Richard, popsters Van Morrison and Leon Russell, and vocal groups the Mills Brothers and the Orioles among the possibilities. The original version by Leadbelly is on *Goodnight Irene* (Tradition/Rykodisc CD 1006).

7. "The Continental"
Words by Herb Magidson and Music by Con Conrad
Copyright © 1934, Harms, Inc.

While much of life in the 1930s was gritty and deprived, life on the silver screen was mostly glamorous. Extravagant Busby Berkeley productions, such as *The Gold Diggers*, paraded glossy beauties in glorious costumes amid fantastic settings. Lush romantic comedies featured the wealthy and elegant, with evening dress the standard attire. Musicals dominated America's movie houses, and somewhere along the way motion picture music came of age.

During the early days of the film industry, songwriters were unseen contract labor. Herb Magidson and Con Conrad fit the typical profile of relocated New York songwriters who could produce well-crafted music, in quantity, under tight time constraints. As movies evolved, their background scores and songs became more central to the overall production, bringing a new appreciation for the men and women who wrote the music. Conversely, the movies reached every corner of the country, enabling them to deliver a song more powerfully than even Broadway could manage. This interdependence was reflected in the addition of a new category for "Best Original Song" to the 1935 awards ceremony of the Academy of Motion Picture Arts and Sciences. The academy had been created in 1929 by Louis B. Mayer and other studio heads, in part to strengthen their hand in dealing with unions. The Academy Awards (which would not become known as The Oscars until the 1940s) were initiated with just twelve categories and not much fanfare, but by 1935, the ceremony had grown into a glitzy, well-attended affair.

And the winner was . . . "The Continental" from the movie version of Cole Porter's musical *The Gay Divorce* (renamed *The Gay Divorcee* to avoid any suggestion that Hollywood endorsed divorce). Some thought it won only because Porter's own "Night and Day" did not qualify as an original motion picture song. "The Continental" was the centerpiece of an incredible seventeen-minute musical production that featured nearly one hundred dancers, an Art Deco background, and Fred Astaire and Ginger Rogers in their first joint appearance in leading roles. The gracefully athletic couple exuberantly danced over furniture and up stairs as the lyrics of the song provided an opportunity to switch styles from Hungarian to Spanish to Jazz. It was a truly spectacular number and audiences loved it, helping to propel Astaire and Rogers to stardom and a long series of similar films.

"The Continental" was quickly recorded by dance bands. Leo Reisman and his Orchestra had a number one hit soon after the movie premiered, and two other versions charted in the same year. Tommy Dorsey and the King Cole Trio both did versions later in the decade. "The Continental" also enjoyed brief popularity as a dance. The sheet music, which featured twenty-seven demonstration photos, was a best-seller.

Many recorded versions of "The Continental" are available; for example, Nelson Riddle's arrangements for *Frank Sinatra Sings Days of Wine and Roses, Moon River, and Other Academy Award Winners* (Reprise 1011). It is also in many song anthologies including *Hollywood Musicals Year by Year, 1927-1939* (Hal Leonard 00311660).

8. "I Get a Kick Out of You"
Words and Music by Cole Porter
Copyright © 1934, Chappell and Company/Harms, Inc.
c/o Warner Brothers Music

A showdown over censorship of the arts and literature had been developing in the United States since 1873 when the New York Society for Suppression of Vice was formed. The 1930 Hawley Tariff Act transferred authority for censorship decisions from the Customs Office to the federal judicial system. The first federal obscenity case, regarding the book *Ulysses*, was heard in 1933. Although federal Judge

John M. Woolsey did not find the book to be obscene, the publicity brought a great deal of attention to the issue.

In addition to watching for "offensive" works of literature, many groups began to scrutinize songs, especially those from Broadway shows and films. The most popular musical of 1934, *Anything Goes*, and the Cole Porter song "I Get a Kick Out of You," were modified to avoid being branded offensive.

The original musical (full of whimsical songs) was a fairly light-hearted story about shipwrecked passengers. After rehearsals had begun, the cruise liner *Morro Castle* burned off Asbury Park, California, and 215 lives were lost. The show's producers, fearing that the topic was too sensitive, had the libretto rewritten.

The new story was adequate, but it was the Cole Porter songs that became most popular. Cole Porter was by no means the typical songwriter of the decade. He studied law at Harvard, served in the French army in the 1920s, and married into a wealthy family. He also learned about the many European vices including champagne and cocaine. When he wrote songs for the Broadway musical *Anything Goes*, Porter naturally wrote using real-life expressions with which he was familiar. In the song "I Get a Kick Out of You," the lyrics explain that the singer gets a "kick" from the person they are serenading. The song also refers to several things the singer does not get a kick out of, and, in the original version of the lyrics, one item was cocaine. Fearing public criticism, he later changed it from cocaine to champagne.

Two film versions of *Anything Goes* were released in 1936 and 1956. The Song "I Get a Kick Out of You" has been recorded by numerous artists and remains a standard of the cabaret singer's repertoire. Sheet music for the song is available in *Music and Lyrics by Cole Porter, Vol. 1* by Hal Leonard (HL 312330).

9. "Tumbling Tumbleweeds"
Words and Music by Bob Nolan
Copyright © 1934, Williamson Music, Inc.

The popular image of a cowboy riding alone across the vast American West owes its puissance more to Hollywood than historical reality. Beginning in silent films with William Hart and Tom Mix, the cowboy was portrayed as the American knight-errant. In the 1930s, the talking movie drew ever-increasing numbers of depression-wracked, entertainment-starved patrons into theaters. For a nickel one could see a cartoon, a newsreel, and two feature films; the first shown was the B film, a cheaply made formula film for which "westerns" were fodder.

The cowboy movie made an awkward transition from silent film to "talkie." At first, only stilted dialogue and the sound of gunfire differentiated the new technology from the old. In the 1935 film *Tumbling Tumbleweeds*, the cowboy lifted his voice in song. Named after the title song, the film was an enormous hit and made a star of Gene Autry, a former railroad telegrapher and radio and record artist. Leaving Chicago for California and a movie career, Autry began listening to the many western groups on West Coast stages and radio programs. One of the most popular of these was the Pioneer Trio: Bob Nolan, Tim Spencer, and Leonard Slye. Performing twice a day on KFWB in Los Angeles, the trio's repertoire included western, folk, and popular songs as well as original compositions by Nolan. Financial difficulties caused the group to break up more than once, and it was during one of these layoffs that Nolan, while earning his living as a caddy at Bel Air Country Club, wrote one of the most famous western songs.

Robert Clarence Nobels was born in New Brunswick, Canada, and was raised in Boston. After World War I, Robert moved with his father, whose lungs were damaged by mustard gas, to Arizona. Young Nolan—the family name was changed by the father—wrote poetry and hoboed after high school. He discovered his singing skills after joining a chatauqua troupe in 1929. In early 1932, he answered a newspaper ad for a singer and met his future Pioneer Trio partners.

On a November day in 1932, Nolan was home, looking out the window at the rain which kept him from caddying at Bel Air. Sadness over an inability to earn a livelihood from music combined with the dreary day caused Nolan to write a bittersweet song, "Tumbling Leaves."

In the fall of 1933, Slye and Spencer convinced Nolan to give the trio one more try. Performing Nolan's composition on the radio garnered the trio many letters asking for that song about the "tumbling weeds." By the autumn of 1935, the trio had become a quintet, with the addition of the Farr Brothers on guitar and fiddle; the group was known as the Sons of the Pioneers and Decca recorded the group singing the reworked "Tumbling Tumbleweeds."

After Autry's *Tumbling Tumbleweeds* created a demand for singing cowboys, Leonard Slye left the Sons of the Pioneers to act in the movies; first as Dick Weston, then, in 1937, under the stage name Roy Rogers. Nolan and Spencer kept the group together for over forty years, making records and appearing in dozens of films, many with their former singing partner Roy Rogers, "The King of the Cowboys."

"Tumbling Tumbleweeds" appears in several music folios including Warner Brothers' *Gene Autry Songbook*. Recorded versions available number over fifty, including those by Autry, Roy Rogers, Patti Page, Bing Crosby, and Kate Smith. The Sons of the Pioneers' version is available on *The Country Music Hall of Fame* (MCA CD 10090).

10. "(The) Great Speckled Bird"
Words and Music by Reverend Guy Smith
Copyright © 1937, M. M. Cole Publishing Company

From the Old Testament Book of Jeremiah, Chapter 12, Verse 9: "Mine heritage is unto me as a speckled bird, the birds round are against her; come ye, assemble all the beasts of the field, come to devour." The image of the unloved surrounded by enemies was the central image of a sacred folk song of uncertain parentage that brought an Appalachian preacher's son to international fame.

Roy Acuff was a failed semipro baseball player earning his living as a fiddler and singer in Knoxville, Tennessee, in 1935. Acuff appeared on WROL radio with a group of local string musicians dubbed the "Crazy Tennesseans," which included local Hawaiian guitar wizard Clell Summey.

Also appearing on Knoxville radio was a singing bible college student, Charlie Swain, who worked in a quartet, The Black Shirts. One of Swain's best songs was "The Great Speckled Bird," which Acuff had recalled hearing in his youth. Wanting to learn all six verses to the song, Acuff paid Swain 50 cents to write them down; the melody was easy to remember, for it was a slight variant of a Carter

Family hit record of the previous decade, "I'm Thinking Tonight of My Blue Eyes."

By 1936, Acuff was singing the song on his radio program when a Vocalion record company scout signed Acuff and his group to a recording contract. Acuff said later that the scout wanted the song, not the singer. The recording of "The Bird" in Chicago in October 1936 was the start of Acuff's legendary career at the Grand Ol' Opry, as a music publisher, and as a Tennessee political figure.

Composer credit for "The Great Speckled Bird" was given, on its first sound recording, to Guy Smith, a radio entertainer from Springfield, Missouri, who worked under the name "Uncle George." Perhaps it was Smith who anonymously submitted the text of the song to the Aurora (Missouri) *Advertiser* on March 26, 1936. By the time the song saw print the following year, Smith had become a reverend, though the denomination is unknown. It is known that at least two related Pentecostal denominations claimed the song as "theirs": the Church of God (Dayton, Tennessee) and the Assembly of God (Springfield, Missouri).

The song had an undeniable impact on poverty-stricken country and gospel audiences by telling the story of the ultimate triumph of the unloved bird that will spread her wings and rise.

Print versions are available in single sheets from a variety of religious publishers, and Hal Leonard includes the song in several of the bluegrass and greatest country hits folios. Recorded versions by bluegrass artists are most common, but the original recording is available on *The Essential Roy Acuff, 1936–1949* (Columbia Legacy CD 48956).

11. "One O'Clock Jump"
Composed by William "Count" Basie
Copyright © 1937, EMI April Music Inc. c/o EMI Music Publishing

The song "One O'Clock Jump" became synonymous with 1930s swing-style jazz. It was performed by most swing bands of the decade and recorded by many of them. The manner in which Count Basie wrote the song was representative of his informal approach to creating music: start playing something on piano and hope that it turns into something. The song also shows the blues, jazz, and vaudeville influences that blended to create his unique style of swing.

Born William Basie on August 21, 1904, in Red Bank, New Jersey, he first studied piano with his mother. After moving to Harlem to seek employment and to enjoy the jazz scene, Basie met piano greats James P. Johnson and Thomas "Fats" Waller. Both Johnson and Waller influenced Basie's early jazz piano style. After they became friends, Waller invited William to sit next to him and play the theater organ for silent films.

He performed in the New York area for several years and then toured with vaudeville shows. After one of his touring shows left him stranded in Kansas City, Missouri, in 1927, Basie found employment playing organ in a theater. He soon joined the Bennie Moten Kansas City Orchestra and remained a band member with the group until Moten died unexpectedly in 1935.

After Moten's death, Basie began playing a cabaret-style club in Kansas City called the Reno. Although many of the key players had played with Moten, it was Basie's band. A local radio station, W9XBY, began to broadcast his band from the Reno. The radio station's signal could be heard as far away as Chicago and the band began to get a regional reputation. The radio announcer also gave Basie the moniker "Count" in an obvious comparison to Duke Ellington.

One evening, the band was performing for a W9XBY broadcast and, with ten minutes left to play, Basie could not think of another song to play. The Count told the show's director that the band would just improvise something. The announcer, however, insisted that he have a name for it. Thinking about his need to perform until one o'clock, Basie called it "One O'Clock Jump."

Amazing as it seems, one of the greatest swing songs ever written was actually improvised during a radio broadcast. Count Basie, known for his ability to establish a strong but unpretentious rhythmic piano accompaniment, began "One O'Clock Jump" and the band followed his lead. By the end of the radio broadcast, the Count Basie Band had a new song that would become their theme song.

"One O'Clock Jump" became so popular that the Bennie Goodman Orchestra, the most popular swing band of this era, and many others recorded it. A recording of this song is available on *Count Basie: The Early Years* (GRP #GRD655).

12. "Hell Hound on My Trail"
Words and Music by Robert Johnson
Copyright © 1978, King of Spades Music

Robert Leroy Johnson was born near Hazlehurst, Mississippi, in 1911, the son of field hands. Like most African American children growing up on a plantation, Johnson probably was familiar with hard work at an early age. Of slight physical stature, he could contribute little to the family workforce. A stern, religious stepfather disapproved of Johnson's interest in music as Robert learned to play blues and reels on his harmonica.

Upon moving to the delta region in the 1920s, Johnson became enthralled with the playing of Charley Patton, Willie Brown, and Son House. By the early 1930s, Johnson was playing guitar, though Robert was so bad that the older musicians would chase him away from the house parties and juke joints where they performed.

Johnson disappeared from the upper delta for several months and he reappeared playing guitar better than anyone in the vicinity. Soon the rumor spread that Robert had gained this ability by selling his soul to the devil in a ritual at a crossroads at midnight.

For several years Johnson lived the life of an itinerant musician, rambling as far as Detroit and New York. In 1936, he was recommended to the ARC Record Company by H. C. Speir, a Jackson, Mississippi, record retailer and talent scout. In November 1936, Johnson made his first recordings in a makeshift studio in San Antonio, Texas. Three days of recording produced a body of work that included future blues standards: "I Believe I'll Dust My Broom," "Sweet Home Chicago," and the evocative "Cross Road Blues," which describes meeting the devil at the crossroads.

Sales of the initial releases on the Vocalion and associated ARC labels were good enough for ARC to record Johnson again in Dallas in 1937. On Sunday, June 20, Johnson started the day with "Hell Hound on My Trail," an evocative song of despair and resignation caused by blues-forced travel and voodoo hexes. Sunday was Johnson's last recording session. On August 16, 1938, he was dead, poisoned by a jealous husband at a juke joint near Greenwood, Mississippi. He was twenty-seven years old.

In December 1938, John Hammond produced the "Spirituals to Swing" concert at Carnegie Hall in New York. The concert was intended to show mainstream America the breadth of African American musical expression, and Hammond wanted Johnson as the exemplar of country blues. Had Johnson lived to make this appearance, one can imagine the career he might have had.

In 1960, Columbia Record Company issued an LP of Johnson's 1930s songs. It was this album that secured Johnson's reputation by influencing a generation of guitar players and singers. Future stars such as Eric Clapton and Keith Richards were profoundly changed when they heard the sophisticated guitar and emotive singing of Robert Johnson.

All of Johnson's twenty-nine recorded songs are available (with guitar notation) in *Robert Johnson at the Crossroads: The Authoritative Guitar Transcriptions* from Hal Leonard. Johnson's original recording can be found on Columbia's *Robert Johnson, the Complete Recordings*, (C2K 64916; two CDs).

13. "Over the Rainbow"
Words by E. Y. "Yip" Harburg and Music by Harold Arlen
Copyright © 1938, Metro-Goldwyn-Mayer Inc.; 1939, EMI–Feist
Catalog Inc.

The song "Over the Rainbow," from the MGM film *The Wizard of Oz*, was more a result of sheer coincidence than any sort of plan. This is a work—one that was almost not released—some critics have called the top song of the century. "Over the Rainbow" became a capstone song for the 1930s because it summarized the escapist optimism of persons who had survived the Depression era.

The 1939 film *The Wizard of Oz* was based on an extremely popular children's book written by L. Frank Baum and published in 1900. Baum eventually wrote thirteen other volumes of the *Oz* series and produced three films based on the books in 1914. Later, in 1925, comedian Larry Semon produced and starred in his own film version of *The Wizard of Oz*.

Because neither of the first two *Oz* film ventures was terribly successful, one might logically assume that films based on *The Wizard of Oz* book had run their course by 1939. But, executives at MGM, eager to emulate the success of Walt Disney's 1937 animated feature *Snow White and the Seven Dwarfs,* hired producer Mervyn LeRoy to produce a new film version of the Baum book with songs by Harburg and Arlen.

Sixteen-year-old Judy Garland's performance in *The Wizard of Oz*—both acting and singing—launched her career. Ironically, she was not originally cast in the role of Dorothy for the film. Both MGM and the film's producer had intended to have Shirley Temple play the part of Dorothy, because she better resembled the young girl with blond curls in the original Baum book. However, Temple was signed to Fox Studios and they would not allow her to work for MGM.

The song "Over the Rainbow" was so well suited for Garland, it became her signature song for decades to come. It was also the most memorable song of the film and continues to be performed and recorded more than fifty years later. It is, therefore, ironic that MGM executives tried to cut the song from the show at one point. They felt that it did not fit with the other songs in the show, all of which were more "upbeat" than the more sensitive "Over the Rainbow." It is quite likely that Arthur Freed, an assistant to the film's producer, was influential in the decision to keep the song in the film, because he had been a successful songwriter himself before pursuing film production.

Although *The Wizard of Oz* did not win an Academy Award (it was eclipsed by *Gone with the Wind*), "Over the Rainbow" won an award for song of the year. Garland's recording of the song on Decca Records was also a hit the same year. Since 1939, this song has been recorded by hundreds of artists and performed by thousands.

"Over the Rainbow" has been arranged for myriad voice and instrument combinations from vocal jazz ensemble to marching band. The most representative recording by Judy Garland is available on *Over the Rainbow: The Very Best of Judy Garland* (MCA CD 112691).

14. "God Bless America"
Words and Music by Irving Berlin
Copyright © 1938, Irving Berlin Music Corporation

In 1938, America again agonized over its role in world affairs. Allies in Europe were sliding into war, confronted by Adolf Hitler's aggression.

Opposing voices called for intervention or isolation. The fear of war was palpable on November 10, the eve of Armistice Day, when America honored nearly 117,000 men killed in World War I, just one generation earlier. When Kate Smith stepped to the microphone for her weekly *Kate Smith Radio Hour* and sang "God Bless America," calls and telegrams poured in. She continued to sing "God Bless America" almost every week for two years and would use it to sell more than $600 million in war bonds. Its lyrics were entered in the Congressional Record, and both political parties used the song as their convention theme in the 1940 presidential election, neither wanting the other to claim its sentiments.

Irving Berlin had already written hundreds of songs by the time Kate Smith was looking for a patriotic number. By most accounts, he was a sincerely patriotic man who was grateful for his adopted home, and who recalled his mother's frequent and fervent declaration: "God bless America." As war approached, he remembered a song he had written in 1918 while an enlisted man at Camp Upton in Yaphank, Long Island, New York. Officers there had assigned him to write a musical for the camp, titled *Yip Yip Yaphank!* The finale was to be a rendition of "God Bless America," but the song was too somber for a comedy show, and was tucked in a drawer and forgotten. When Kate Smith came calling, Mr. Berlin had just the song she needed. He tinkered with his original lyrics, both before and shortly after the historic first performance, to produce the patriotic hymn that is known by virtually every American.

Kate Smith predicted that the song "will be timeless—it will never die—others will thrill to its beauty long after we are gone" (Hayes 1995, 52). She was correct. The song had such an impact that there was a campaign to have it declared the national anthem, though neither Smith nor Berlin supported the idea. Berlin granted exclusive performance rights for the song to Smith, and she recorded a version with the "Star Spangled Banner" on the opposite side, but others clamored to perform it as well. In 1940, Berlin formed the God Bless America Foundation, and assigned all future royalties to the Boy Scouts and Girl Scouts of America.

Not everyone revered "God Bless America" when it first washed over the nation. Some objected to its mix of politics and religion. Some found it too martial and a few argued that an immigrant Jew was not the appropriate composer for such a work. In 1944, Woody Guthrie countered in a song with the refrain "God blessed America for me" that would evolve into his anthem for the political left, "This Land Is Your Land."

Conceived in World War I and embraced in World War II, "God Bless America" would be the soundtrack for the nation's response to a terrorist attack that leveled New York's World Trade Center on September 11, 2001. Beginning with a bipartisan performance by Congress on the steps of the Capitol, it became a hymn of consolation and defiance as Americans faced a new era.

"God Bless America" is available in many sheet music editions. The memorable version performed at 9/11 memorial services by New York Police Department member Daniel Rodriguez is his *God Bless America* (Manhattan Records CD 72438 776842 0).

15. "Flying Home"
Words (added later) by Sydney Robin and Music by
Benjamin "Benny" David Goodman and Lionel Hampton
Copyright © 1939, Ragbag Publishing c/o Jewel Music Publishers

Because of the solemn mood of the nation, the effervescence of the 1920s gave way to a more serious sensibility as the 1930s began. The nation looked toward social reforms to help create jobs for and restore dignity to otherwise proud citizens. The jazz sounds that symbolized a decade of bootleg liquor and seemingly endless parties gave way to more orderly popular music as the Roaring Twenties came to a close.

As some of Franklin Delano Roosevelt's programs began to succeed in giving the nation a new sense of optimism, a new youth movement emerged. After Prohibition was repealed in 1933, new venues for entertainment began to appear. Hotel ballrooms, restaurants with dance floors, and other "dance emporiums" replaced illegal speakeasies. Americans, especially young ones, were eager to enjoy life.

A new type of dance music was also emerging. Music was more accessible than ever before due to the rapid development of radio and film. By 1935, swing was the most popular form of music in the nation. Although it is a genre that has been referred to as "jazz" or "big band jazz," it was really a form of popular music that used elements of jazz such as improvised solos.

Although clarinetist and bandleader Benny Goodman was influenced by many of the great New Orleans–style jazz artists, he represented a very different breed of musician. Born in Chicago, Goodman received music instruction at his synagogue and he performed in the Jane Addams Hull House Band. He later studied music at Austin High School on Chicago's North Side, a school that became famous for training big band musicians.

Because of his ability to read and write traditional music notation, Goodman crossed the line between classical and popular music. As he evolved as a musician, he was as comfortable performing a concerto in front of a symphony orchestra as he was playing an improvised solo with his big band. In 1934, he created his first big band: three saxophones, three trumpets, two trombones, piano, bass, and drums. With the help of booking agent Willard Alexander, Goodman took the band on the road for a national tour. Although the band met with mixed reviews throughout the tour, their final stop at the Palomar in Los Angeles left an indelible mark on the music of the 1930s. Benny Goodman was dubbed the "King of Swing" and the new style of energetic jazz–influenced instrumental music came to be known as "swing."

Goodman is also credited with helping break down the color barrier in music of the era. Although black musicians and white musicians performed together from time to time on riverboats or in black-and-tan shows, major show bands were racially segregated. In 1937, however, Benny Goodman hired drummer and vibraphonist Lionel Hampton to replace Gene Krupa who had left the band. Hampton, who was African American, later recorded and composed with Goodman.

In 1939, Benny Goodman and Lionel Hampton collaborated on a swing composition called "Flyin' Home." They recorded it using the Goodman Sextet with Hampton playing the solo that has become a swing classic. Hampton enjoyed the song so much that he adopted it as his theme song when he became a leader of his own big band.

Lionel Hampton continued to perform "Flyin' Home" during his tours that continued until the 1980s. It has been recorded numerous times by jazz combos and big bands.

This song is available on *Flyin' Home (1942–1945)* by Lionel Hampton (MCA Records ASIN B000008B58 CD).

1940–1949

Swinging into a Second World War

The most significant life-changing event of the 1940s was the second world war of the century. Roosevelt signed legislation in 1939 that repealed the Neutrality Act of 1937, thereby allowing the United States to give aid to Allied forces in Europe. It also signaled that he knew the likelihood of America entering the war allied with France and England. When Germany, Italy, and Japan formed an allegiance of Axis powers, war became even more likely.

After Japanese airplanes attacked U.S. forces at Pearl Harbor on December 7, 1941, Roosevelt had no choice but to declare war on Japan and the Axis allied countries. Sadly ironic, American bombs ended the war as quickly as Japan's bombing raid forced the United States to enter the world conflict. As devastating as World War II was prior to August 6, 1945, no one could possibly have imagined the destructive force of the atomic bomb dropped on Hiroshima that day. It killed eighty thousand people and severely injured many more. The extreme heat of the A-Bomb destroyed the entire city. On August 9, the day following the destruction of Hiroshima, Russia declared war on Japan. On August 10, the United States dropped a second atomic bomb on Japan, this time on Nagasaki. Later that day, Japan agreed to an unconditional surrender.

As the war ended, Americans were stunned to learn of the Holocaust in Europe. In addition to the 50 million soldiers who lost their lives on battlefields, 6 million Jewish civilians died in Nazi concentration camps. Shocked at the horror of genocide, Americans asked why leaders of the Allied nations, especially U.S. politicians, had turned their backs on these atrocities. World courts would spend the next fifty years pursuing perpetrators of crimes against Jews.

The war caused significant changes in the way society looked at gender roles and sexual standards. As many young soldiers left for Europe, their last stop was at the justice of the peace. Marriages increased by 20 percent as the war began to escalate. Females who volunteered to dance with soldiers, V-Girls, gave a patriotic legitimacy to public flirtation. As more males enlisted and traveled overseas, females moved into factories and offices to assume jobs considered "mens' work" until the war. At the height of the war, women typically outnumbered men in factories.

While females were developing new gender roles at home, males were overseas for long periods of time. Many American soldiers admitted having sexual encounters in the foreign countries they visited during the war. In 1946, the number of divorces totaled 500,000, perhaps due to confessions of infidelity. In the postwar 1940s, 750,000 babies were born out of wedlock. The war had precipitated a sexual revolution.

Entertainment media—recordings, radio, television, and film—developed throughout the decade. Radio became the center of many U.S. households during the 1940s. Families huddled around electronic devices listening to news about the war and enjoying their favorite comedians and musicians. Big bands dominated radio airplay until August 1, 1942, when the musicians union imposed a ban on recordings due to a disagreement over royalties paid to musicians. By the time they settled the ban in 1944, vocalists had become the prototypical featured performers on radio. As vocalists, called "crooners," became increasingly popular, big band instrumental recordings lost their appeal and sales declined.

Future television behemoths NBC and CBS began broadcasting nationally in 1941. Regular network programming, begun in 1948, included *Texaco Star Theatre* (hosted by Milton Berle) and Ed Sullivan's *Toast of the Town*. Competition between television and film became heated as the decade came to a close. One thing became quite clear: Both of these media had become woven into the fabric of our culture.

SONGS

1. "In the Mood"
Words by Andy Razaf and Music by Joe Garland
Recorded by Glenn Miller Orchestra, 1940
Copyright © 1939, Shapiro, Bernstein and Company, Inc.

"In the Mood," a song that became associated with the Glenn Miller Orchestra, was descriptive of the time period between the Great Depression and World War I and the U.S. entry into World War II. It was a time of optimism when people from all social strata believed that the worst was behind them. Like the Pied Piper, trombonist and big band leader Glenn Miller moved people to celebrate the brief renaissance. And unlike many of his contemporaries, he was more interested in providing music that was entertaining and danceable than complex jazz. As a result, his orchestra became the most popular swing band from 1939 until his death in 1944.

Miller was born in Clarinda, Iowa, and grew up in Fort Morgan, Colorado. He attended the University of Colorado briefly, and then worked with various big bands from 1926 to 1937. In 1938, he formed his own big band and began performing at the Glen Island Casino in New Rochelle, New York, during the summer. Broadcasts from the casino helped promote the band's music and eventually got them a recording contract with Bluebird Records.

The Glenn Miller Orchestra became an instant success, especially with young listeners eager to dance, resulting in a nonstop string of hit records. "In the Mood" became the top-selling swing record to date and remained associated with the Glenn Miller Orchestra. The band's popularity remained strong until Miller disbanded the group to enlist in the armed forces in 1942. Glenn Miller formed the Army Air Force Band and used his tremendous popularity to entertain and motivate the troops. His live performances and radio broadcasts ended when a plane he was flying in disappeared on December 15, 1944. Neither his remains nor the wreckage of the plane was ever found. The passing of this beloved entertainer was a metaphor for the nation's loss of the comfort and security of isolationism. There was only slight consolation in the Glenn Miller Orchestra continuing under the leadership of Jerry Gray and Ray

McKinley and the emergence of the United States as postwar world superpower.

There were three films about Glenn Miller: *Sun Valley Serenade* (1941); *Orchestra Wives* (1942); and *The Glenn Miller Story* (1953, starring Jimmy Stewart). All of the Glenn Miller Orchestra recordings for the years 1938 to 1942 are available on *Complete Glenn Miller, Volumes 1–13* (Bluebird Records).

2. "I'll Never Smile Again"
Words and Music by Ruth Lowe
Recorded by Frank Sinatra, 1940
Copyright © 1939, MCA Music, Inc.

Ruth Lowe was born in Toronto, Ontario, Canada, in 1914. Her father, a struggling grocer, moved the family to Los Angeles briefly during Ruth's early teen years. The family's economic circumstances did not improve, and by 1931, they were back in Toronto. When her father died, Ruth assumed support of the family and secured a job demonstrating sheet music at the Song Shop on Yonge Street.

At night, Lowe performed in Toronto night clubs and on the radio stations CKNC and CKLC where she became the staff pianist. In 1935, bandleader Ina Ray Hutton brought her all-girl jazz band, the Melo-dears, to Toronto. A last-minute emergency left Hutton without a pianist and Lowe was hired. For two years, she traveled with and composed and arranged for Hutton. It was during this time that she met Chicago music pitchman Harold Cohen.

Cohen was the great love of Ruth's life. They married in Chicago in 1937 and Ruth quit the Hutton band. The marriage lasted only thirteen months. In 1938, Cohen died suddenly of a kidney ailment and Lowe returned to Toronto, brokenhearted. She found a job as a staff pianist at the Canadian Broadcasting Corporation (CBC) and wrote songs, one of which, "I'll Never Smile Again," best expressed her emotions. Bandleader Percy Faith, a fellow staffer at the CBC made a reference recording of the song in the CBC studio.

A few months later, Lowe gave a copy of Faith's recording to a friend playing in the Tommy Dorsey Orchestra, which was appearing at the Canadian National Exhibition. Dorsey had a new male vocalist who was prodding the bandleader for more of the spotlight. Frank Sinatra loved singing ballads.

At a New York recording session for RCA Victor in April 1940, Dorsey had complete takes of the four tunes scheduled. With twenty minutes left over, the orchestra, with Sinatra singing the solo, had time to put down three takes of "I'll Never Smile again." RCA considered none of the takes technically acceptable, so a month later the song was recut in one take.

The record hit the Billboard charts in June 1940. It spent twelve weeks in the number 1 position and went on to eventually launch Sinatra to solo stardom. Sinatra also performed the song in the film *Las Vegas Nights* with Dorsey's band, but it soon became apparent to everyone that Sinatra was destined to be more than a band singer.

"I'll Never Smile Again" became the best-selling song of the 1940s. Lowe moved to New York where she wrote songs for several years, though none achieved the same success as "Smile." She remarried and moved back to Toronto where she lived as a homemaker and mother until her death in 1981.

"I'll Never Smile Again" is available in seventeen different folios from Hal Leonard Publishing, most in piano/vocal arrangement. Sound recordings by more than thirty artists are listed, but the original hit is still definitive on various Tommy Dorsey reissues including *The Best of Tommy Dorsey* (RCA CD 51087).

3. "Strange Fruit"
Words and Music by Lewis Allan (née Abel Meeropol)
Copyright © 1939, Edward B. Marks Music

In Greenwich Village, New York, in the late 1930s there was a venue where sophisticated, mostly white, often leftist, audiences could hear the leading jazz performers of the day, both black and white. In 1939, the headliner was Billie Holiday, who at the age of twenty-four was already toughened by a rough childhood and life on the road as the lone black member of Artie Shaw's band. At Café Society she was not paid well ($75 a week for seven nights of work), but she could stay put and play to appreciative audiences.

It was at Café Society that Abel Meeropol came to her with a poem set to music that painted a stark image of a nearly forbidden

topic, lynching. A Tuskegee Institute study of the period has estimated that between the years 1890 and 1940 nearly four thousand
people were lynched in the United States, 90 percent of them in the
South and 80 percent of them black (Marqolick 2000, 34). That reality was far from the minds of the comfortable jazz lovers at Café Society, until Billie Holiday presented her chilling rendition of
Meeropol's song. When she moaned of swinging black bodies that
seemed like a metaphor for fruit, the impact was immediate. Patrons
sat in stunned silence, reacting to Billie's visceral delivery of the
song. The scene would be repeated at the end of every set, every
night, for the remainder of Holiday's engagement at Café Society, at
most engagements throughout her high ride in the 1940s, and to the
end of her tumultuous career in 1959, when heroin and hard living
claimed her.

The composer of the song, who used the pen name of Lewis
Allan, was a politically active high school teacher and a prolific
poet/lyricist. He wrote the song after seeing a gruesome photograph
of a lynching in a civil rights magazine. Though he had other successes and eventually left teaching to try his hand in Hollywood,
"Strange Fruit" is Meeropol's legacy. He and his wife (who later
adopted the children of the executed spies Julius and Ethel Rosen-
berg) had performed the piece at political gatherings, and it appeared in a union publication, but attracted little attention before he
brought it to Barney Josephson, owner of Café Society, expressly for
Billie Holiday. The music was reworked by pianist Danny Mendel-
sohn, perhaps with help from Holiday or others, but the lyrics stood
as written.

When the song gained immediate celebrity, Holiday talked to
her label, Columbia, about a recording, but neither the company
nor her producer, John Hammond, would touch it. Unwilling to set
it aside, she found an ally in record dealer Milton Gabler who got
permission from Columbia for a recording to be released on his own
Commodore label. The recording was not a hit by most measures,
and it had little impact beyond the politically charged environment
of New York, but it sold steadily. By 1945, roughly fifty thousand
copies were in circulation. Few radio stations would play the song,
but the reverse side, "Fine and Mellow" by Holiday and Gabler, was
enough to get it on certain jukeboxes. The sheet music never sold

well, perhaps because so few felt they could attempt a performance. Of Holiday's contemporaries, only Josh White and Nina Simone regularly sang "Strange Fruit." Billie's performances assured the song's immortality. During her lifetime, fans constantly requested the piece and "Lady Day" obliged, though she said that it never ceased to depress her. Decades after her death she remains in the top ranks of jazz vocalists, her legend indelibly linked to Abel Meeropol's "Strange Fruit."

"Strange Fruit" is available in several song collections including *Lady Day Sings the Blues* (Hal Leonard 00357202). For a recorded version, try Holiday's *Complete Commodore Recordings* (Commodore CD 401).

4. "When You Wish Upon A Star"
Words by Ned Washington and Music by Leigh Harline
Copyright © 1940, Irving Berlin, Inc., later Bourne Music Company

Jiminy Cricket, the unlikely hero of the animated classic *Pinocchio* that many consider Walt Disney's most masterful production, opens the film by reminding children everywhere that they need only wish upon a star to have their dreams come true. The entertainment world had praised Disney's first feature-length film, *Snow White and the Seven Dwarfs*, when it was released in 1939, but he considered it an arduous learning exercise. It was his second film that would combine all the visual, musical, and narrative elements that are the hallmark of the best Disney animated films.

By 1940, the Disney Company occupied sprawling new studios in Burbank, California, employed eleven thousand people, and could apply unsurpassed technical capabilities to *Pinocchio*. The new multiplane camera produced lush, lifelike colors in three-dimensional settings. The story would build a series of exciting episodes (Lampwick becomes a donkey) to a dramatic apex (Monstro swallows Geppetto) and an emotional reward (Pinocchio becomes human), not unlike an opera. More important, instead of just a sequence of songs, the film had a rich musical score with themes for each major character.

The first of these was "When You Wish Upon a Star," performed in the smooth tenor of Cliff Edwards, who also did the speaking voice of Jiminy Cricket. He sang it twice, at the beginning and as a reprise at the end of the film, but instrumental variations were used whenever Jiminy was in the scene. Edwards had enjoyed a career in vaudeville, touring as "Ukulele Ike" in the early 1920s, then appeared in Broadway musicals before becoming a minor film star in the 1930s. His career had just about eclipsed when it was revived by a cricket.

Both "When You Wish Upon a Star" and the musical score for *Pinocchio* won Academy Awards, and the song was recorded by many performers. Glenn Miller and his Orchestra had a number 1 hit shortly after the film's release, and Edwards's own recording (with "Give a Little Whistle" on the flip side) also charted. The music of *Pinocchio* was a collaborative effort but the most significant contributor was composer Leigh Harline, who had been with Disney since 1932 and had worked on the score of *Snow White*. While creating "When You Wish Upon a Star," he worked with Ned Washington, a prolific New York lyricist who moved west in 1935 to make his mark in the movies. Among Washington's many works were "Baby Mine" from *Dumbo* and "Do Not Forsake Me" from *High Noon* (1952), which earned him another Oscar.

"When You Wish Upon a Star" eventually became the theme song of the Disney Company. It was used for Disney's television show, at its theme parks, in advertising, and, finally, on its hugely successful video rereleases. At that point it ran afoul of copyright law. Disney did not have its own publishing company in the early 1940s, so the song had been published by Irving Berlin Music and later assigned to the Bourne Company. Disney's license was only for motion pictures. A protracted court case in the 1990s was finally settled, largely in Bourne's favor, and has served as important case law for the entertainment industry.

This song is available on many recordings by contemporary and period performers. For the original version, try *Classic Disney: 60 Years of Musical Magic* (Disney CD set 860). It is also available in sheet music as Bourne Music item number 144941.

5. "You Are My Sunshine"
Words and Music by Jimmie Davis and Charles Mitchell
Copyright © 1940, Peer International Company; Southern Music
Publishing (sole selling agent)

Jimmy Davis's life was a model for how a child from a poor share-cropper family can rise to the highest levels of success in America. His signature song, "You Are My Sunshine," reflected his outlook on life and love.

Davis was born in 1902 into a family of eleven children, each of whom was expected to pull his weight by helping his parents run a small cotton farm in northern Louisiana while living in a humble rented home. Unlike most children of cotton sharecroppers, Jimmy was not satisfied to follow in his father's footsteps. He used his singing talent to work his way through Louisiana College, where he sang in the Men's Glee Club on campus and street corners in town.

After graduation, Davis moved to Shreveport, Louisiana, and taught at Dodd College, a school for women. He began to write popular and country songs that he sang on KWKH, a local radio station. A talent scout heard Jimmy singing on the radio and told a Decca Records executive in Memphis that Davis had potential as a recording artist. Jimmy soon signed a recording contract with Decca and his rare combination of warm personality, exceptional songwriting skills, and pleasant singing voice helped make him one of the most successful persons in the music industry.

Jimmy Davis became as successful in politics as in music. He eased into politics by running for police commissioner of Shreveport. To set himself apart from his opponent, he sang at his campaign rallies. After noticing the tremendous crowd reaction he received when he sang "You Are My Sunshine," a song he cowrote in Shreveport with Charles Mitchell, he started a tradition of ending each show with the positive-message ballad.

The royalties he earned from his signature song also contributed to his political success. "You Are My Sunshine" became quite popular and eventually was recorded by over 350 different artists in almost every conceivable genre of music. A diverse range of artists, including Bing Crosby, Guy Lombardo, Ray Charles, and Aretha Franklin, have recorded the song.

After the scandal-ridden administration of Louisiana Governor Huey Long ended, Davis decided to run for governor. Using his proven style of campaigning, Jimmy Davis focused on a positive future for the state and, of course, ended each campaign rally by singing "You Are My Sunshine." He won the governorship and served two terms. Not only did he become an extremely popular governor, he was also asked to tour the country promoting sales of U.S. Savings Bonds. Maintaining his paradoxical lifestyle, Davis met with presidents from Truman through Kennedy, yet continued to sing in honky tonks throughout his life.

The one dark moment in his life came in 1967 when Alvern, his wife and inseparable lifemate of many years, died of breast cancer. It was the one moment when the angels took Jimmy Davis's brightest ray of sunshine away.

A representative recording of "You Are My Sunshine" can be heard on the *Country Music Hall of Fame Series* (MCA, 1991, produced by the Country Music Foundation). Sheet music is available in the song folio *Great Gospel Songs of Jimmy Davis* (Hal Leonard 313161).

6. "White Christmas"
Words and Music by Irving Berlin
Copyright © 1940, Irving Berlin

Referring to "White Christmas" as a successful song is truly an understatement. From the moment it was first heard in the 1942 film *Holiday Inn,* starring Bing Crosby and Fred Astaire, it became a perennial favorite with Americans. Ironically, the film containing "White Christmas," a song now associated with the Christmas holiday season, was released in August 1942.

A well-crafted song and the ideal crooner, Bing Crosby, combined to create a song for wartime America. "White Christmas" describes someone in the warm climate of southern California daydreaming about the snow-covered environment back home during the holidays. It touched many Americans, because it evoked emotions many families were experiencing as they wondered how many more holidays they would spend without their loved ones who were fighting a war in the Pacific arena. After the song began getting airplay on Armed Forces Radio, it quickly became the most frequently requested song by soldiers.

How popular has "White Christmas" been over the years? It won an Academy Award for best song from a film in 1942, the year that it also rested confidently at the top position on the Hit Parade record chart for eleven weeks. Since that time, there have been over five hundred different recorded versions of the song. In 2001, the American Society of Composers, Authors and Publishers (ASCAP), named it the most performed song of the century. As of 1963, it had sold over 45 million records. The continuing popularity of the song inspired the release of a second film, this one entitled *White Christmas,* in 1953.

Aside from the commercial success of the song and the films in which it appeared, there remains some controversy regarding symbolism contained in the original film. Bing Crosby appeared in black face and sang a duet with the character Mamie in a segment of the film celebrating freedom. He also used slang that was typically associated with African Americans rather than whites at that time. Although his donning of makeup to appear black would be considered disrespectful today, it was not necessarily a derogatory gesture back then. In fact, that part of the film seemed to show a comradeship for African Americans that offended racists at that time.

In addition to the symbolism one might extract from the blackface scene, there were two principal female characters in the film: Linda Mason and Lola Dixon. Was this a subtle reference to the Mason–Dixon line and the tension between Linda and Lola that resolves at the end of the story? Or was this simply coincidental? We will probably never know for sure, but one additional coincidence gives life to the theory of hidden messages in the film. Bing Crosby, a northerner, was married to Dixie Lee, a southerner from Memphis, Tennessee.

The song "White Christmas" has been recorded by more artists than any other song in the history of the recording industry. The prototypical rendition is by Bing Crosby on *Bing Crosby: A Centennial Anthology of His Decca Records* (MCA CD 113222.2). Sheet music is widely available in song folios such as *Irving Berlin: White Christmas (Movie Vocal Selection)* (Hal Leonard 313165).

7. "Boogie Woogie Bugle Boy"
Words and Music by Don Raye and Hughie Prince
Copyright © 1941, MCA, Inc.

In 1931, a trio of sisters entered a singing contest in their hometown of Minneapolis, Minnesota. The youngest of the Andrews Sisters,

Patty, was only eleven at the time but the ensemble was striving to echo the jazz-tinged harmonies of the popular Boswell Sisters. The oldest of the Andrew Sisters, La Verne, soon convinced the entire family that the girls should drop out of school and go on the vaudeville circuit. The timing was unfortunate: they toured in 1932 at the very end of vaudeville's run, when, as Maxene later recalled, they "closed every RKO theater in the Midwest" (Andrews 1993, 7). The next year they began singing for a succession of bands but with little financial success. In 1937, they had a brief radio appearance with the Billy Swanson Band at the Edison Hotel in New York. He fired them after one song, but Decca executive Dave Kapp heard them and later signed them to a recording contract. The result was a collaboration that would put ninety singles on the pop charts over the next fourteen years. Their success started with the unlikely Yiddish song "Bei Mir Bist Du Schon," which went quickly to number 1.

None of the sisters were musically trained but each had a good ear, and the three sibling voices achieved a distinctive harmony that was well suited to the pop stylings of many big bands. Their swinging demeanor on stage was also distinctive. As Maxene noted, "[H]armony groups never moved, but we never could contain ourselves" (Hall 1989, 173). What really established the Andrews Sisters as the most successful of all sister groups was their hardworking performances during World War II. They were quick to sign on when the United Service Organization (USO) was formed in 1941 to take music to the troops. That same year they appeared as themselves in the low-budget hit movie *Buck Privates*, a humorous look at Army life that introduced the comedy team of Bud Abbott and Lou Costello in which they sang the catchy song "Boogie Woogie Bugle Boy." The lyrics tell of a Chicago trumpet player who is drafted into the Army, where he has to be satisfied with jazzing up reveille. The song made light of a very real problem in the entertainment world as bands were torn apart by Selective Service Boards. More films followed, and throughout World War II, the lively Andrews Sisters, who were nicknamed "The Jive Bombers," were seemingly everywhere—on radio and records, in films, in theaters across the country, and on the touring troop shows.

The song was one of many pop songs from the swing era that loosely referenced the percussive, blues-based boogie-woogie piano style of earlier decades. Others included "Beat Me Daddy Eight to the Bar," "Scrub me Mama, with a Boogie Beat," and "Rhumboogie," all by composer Don Raye and/or lyricist Hughie Prince and all hits for the Andrews Sisters. Both men wrote for the movies but not much is known about how they collaborated. Raye transplanted himself to Hollywood to work for the studios while Prince maintained his New York base. Because of its nostalgic connection to World War II, "Boogie Woogie Bugle Boy" has proven to be the Andrews Sisters' most durable hit. It was later revived on stage by Bette Midler, including one memorable performance with Patty and Maxene. Her success with the song helped fuel a retrospective interest in the Andrews Sisters as well.

"Boogie Woogie Bugle Boy" is available in many song anthologies, including *I'll Be Seeing You: 50 Songs of World War II* (Hal Leonard 00311698). The Andrews Sisters' version is found on nearly a dozen recorded anthologies as well, including Bette Midler's *The Divine Miss M* (Atlantic CD 82785).

8. "Tell Me Why You Liked Roosevelt"
Words and Music by Otis Jackson
Copyright © 1946, Otis Jackson

In April 1946, the Evangelist Singers, a male vocal group from Detroit, went into a recording studio to cut some songs for the Hub and Chicago labels. Acting as booking agent for the gospel group was a thirty-four-year-old Georgia native, Otis Jackson. Not much is known of Jackson's childhood, but by 1944, he was married, living in Jacksonville, Florida, and promoting gospel music programs. He was, variously, a disc jockey, singer, pianist, and songwriter.

Most likely, Jackson met the Evangelists by booking them in Jacksonville. In the spring of 1946, Jackson was not only promoting the group, he was the lead singer for their signature song "Tell Me Why You Liked Roosevelt." Recorded a year after the president's death, the song is a remarkable tribute from the African American community. The verses consist of a dozen rhyming couplets delivered in the chanted manner of a sanctified preacher. The chorus, a call-and-response melodic phrase, asks the title question three times (call), followed by the response, which indicated Roosevelt's affinity for the poor.

The first verse details the circumstances of Roosevelt's death, including mention of the famous unfinished portrait the artist Elizabeth Shoumatoff was working on at Roosevelt's Warm Springs, Georgia, home. The time and cause of death—cerebral hemorrhage—and Dr. Bruen's attendance are also stated.

Subsequent verses look back at the difficulties blacks faced before Roosevelt's first term, and the wonderful improvements thereafter. Specific couplets mention General Benjamin O. Davis, the first Negro General of the United States, Madame [Mary McLeod] Bethune, the First [African American] Lady of the Land, and Mr. [Arthur] Prettyman, who was Roosevelt's valet and was remembered in the president's will.

The recording, released on both sides of a 78 rpm disc, "Tell Me Why You Like [*sic*] Roosevelt, Part 1 and Part 2" resonated deeply in the black community, so much so that the song was recorded a half dozen times in the following decade. The Soul Stirrers, a Texas group that gave the young Sam Cooke his start, recorded "Roosevelt" in 1947; the Reliable Jubilee Singers in 1947; and the National Clouds of Joy, with Jackson singing an expanded text, in 1949.

Otis Jackson continued his music activities through the 1950s. He composed topical songs, for example, "Korea (Fightin' in the Foreign Land)," "I'm So Grateful to the N.A.A.C.P.," and "The Life Story of Madame Bethune." Jackson died in March 1962 at the age of fifty.

Sheet music for "Roosevelt" is long out of print, but several recorded versions are available. One is by Memphis' Jesse Winchester in his *Best of* collection (Rhino CD 70085).

9. "Ornithology"
Music by Charlie Parker and Benny Harris
Copyright © 1946, Atlantic Record Corporation

"Ornithology" was first recorded in 1946 (Dial Records). An alternate version of the same recording was released under the title "Bird Lore"; an earlier version, entitled "Thriving from a Riff," was recorded in 1945 (Savoy Records). "Ornithology" borrows from the song "How High the Moon," a Benny Goodman hit in 1940.

"Ornithology" is a song that, along with several other masterpieces by Charlie Parker (nicknamed "Bird" or "Yardbird" by fellow musicians) and Dizzy Gillespie, created a new school of jazz that came to be called "bebop." As big bands became increasingly associated with popular songs of the day, bebop signaled a separation between pop and jazz. While big band music was directed toward radio broadcasts and dancing, bebop was performed for those who wanted to listen in smaller club environments, often smoke-filled bars. Big bands used precisely conceived instrumental arrangements; bebop combos improvised most of the night.

One distinguishing characteristic of early bebop jazz was the machine-gun speed of melodic lines that required virtuoso talent. And it was Parker's saxophone performances that were so impressive that he earned the title of the finest jazz sax player who ever lived. Parker's music differed from all earlier styles of jazz because it departed radically from the more traditional harmonies and melodies of earlier jazz. A typical Parker solo included complex melodic lines that seemed to be filled with millions of notes. He also developed melodic lines using long leaps and expanded harmonies.

Parker's tormented personal life was a tragic contrast to his professional success. He was born in Kansas City, Missouri, on August 29, 1920. He quickly fell in love with the great jazz music he heard throughout Kansas City and began to study music. At the age of sixteen, he dropped out of high school to pursue a career in jazz.

Because Parker's mother worked during the day, he could practice music and, unfortunately, experiment with drugs, such as heroin, when unsupervised. His early experimentation with drugs developed into a serious addiction as he grew into adulthood. His fascination with drugs was exacerbated by the environment in which bebop jazz evolved. The beat poets, hipsters, and avant-garde intellectuals who attended jazz clubs reinforced the notion that drugs somehow helped one to be more creative. At the youthful age of twenty-two, Parker had already been fired from several engagements for his drug problem and "unusual behavior."

By the time Parker recorded "Ornithology," he had already established his famous style of saxophone playing and his infamous reputation for unorthodox behavior. In 1946, he suffered a nervous breakdown and was institutionalized. In 1954, after being admitted to Bellevue Mental Institution in New York City twice, Parker attempted suicide. On March 12, 1955, Charlie Parker died after refusing to be hospitalized for what he thought was an ulcer attack. An autopsy revealed that he died of lobar pneumonia and the long-term effects of heroin and alcohol. His last performance was at Birdland, a club in New York named after him.

Charlie Parker's composition "Ornithology" was inducted into the Grammy Hall of Fame in 1989. Although many jazz artists have recorded this work, a representative recording by Bird himself is available on *Complete Dial Sessions* (February 5, 1946–December 17, 1947; Stash Records).

10. "Lovesick Blues"
Words and Music by Irving Mills, Cliff Friend, and Hank Williams
Copyright © 1922, Mills Music, Inc.

"Lovesick Blues," the song which launched Hank Williams's career in 1949, was the first number 1 hit by the country giant. An American icon now known as much for his songwriting as his singing, Williams' beginning with a recycled Tin Pan Alley flop is ironic.

In 1922, the blues craze was in full bloom and any song with the word in the title could be sold—or so it seemed. In reality, "Lovesick Blues" was pure pop with not one blues tone in it. Conservatory-trained pianist, composer, and lyricist Cliff Friend had been writing specialty songs for Broadway stars such as Al Jolson and Eddie Cantor for years. In 1922, he got involved with publisher, band promoter, and song plugger Irving Mills, and a show aptly named *O-oo Ernest*. Friend (Mills's name on the copyright probably reflects a business arrangement) wrote "Lovesick Blues" for the show, which was not very successful. The song remained unheard for a few years until vaudevillian Emmett Miller incorporated it in his black-face act, adding trick yodels to the song. He recorded the song twice for Columbia in the 1920s. Hank Williams had one of the Miller records in his collection.

In the late 1930s, when teenage Hank Williams was singing on the street corners of Montgomery, another Alabamian, Rex Griffin, resurrected "Lovesick Blues." Simplifying the harmony and making the verse into a chorus (probably as the result of incorrectly remembering the original arrangement), Griffin recorded the altered version for Decca. Hank Williams also had this record in his collection.

In 1947, Williams, under the wing of publisher Fred Rose, signed a recording contract with MGM Records. Williams agreed to write several songs and audition them for Rose who would select the best for the recording session. Rose would then publish the songs through Acuff–Rose Music, the successful firm he had established in Nashville in partnership with Roy Acuff in 1942.

The Rose–Williams method was not working well; by the winter of 1948, the seven issued MGM records had sold poorly, and Hank Williams was still virtually unknown outside Louisiana and Alabama. Williams's personal struggle with alcoholism and his stressful marriage had blocked his writing, which, thus far, showed promise with songs like "I Saw the Light" and "Honky Tonk Blues."

On December 22, 1948, in a Cincinnati studio, Williams and a group of local studio players recorded three forgettable songs. Needing a fourth to complete the three-hour session, Williams suggested "Lovesick Blues." Rose's reaction was to leave the studio. The musicians shared Rose's opinion of the song, but Williams had been singing the song onstage to fervid audience reaction. He had a hunch.

MGM released "Lovesick Blues" early in 1949. By February 11, it was number 1 on the Billboard chart. Williams was getting calls for live appearances from all over the country. The Grand Ole Opry invited him as a guest, where he encored six times and earned the nickname "The Lovesick Blues Boy." Fred Rose, doubting his ability to spot a hit song for the first time in his long career, was, nevertheless, pleased to have a valuable copyright in his catalog. Williams claimed he had bought the rights to the song from Rex Griffin and Rose was, therefore, free to publish "Lovesick Blues."

Irving Mills was not a man to overlook any infringement. Surprisingly, and with uncharacteristic generosity, Mills allowed Williams and Rose to share in the composer and publisher's revenue generated by the hit record. Perhaps Mills felt the money a windfall from an unlikely source. Or perhaps Rose threatened to pull the record from the market. The result was a country music standard fashioned from a pop music failure.

"Lovesick Blues" is printed in *The Hank Williams Songbook* (Hal Leonard 00699255). In addition to Hank Williams's rendition, well over fifty recordings are available, including those by Dolly Parton,

Frank Ifield, Leon Redbone, and a rhythm and blues version by Etta James. The original pop version by Emmett Miller is on *The Minstrel Man from Georgia* (Columbia CD 66999).

11. "Run Joe"
Words and Music by Walt Merrick, Joe Willoughby, and Louis Jordan
Copyright © 1947, Cherio Corporation

Louis Jordan was born in Brinkley, Arkansas, in 1908. His father, a professional musician, taught young Louis saxophone and clarinet. After playing in Arkansas, Jordan moved to Philadelphia and played with jazz violinist Stuff Smith before joining the reed section of drummer Chick Webb's big band.

In New York, in 1938, Jordan formed his own small combo: two reeds, one brass, three rhythm. Though the big bands of the era were known as "swing" bands, Jordan's style became known as "jump" music because of the shuffle rhythms and melodic riffs played behind the vocal phrases.

By the early 1940s, Louis Jordan and his Tympany Five were known as an entertaining and popular live act. Whites and blacks attended shows at clubs in Illinois, Iowa, Missouri, and the Dakotas equally. As records made for the Decca Company broadened Jordan's audience, especially novelties like "Five Guys Named Moe," "Knock Me a Kiss," and "Choo Choo Ch'Boogie," the band toured the segregated South, where they performed two nights at each venue—one night for blacks, one for whites.

Jordan's popularity led him back to New York where successful engagements at the Apollo and Paramount Theaters secured his reputation with uptown and downtown audiences. By 1946, Jordan was one of Decca's best-selling artists with songs like "Caledonia," "That Chick's Too Young to Fry," and "Let the Good Times Roll" found on jukeboxes across America. Decca's appetite for songs seemed insatiable, and writing or acquiring new material was becoming difficult. Jordan, with few exceptions, refused to "cover" hits by other artists; he wanted to create the hit and let the others cover him.

Dr. Walter Merrick, Louis's physician, was a native of St. Vincent, a small Caribbean island. In 1928, while in medical school in Washington, D.C., Merrick had written an operetta, *Black Empire*, but had forsaken music upon graduation. Now, with so famous (and accessible) a patient, Merrick teamed with a lyric-writing Trinidadian friend, Joe Willoughby, to write a popular song in a style that might appeal to Jordan.

"Run Joe" tells the story of Moe and Joe who run a candy store, which is a front for a fortune-telling scam. In seven verses, Moe, captured by police, tells Joe to arrange Moe's bail, destroy the evidence, and secure a lawyer. The lyric is in Caribbean dialect, and the sheet music gives "Rhumba Calypso" as rhythmic guidance. The song reflects the storytelling style popular in the island calypso tradition.

Jordan did such a convincing Decca recording of "Run Joe," that for years afterward, fans were sure he was born in the islands. The record was an enormous hit, preceding by a decade Harry Belafonte's calypso successes. Jordan also prefigured elements of rhythm and blues: a small group led by honking saxophone, shuffle rhythms, and repeating instrumental figures behind the vocal.

While "Run Joe" is not available in sheet music, many recordings by artists as diverse as The Kingston Trio, The Skatalites, The Dirty Dozen Brass Band, Maya Angelou, and The Neville Brothers can be purchased. Jordan's original hit can be found on *The Best of Louis Jordan* (MCA CD 4079).

12. "Blue Moon of Kentucky"
Words and Music by Bill Monroe
Copyright © 1947, Peer International Corporation

Kentuckian Bill Monroe wrote "Blue Moon of Kentucky" while driving north from an engagement in Florida in 1946. He was thirty-five years old and had been a country music star for ten years. With his brother Charlie, he had risen to stardom as half of the Monroe Brothers. In 1939, they split and Bill formed his Bluegrass Boys band and secured a spot on the Grand Ole Opry, the nation's premiere country radio show.

The Monroe Brothers had made their reputation singing traditional folk and gospel material. Bill, determined to be successful without his older brother, began creating a distinct repertoire and style. Asked about the inspiration for his most famous song in a *New York Times* interview of June 9, 1994, the laconic Monroe would only say, "I thought the words 'blue moon' would be good to put in a song."

Indeed, they are. Several popular songs from the 1920s and 1930s had used the image. "Once in a Blue Moon" from 1921 (published by Irving Berlin) put the literal meaning of the phrase in popular music; and Richard Rodgers and Lorenz Hart's "Blue Moon" of 1934 used blue in its emotional sense. Monroe's use followed Hart's.

In 1947, Columbia Record Company released Monroe's wistful waltz about a false lover, and while it was well received by the country music audience, it did not achieve the success of his other "Kentucky" song, "Kentucky Waltz" (1946), which had peaked at number 3 on Billboard's juke box chart. However, Monroe had begun composing a body of works that would eventually number into the hundreds. Although not as immediately successful as "Kentucky Waltz," "Blue Moon Kentucky" went on to become Monroe's best-known song thanks to a young man in Memphis.

Elvis Presley grew up in a poor family in Tupelo, Mississippi, and Memphis, Tennessee. He was twelve years old when "Blue Moon of Kentucky" was released and he undoubtedly heard Monroe perform it many times on the Grand Ole Opry. By 1954, Presley, an aspiring singer, had captured the interest of Sun Records' owner Sam Phillips.

In the summer of 1954, Presley, along with a bassist and lead guitarist, took "Blue Moon of Kentucky" from a rural lament to an urban frenzy. Played in 4/4 time with a slapped bass line, electric guitar breaks, and echo-drenched vocals, "Blue Moon of Kentucky" became the B side of Presley's first Sun release. It caused a sensation, first regionally, then nationally. Eventually Presley left little Sun Records to sign with the industry giant RCA Victor.

That fall, with "Blue Moon of Kentucky" climbing the country charts, the Grand Ole Opry called on Elvis for a guest appearance. Elated and apprehensive at the same time—Sam Phillips had heard that Monroe was so upset with the Sun version that he threatened bodily harm to the singer and his label owner—the Presley trio and Phillips headed to Nashville.

The rumors of Monroe's anger were not accurate. Backstage at the Opry, Monroe complimented Elvis. Monroe had been playing

Elvis's version of his song for other Nashville artists, telling them they had better record the song if they wanted to sell some records.

Bill Monroe was elected to both the Country Music Hall of Fame and the Rock and Roll Hall of Fame. "Blue Moon of Kentucky" is often cited as a wellspring of rock and roll. Monroe is said to be the only American musician to have created a new genre during the twentieth century: bluegrass.

"Blue Moon of Kentucky" is available in at least twenty song folios of country and Elvis standards. Recorded versions are also plentiful including versions by Elvis and Ray Charles. Bill Monroe's original recording is on *Country, the American Tradition* (Columbia/Sony CD 65816).

13. "Boogie Chillun" (Hooker also referred to different versions under the titles "Boogie Chillen," "Boogie Chillen 2," and "Jump Chillun")
Words and Music by John Lee Hooker and Bernard Besman
Copyright © 1948, La Cienega Music

The song "Boogie Chillun," with its simple lyrics and skeletal guitar accompaniment, would seem to be the most unlikely start of a long and prolific recording career for blues artist John Lee Hooker. Hooker recorded the song during a period when sweet, romantic-sounding songs by artists such as Nat "King" Cole were considered the norm for commercial recordings by African American artists.

Hooker recorded the song only one month after signing with Modern Records, a West Coast label. When he recorded the song, John Lee used a simplified guitar tuning (open tuning) idiosyncratic to rural blues stylists. Because of his unorthodox rhythmic style, the label opted to record him without a backup band. A bluesman singing an up-tempo song with only his own electric guitar and foot tapping as accompaniment? These were hardly the characteristics of commercially successful songs of that era.

Hooker was born in Clarksdale, Mississippi, in 1920. He learned to play guitar from his stepfather Will Moore, who was a friend of blues legend Blind Lemon Jefferson. When he reached the age of fourteen, Hooker ran away from home and moved to Memphis in search of work as a performer. After a short time, he moved to Cincinnati where he performed with gospel quartets and continued to develop his unique guitar style.

After living in Cincinnati for ten years, he moved to Detroit in 1943. Hooker found a day job as a custodian in an automobile factory but soon was able to establish himself as a club performer. Because of his regional fame as a club performer, he was discovered and signed by Modern Records. After the modest success of "Boogie Chillun," John Lee recorded four more songs, each of which became extremely successful: "Hobo Blues," "Hoogie Boogie Blues," and "Crawlin' Kingsnake Blues" (all were 1949 hits), and "I'm in the Mood for Love" (1951 number 1 on the charts).

But it was "Boogie Chillun" that first commanded the attention of many famous rock stars over the next fifty years. Artists and bands who have acknowledged his tremendous influence on their careers include Bonnie Raitt, Bruce Springsteen, the Rolling Stones, Van Morrison, and ZZ Top, to name just a few. In 1961, The Rolling Stones, at the time a relatively unestablished band, was the opening act for John Lee Hooker's European tour.

Controversy surrounding the song "Boogie Chillun" resulted in a lengthy court battle between ZZ Top and La Cienega Music, publisher of the song, that eventually went before the U.S. Supreme Court. Bernard Besman, credited as cowriter of the song with John Lee Hooker, became sole proprietor of La Cienega Music and controlled the copyright. He believed that the ZZ Top song "La Grange" was so similar to "Boogie Chillun" that it infringed on the copyright. Although "La Grange" was recorded in 1973, Besman did not become aware of it until 1991. He filed a lawsuit that was not resolved until 1997. After years of litigation and thousands of dollars in legal fees, ZZ Top and La Cienega Music agreed to an out-of-court settlement. They also agreed that neither party would discuss the terms of the settlement.

John Lee made a brief cameo appearance as a street singer in the 1980 film *The Blues Brothers*, a simple feat, but representative of his continuous image as the rock stars' star. He released an album of duets with various other artists on *The Healer* in 1989. Artists and bands with whom he sang included Santana, Los Lobos, and Robert Cray. His duet with Bonnie Raitt, a reprise of his 1949 hit

"I'm in the Mood," garnered him a Grammy for traditional blues recording.

John Lee, determined to circumvent exclusive recording contracts he signed, recorded under many different pseudonyms. In the first six years of his career, he recorded under ten different pseudonyms for twenty-one different labels. Names he created included Texas Slim, John Lee Booker, Delta John, Birmingham Slim, and Boogie Man.

The record "Boogie Chillun" was inducted into the Grammy Hall of Fame in 1999. Hooker was inducted into the Rock and Roll Hall of Fame in 1991 and he received the Lifetime Achievement Award from the National Academy of Recording Arts and Sciences in 2000. John Lee Hooker died peacefully in his sleep on June 21, 2001.

Because John Lee Hooker had a long and prolific career, there are many recordings of him performing "Boogie Chillun." One authentic rendition is available on *The Ultimate Collection (1948–1990)* (Rhino Records R2-70572).

14. "Rudolph the Red Nosed Reindeer"
Words and Music by John D. Marks
Copyright © 1949, St. Nicholas Music, Inc.

Johnny Marks was a Phi Beta Kappa graduate of Colgate University and a songwriter in the famous Brill Building of New York when, in 1949, he sent off demo copies of a catchy little Christmas song he had written. Marks would later recall that he had the story of Rudolph in his head for ten years after the poem was written by his brother-in-law, copywriter Robert L. May, for a 1939 Montgomery Ward store brochure. When he finally set the poem to music he sent copies to Bing Crosby, Dinah Shore, and other star vocalists of the day. As an afterthought he sent one to cowboy singer Gene Autry, who had recently scored a hit with his own "Here Comes Santa Claus."

Gene Autry did not think much of the song but his wife Ina liked it. So, when he was caught in the studio with three Christmas songs recorded and ten minutes remaining before his union musicians clocked out, he hastily distributed copies of "Rudolph" and recorded it in one take. Nobody remembers the A side of the record

("He's a Chubby Little Fellow"), but "Rudolph" sold 2.5 million copies in the first year and more than 12.5 million in the next two decades. Other versions were recorded by hundreds of artists in dozens of languages, making it one of the most recorded songs of the twentieth century.

The song about the misfit deer marked Gene Autry's move from cowboy film star and country singer to mainstream pop singer. He started his career in the early 1920s with a traveling medicine show, went into radio on the advice of Will Rogers, and ended up at the head of an enormous entertainment empire. As he noted, "The war, and a new generation of war babies, caused the children's songs that kept my popularity as a recording star high at a moment when it could have waned" (Autry 1978, 30). He followed his unexpected success with "(Here Comes) Peter Cottontail" and "Frosty the Snowman" the following year.

"Rudolph the Red Nosed Reindeer" was also very good to Johnny Marks, who formed his St. Nicholas Music Company for the purpose of publishing the song and collecting the royalties. His colleague in the Brill Building, Dick Jacobs, had done the arrangement for free with a promise of double union scale if it was successful. Jacobs later noted that he also got "a handsome bonus" (Jacobs 1994, 205). Christmas and kids' songs anchored Johnny Marks's career. He also produced "Rockin' around the Christmas Tree," "A Holly Jolly Christmas," and the "Ballad of Smokey the Bear." "Rudolph" was just one of the many songs written and recorded for the millions of children born in the late 1940s and the 1950s who would become known as the "baby boomers."

"Rudolph the Red Nosed Reindeer" is available as sheet music (Warner Brothers 6707 RP2X) or in the *Gene Autry Songbook* (Warner Brothers PF9708). For a different take on the song, try *Spike Jones' Greatest Hits* (RCA CD 67814).

15. "Some Enchanted Evening"
Words by Oscar Hammerstein II and Music by Richard Rodgers
Copyright © 1949, Williamson Music, Inc.

Rodgers and Hammerstein were the emperors of Broadway in the 1940s and 1950s. Following the astonishing success of *Oklahoma*

(1943), which ran for 2,212 performances, their major hits included *Carousel* (1945), *The King and I* (1951), *Flower Drum Song* (1958), and *The Sound of Music* (1959). There were minor hits along the way as well and the duo kept as many as four New York shows running simultaneously. But it was *South Pacific* (1949) that both critics and audiences lauded as their best work.

The most memorable song of that extraordinary show was "Some Enchanted Evening," composed by Rodgers specifically for the magnificent voice of Ezio Pinza, a famous basso from the New York Metropolitan Opera who unexpectedly became available to do a musical. Early in act 1 the song introduces the possibility of romance between French planter Emile de Becque (Pinza) and plain-spoken nurse Nellie Forbush (Mary Martin) of Little Rock, Arkansas. The pairing of the aging Pinza with the sprightly but vocally overmatched Mary Martin was risky, but it worked. Their romance advanced the play's theme of racial prejudice. Nellie finds herself falling for de Becque but is repulsed because he has fathered mixed-race children by a Polynesian woman. It is a prejudice that "is born in me" she explains. Only when Emile is in grave danger on a military mission does Nellie realize she can overturn her ingrained bias. As expected for the period and genre, a happy ending follows.

South Pacific was the first show completely under the control of Rodgers and Hammerstein as producers. It was based on a collection of short stories by James Michener that recalled his experiences while stationed on a Pacific island during World War II. Both Michener's book and later the play won the Pulitzer Prize. The show was considered daring in its treatment of recent history, and in its challenge to racial divisions. Audiences were also eager to see if the touted opera star (who had never fully mastered English) could succeed in a lighter work. Speculation and publicity drove advance ticket sales to more than $1 million at a time when an orchestra seat cost $6. The musical ran for 1,925 performances on Broadway and more than 800 in London, with many more by the touring company. In 1958, a successful motion picture version was produced, though with a complete change of cast.

"Some Enchanted Evening" was an immediate hit. Perry Como had a number 1 record on the Billboard charts less than a month after the play opened. Six other versions, including one by Pinza, charted before year's end. An LP recording with the original cast was released later in the year, and was also a top seller.

"Some Enchanted Evening" is available in many anthologies of show tunes. A folio of vocal selections from *South Pacific* is available (Hal Leonard 0312400) as is a single sheet (Hal Leonard 00305105). For a recorded version, try the original cast album (TNK–Columbia CD 60722).

1950–1959

Teens Rock the Boat

The wave of births that occurred in the United States during and immediately following World War II was unlike anything the nation had experienced in its history. The generation that came to be called "baby boomers" adopted its own pop cultural icons, especially those in the music industry. Music of this generation was intentionally anti-establishment. Parents, educators, the clergy, and anyone who respected established formalities of previous generations tended to shun rock 'n' roll. It was the rebellious nature of this music that gave teenagers ownership of it.

Although the United States had weathered the storms of two world wars, a new war, called the "Cold War," was born soon after World War II. The communist People's Republic of Korea (Northern Korea) invaded the democratic Republic of Korea (Southern Korea). The United Nations Security Council protested the invasion and sent U.N. forces to Korea under the command of U.S. Army General Douglas MacArthur. Although the U.S. government called it a "police action," private citizens knew that there was a war in Korea until North and South Korea reached a peace accord in 1953.

The Soviet Union launched *Sputnik,* the first satellite to orbit the earth, in 1957. The United States launched its first satellite one year later. As communism seemed to spread throughout the world—China, Cuba, Korea, Vietnam—the fear of nuclear warfare affected

U.S. military strategy. The United States developed the hydrogen bomb and successfully tested one in 1952. Both the space race and the nuclear arms race had begun.

In a knee-jerk reaction to the threat of communism, Senator Joseph A. McCarthy led a campaign to rid the nation of communists. Many people in the media and the entertainment industry were blacklisted and McCarthyism destroyed some careers. By 1954, other members of the Senate recognized the damage that McCarthy's overzealous tactics were causing and he was condemned by his own legislative body.

There was a new awakening of the civil rights movement in this decade, no doubt buoyed by the template for desegregation created by *To Secure These Rights*, a document drafted by the 1947 President's Committee on Civil Rights. In the landmark case *Brown v. Board of Education of Topeka*, the U.S. Supreme Court ruled in 1954 that "separate but equal" educational systems were no longer legal in this nation. The 1957 Civil Rights Act authorized the creation of the U.S. Commission on Civil Rights, a governmental entity that would have a tremendous impact on social reform for the next twenty years.

The role of women in the country continued to evolve due in part to the large number of females in the workforce. Employment of women reached a high point in 1951, even surpassing the war years. The affluence brought on by two-income families helped motivate urban flight to the suburbs. It also forced marketing executives to pay particular attention to the spending habits of females and teenagers. Music, films, television, and radio also reflected the growing necessity to recognize demographic subgroups based on age and gender.

Television emerged as the dominant news and entertainment medium in the 1950s. By 1952, there were more than two thousand new television broadcasting stations in the United States. In response to the competition it felt from television, the film industry created wider screens and better audio sound systems for theaters. Epic films, such as *The Ten Commandments* and *Ben Hur*, took advantage of the new technology.

The number of record labels soared during the decade. Unlike previous decades, when a handful of major record companies dominated the landscape, hundreds of record labels—many specializing in one genre or subgenre of music—developed and flourished in the 1950s. In response to the seemingly unsatiable appetite of teenagers for dance music, radio personalities (called "disc jockeys" or "DJs") made personal appearances at sock hops and concerts. The persona of some DJs reached celebrity status. A local show first produced in Philadelphia, called *American Bandstand*, capitalized on the sock hop craze. The show, and its host Dick Clark, set the standard for youth-oriented music shows on television. Rock 'n' roll was here to stay.

SONGS

1. "Mona Lisa"
Words and Music by Jay Livingston and Ray Evans
Copyright © 1949, Famous Music Company (in Italian);
1950, English version recorded

In January 1950, as America marked the midcentury point, smooth pop vocalists and survivors from the big band era dominated popular music. Bing Crosby and Perry Como led the weekly rosters of *Your Hit Parade*, trailed by the orchestras of Tommy Dorsey, Freddy Martin, Gordon Jenkins, and others. Female vocalists were represented by Jo Stafford and Teresa Brewer. It was an era that critic Henry Pleasants has termed "the white time" (1974, 214). But by the middle of 1950, a black balladeer emerged to be "much popper than any of them" (Christgau 1998, 18), and he would come from the unlikely world of jazz.

Nat Cole was an acclaimed jazz pianist with his own King Cole Trio before he "crossed over" (before anyone knew what crossed over meant) into the pop world. He was born Nathaniel Coles in Montgomery, Alabama, in one of the later years of the first decade of the twentieth century (the year is open to question) but was raised in Chicago, where he sang and played organ in his father's church. He founded his first combo, The Rogues of Rhythm, while still in his teens and came under the influence of Earl Hines.

In 1936, he joined the road company of a revival of Sissle and Blake's *Shuffle Along* as bandleader. The show folded in Los Angeles, where Coles worked as a solo act until he formed a trio to please a jazz club owner. It was the club owner who reportedly dropped the "s" from Coles's name and called it the King Cole Trio. That trio, which featured Oscar Moore on guitar and Wesley Prince on string bass, was an immediate success and is often credited with establishing the small jazz combo trend at a time when large orchestras were the prevalent form.

In 1944, the group had their first big hit on Capitol with Cole's own "Straighten Up and Fly Right." At the heart of the trio's success was Cole's brilliance on the piano. He would ride that success until 1950, when a tune that he did not like very much would motivate him to leave the jazz life behind for a whole new level of celebrity and financial success.

Jay Livingston and Ray Evans were already a successful song-writing team when they wrote "Mona Lisa" for a forgotten Paramount movie titled *Captain Carey, U.S.A.* Alan Ladd starred as an intelligence officer for whom snippets of "Mona Lisa," in Italian, served as a secret code. The movie was not very successful, but the song won an Academy Award.

Eager to get a major artist to record their song, the composers promoted the English-language version to Perry Como, Vic Damone, and Frank Sinatra, all of whom turned it down. Cole was not interested either, but allowed Livingston and Evans to come to his house to demonstrate it. He was persuaded to record a Nelson Riddle arrangement of the song with his trio, but then did not like the results, so he shelved it until he needed a B side for what he believed was a sure hit, "The Greatest Inventor of All," a spiritual.

To his amazement, disc jockeys preferred the B side and strong airplay propelled "Mona Lisa" to number 1 on the Billboard chart. It sold more than 1 million records in 1950 alone, 3 million overall, and would stay on the charts for twenty-seven weeks. Eight other artists, including country singer Conway Twitty, put a version on the charts in the 1950s. The song marked a watershed for Cole as his sensual, liquid baritone enchanted mainstream America and launched him as a popular vocalist. He gradually left his trio and his piano stylings behind and worked constantly as a solo vocalist until his early death from lung cancer in 1965. Cole's work from both the jazz years and the following period enjoyed a revival when his daughter Natalie released her tribute album *Unforgettable with Love* in 1991. The album is most noted for its title duet, in which Natalie paired her voice to her father's 1951 recording.

"Mona Lisa" is available in sheet music form (Hal Leonard 00353190) and in many song anthologies. For a recorded version, try Cole's *Greatest Hits* (Capitol CD 29687).

2. "I'm Movin' On"
Words and Music by Hank Snow
Copyright © 1950, Unichappell Music, Inc.

"In my opinion, the 1950s was the heyday of good, down-to-earth country. My timing was perfect" (Snow 1994, 366). Hank Snow catapulted to success in country music just as the decade began, with the first of his eighty-five hit singles. He performed into the 1990s and died just days before the century's end. Along the way he earned accolades for his distinctive singing, songwriting, and guitar playing, and also for his substantial success as a recording industry executive. He took perhaps the greatest pride in holding to traditional country music while others went first to rockabilly, then orchestrations and strings, and then to what Snow termed a "Fifth Avenue charade." In 1985, he declared, "I'm glad my time is done with recording. I got out at the right time" (Edwards 1985).

Hank Snow's timing may have been good but his success was hard-won. Born as Clarence Snow in Nova Scotia, Canada, in 1914, he suffered at the hands of his abusive grandparents and stepfather. He ran away repeatedly—the last time to join the fishing fleet at the age of twelve—and would later build his career on songs about traveling. Still, his mother's influence was strong; it was she who exposed him to the music of Jimmie Rodgers, his greatest influence. Before he was twenty, he bought a guitar and began singing on radio in Halifax for a show sponsored by Crazy Water Crystals, a laxative. He recorded for RCA's Bluebird label in Canada, but was rarely heard by country fans across the border.

Snow and his wife Minnie decided to try their luck in the United States in the mid-1940s, first in Hollywood, then on West Virginia's *Wheeling Jamboree*, and finally in Dallas on the *Big D Jamboree*. He was one of the last country stars for whom live radio was the critical pathway to stardom. His friendship with Texan Ernest Tubb led to a coveted spot on Nashville's *Grand Ole Opry* but he nearly lost it just months later when audiences failed to warm to him. His first hit song saved him.

Steve Sholes, famous artist and repertoire man for RCA Records, brought Snow to Chicago for an audition in 1949. Snow played a song that he believed had great promise, but which Sholes dismissed, preferring to release "The Marriage Vow" instead. The record did not sell well but it got Snow a second chance a year later, when he again auditioned "I'm Movin' On." This time Sholes bit and the song went to number 1 on the Billboard chart (termed the "folk chart" at the time), and stayed on the chart for nearly a year. Snow's membership in the Opry was secure. He performed there for forty-six years, lived at his "Rainbow Ranch" near Nashville for fifty years, and was wed to Minnie for sixty-three years. He had at least one song on the charts for each of five decades.

"I'm Movin' On" was recorded by many performers, including Elvis Presley and Ray Charles, but it was always Hank Snow's theme song. "I'm Movin' On" is available on *Decade Series: The 1950's* (Hal Leonard 00690543). To hear Hank sing it, try *The Essential Hank Snow* (RCA Nashville 66931).

3. "Rocket 88"
Words and Music by Jackie Brenston
Copyright © 1951, Hill and Range Songs, Inc.

By 1950, the recording industry, which had suffered shortages of man-ufacturing materials and a musicians' strike in the 1940s, was back on its feet. The large, corporate-owned labels were challenged by inde-pendents such as Mercury, Atlantic, and a host of regional imprints.

In Memphis, an engineer at WREC radio, Sam Phillips, started the Memphis Recording Service in January 1950. He recorded big band broadcasts from the Peabody Hotel, transcription programs for public service agencies, weddings, and political speeches. That sum-mer, he decided to try the record business.

Phillips Records was out of business by September, having is-sued only one single. Sam Phillips found the business perplexing; copyrights, royalties, manufacturing, and distribution were new ground for the engineer and music lover. He did, however, meet and solicit advice from other record men. The Bihari brothers, owners of Los Angeles' Modern and RPM labels, liked Sam and tried to help him. They were also interested in the talent to be found in the Memphis area, and after Phillips Records' demise, they struck a deal with Sam. Phillips agreed to provide master recordings for issue on RPM.

Over at WDIA radio, the South's first all-black station, a disc jockey and entertainer named B. B. King was attracting local attention. Phillips signed King to a recording contract and subsequently recorded and sold masters of King's music to RPM in 1950 and 1951. King, happy to be a recording artist, told Ike Turner, bandleader and disc jockey at WROX in Clarksdale, Mississippi, about the Memphis Recording Service. Turner took the advice of B. B. King and headed to Memphis to record for Phillips.

Driving to Memphis for a recording session in early March 1951, Ike Turner and his Kings of Rhythm, a quintet which included Ike's cousin Jackie Brenston, suffered a mishap when guitarist Willie Kizart's amplifier and speaker cabinet fell off the top of the car. Unable to fix the damaged speaker, Turner's rhythm and blues group entered the studio on March 5 and recorded an ode to a popular automobile of the day, the Oldsmobile Rocket 88. Kizart, playing a boogie-woogie phrase though the distorted amp, created an unusual guitar sound. Singer Brenston had modeled his vocal styling for the song on the jump blues made popular by Louis Jordan and others in the 1940s. The "fuzztone" guitar and Brenston's fervent vocals made the session unique. Phillips would later declare it the first rock 'n' roll record.

Sam Phillips had become acquainted with Leonard Chess, who was often in Memphis on business for his Chicago-based Aristocrat and Chess labels. Phillips made a deal with Chess to release "Rocket 88." This fundamental business blunder would eventually cost Phillips dearly.

Ike Turner was outraged when his song was released by Chess (number 1458) in April 1951. The label read: "Rocket 88" by Jackie Brenston and his Delta Cats. By the time the record hit number 1 on the charts in June, the Bihari brothers were so upset with Phillips that they signed B. B. King directly to their company and hired Ike Turner as their representative in the South. As a talent scout, Turner was very successful, discovering and grooming many artists including a young woman from Nutbush, Tennessee, Annie Bullock. After marrying Ike, she would become Tina Turner.

Phillips did not only lose his connection to his local artists and RPM Records. In less than a year, Chess realized he could deal directly with the Memphis musicians. He convinced Howlin' Wolf, who Sam Phillips thought his most important discovery, to move to Chicago and record exclusively for Chess. By 1953, Phillips was isolated from all avenues of distribution of the southern music he so loved. He was forced by circumstance, and quite against his will, to start his own label again. This time he called it Sun Records.

"Rocket 88" is in print in *The History of Rock* (Hal Leonard 00490216). More than thirty sound recordings of "Rocket 88" are available. The original version can be found on *The Sun Records Collection* (Rhino CD 71780; three CDs).

4. "(We're Gonna) Rock around the Clock"
Words and Music by Max C. Freedman and Jimmy DeKnight
Copyright © 1952, Myers Music

The simple two-minute, eight-second recording of "Rock around the Clock" released by Bill Haley and His Comets (often incorrectly referred to as Bill Haley and *the* Comets) in 1954 helped alter the music industry forever. It was the first rock 'n' roll record to reach number 1 on a national chart and, by doing so, established rock 'n' roll as an economically viable commodity. Interestingly, if it were not for one of its songwriter's persistence, the song would never have been a hit record.

Jimmy DeKnight was the stage name used by songwriter, publisher, and promoter James E. Myers. He began writing "Rock around the Clock" in 1952 and later sought the assistance of Max C. Freedman to finish it. Myers, a musician who loved big band jazz more than anything, had no intention of writing a rock 'n' roll song; he merely wanted to write something more upbeat than the typical songs of the day. Decca Records apparently did not realize that this would be a landmark rock 'n' roll smash either, because they included "fox trot" on the label of the original release.

Myers took his completed song first to a local Philadelphia bandleader Sunny Dae and His Knights. Sunny Dae's release was a failure in the marketplace, but Myers was determined to get the song into the national limelight. Because Bill Haley and His Comets had a recent national hit single called "Crazy, Man, Crazy," Myers played them the song and encouraged them to record it. Although Bill Haley liked the song and wanted to record it, his label refused to let him record the song. After he switched to Decca Records, Haley recorded the song. In 1954, however, it was released as the B side of a song called "Thirteen Women," a song that did poorly in the marketplace.

Determined to promote his song, Myers sent copies of the Bill Haley recording to Hollywood film studios. The song was played during the opening credits of the 1955 film *Blackboard Jungle*, starring Sidney Poitier. The film dealt with juvenile delinquency and racial tensions, two bold themes at the time. The song became associated with rebellious teens because of its association with the film. Sales of "Rock around the Clock" increased dramatically as a result of the film.

This song helped define the genre called "rock 'n' roll." In addition, Bill Haley can be considered the first international rock 'n' roll star. "Rock around the Clock" was one of the best-selling records of all time (with sales estimated at more than 100 million copies). This song inspired many subsequent performers, including John Lennon and Elton John. Bill Haley and His Comets gave teens more than this hit song. They gave them a new musical identity that would define their generation for years to come.

There are many recordings of "Rock around the Clock" available. The original Bill Haley rendition is available on *From the Original Master Tapes* (MCA Records, 1985).

5. "I Got a Woman"
Words and Music by Ray Charles and Renald Richard
Copyright © 1954, Unichappell Music, Inc.

In October 1954, Ray Charles and his six band members were driving north from Tennessee. Near South Bend, Indiana, a gospel song with a solid beat came on the radio. Charles and trumpeter Renald Richard began making up secular lyrics as they sang along. Charles began with the title phrase. Richard answered with the next. Intrigued by what they had done, Charles asked Richard if he could compose a complete lyric. The next day Richard delivered it to Charles, who set the words to a gospel-tinged melody inspired by the song on the radio. "I Got a Woman" was to be the struggling Ray Charles's first number 1 record and would establish "Brother Ray" as the "Genius of Soul Music."

Ray Charles Robinson was born September 23, 1930, in Albany, Georgia, and shortly after Ray's birth, Bailey and Aretha Robinson moved to Greenville, Florida. Bailey was a railroad worker and absentee father, and young Ray grew up in rural Florida listening to gospel, blues, and country music. R. C. Robinson, as he was known at the Florida School for the Deaf and Blind, was losing his sight to glaucoma. By age seven, he was totally blind and enrolled at the school where he received instruction in Braille and music. At fourteen, he was dismissed from the school as an "unsatisfactory student" and sent out to make his own way.

For three years, R. C. played around north Florida with dance bands, jazz bands, and even an all-white country band. Seeking a change, he took a bus to Seattle in the spring of 1948 where he joined Gossie McKee, a guitar-playing former bandmate from Florida. The trio they put together was a direct copy of the "King" Cole Trio, with R. C., now known as Ray Charles, imitating Cole.

By the early 1950s, Charles was working the rhythm and blues circuit with a six-piece combo in the style of Charles Brown. The late-night drives between one-nighters gave ample opportunity for Charles to indulge his love for gospel singing. He especially liked to hear Archie Brownlee, lead singer of the Five Blind Boys of Mississippi, when their records came on the car radio.

Renald Richard was a trumpeter from New Orleans playing in Charles's band. A composer and arranger in his own right, Richard would not stay with Charles long. In the mid-1950s, he returned to New Orleans where he played on many record sessions, including Little Richard's landmark rock record "Tutti Frutti." Richard is likely most responsible for the form and lyric content of "I Got a Woman," but it was Charles who, to be successful, needed to find his own "voice." Combining those sexually anthemic lyrics with a pure gospel vocal fervor gave Charles what he needed. However, Charles was criticized by the African American church for using gospel music as the foundation for secular music. He was even criticized by other secular performers for commercializing religious music. Nevertheless, Ray Charles exploited his newfound style with subsequent releases on the Atlantic Records label; "This Little Girl of Mine," "Hallelujah I Love Her So," and "What'd I Say" changed rhythm and blues into soul music and paved the way for the Motown sound of the 1960s.

"I Got a Woman," as an Elvis Presley cover version, is in several Presley folios by Hal Leonard. Hal Leonard also includes it in the folio of music from the *Mr. Holland's Opus* soundtrack. Ray Charles's version is in the Warner Brothers folio *Classic Songs of the 50's.*

Dozens of recorded versions are available, including those by Elvis, Them (featuring Van Morrison), The Monkees, the Shirelles, and Bobby Darin. Jazz organists Jimmy Smith and Jimmy McGriff and bluesmen Howlin' Wolf and Snooks Eaglin have recorded the song. The original is on *The Best of Ray Charles: The Atlantic Years* (Rhino CD 71722).

6. "Love Is a Many-Splendored Thing"
Words by Paul Francis Webster and Music by Sammy Fein
Copyright © 1955, Miller Music Corporation

Paul Francis Webster was a New York lyricist who worked with composer Sammy Fein to create the title song for the film *Love Is a Many-Splendored Thing.* The film and song represented the short-lived postwar period when parents and their teenage children shared the same social values and musical tastes. Sandwiched between the big band–era crooners and frenetic rock 'n' rollers, these pop vocal groups were characterized by clean-cut images—singers who looked as pleasing as they sounded. As affluent white-collar families fled noisy urban life for the quiet environment of suburbia, they were attracted to equally unobtrusive, yet pleasant, harmonies of pop acts such as the Four Aces.

The first half of the decade was, in some ways, the silence before the storm of generational differences. During this conservative period of McCarthyism, fears of a third world war and white flight from inner cities, families enjoyed a sense of comfort in activities shared by the nuclear family. Television shows were family oriented; films were wholesome; and radio, now more dependant on spinning records than producing variety shows, was programmed for all ages.

Male vocal groups such as the Four Aces had an all-American image that appealed to all age groups. Another group, called the Four Freshmen, was based on the collegiate look that was now familiar to larger numbers of young adults, many of whom took advantage of financial aid for ex-GIs. Most of the four-part groups used close harmonies similar to barbershop quartets, gentle lyrical melodies, and lyrics that typically glamorized love.

The Four Aces, a prototypical four-part harmony group, singing the syrupy sweet Webster–Fein collaboration "Love Is a Many-Splendored Thing," yielded a hit that reached the number 1 spot on the Billboard pop chart. It remained in the top 10 for an impressive sixteen weeks. Although the four-part harmony groups continued throughout the decade, this song signaled the end of homogeneity in musical tastes between the generations. Over the next few years, teens would fight to distinguish themselves from their parents by turning from groups like the Four Aces to rock 'n' roll artists.

This song is available in sheet music in the folio *All Time Favorite Movie Classics* (Warner Brothers MF 9706) and on *Forever Plaid: Original Cast Recording* (RCA Victor 9026607022).

7. "Day-O (the Banana Boat Song)"
Words and Music by Irving Burgie, William Attaway, and
Harry Belafonte
Copyright © 1955, Shari Music Publishing Corporation

At the start of 1957, America was beginning a love affair with calypso music, a pop culture fad only surpassed by the hula hoop the following year. The main player in calypso's challenge of Elvis's pop music domination was a twenty-nine-year-old jazz and pop singer named Harry Belafonte.

Belafonte was born in New York City in 1927 to a Jamaican mother. He spent his preteen years with grandparents in Jamaica. It was on the streets of Kingston where he first heard calypso.

Calypso is a Caribbean music genre that quickly spread from Trinidad in the early part of the century. A form of improvised social and political commentary, calypso was performed during Carnival, the festival that precedes Lent. Colorful calypsonians such as Lord Executioner, Roaring Lion, and Attila the Hun delighted listeners throughout the region.

Postwar Americans, especially two income families, could afford to vacation in exotic beach locations like the islands in the Caribbean. Some ex-GIs had seen firsthand examples of lush tropical isles. Exotic tourist spots such as Trinidad conjured up visions of beautiful beaches and twenty-four-hour celebrations, something Americans longed for. While they waited for their dream vacation on the beach, patient U.S. workers listened to calypso.

Belafonte took acting classes at the New School after World War II. Also attending classes were Marlon Brando and Sidney Poitier. Finding no work as an actor, Belafonte began singing at Manhattan's Royal Roost jazz club, where the house band included Charlie Parker, Max Roach, Bud Powell, and Miles Davis. Clarinetist Tony Scott often backed Belafonte and eventually became the arranger for Belafonte's best-selling RCA albums.

Living in Greenwich Village, Belafonte was exposed to folk music of all kinds. A Jewish cantor taught him "Hava Nagila," and performers such as the Weavers, Burl Ives, and Josh White Jr. influenced young Belafonte, especially regarding folk music.

By the early 1950s, he was finding success as a popular interpreter of folk songs and, in October 1955, NBC booked him as a guest on the *Colgate Comedy Hour*. In collaboration with one of the show's writers, Bill Attaway, Belafonte planned a twenty-minute segment of Caribbean music. Attaway called in his friend Irving Burgie, a Julliard-trained composer and guitarist, who, under the professional name Lord Burgess, wrote several songs for Belafonte's appearances. Burgie took "Day-O," originally a West Indian song sung by dockworkers, and rewrote it for American tastes.

Within days of the television broadcast, RCA Victor invited Belafonte to a studio to record an album of Caribbean songs, eight of which were written by Burgie. Not released until the end of 1956, the album, *Calypso*, with backing by Tony Scott and his orchestra, became a hit. It stayed at the top of the charts for thirty-one weeks and sold a million and a half copies in 1957. "Day-O" was issued as a single following the release of a cover version entitled "The Banana Boat Song," by the folk group the Tarriers. Belafonte's single soon pushed the cover off the airways.

Belafonte had continued success as a singer and, in 1957, as an actor, starring in the feature film *Island in the Sun* with a title song by Burgie. Although "Day-O" was not the first calypso-derived song

("Rum and Coca Cola" was a hit in 1944) or Belafonte the most authentic singer of Caribbean songs, they reshaped and injected an ethnic art form into mainstream culture.

"Day-O" is available in piano/vocal sheet music (Hal Leonard 2504171). As "The Banana Boat Song," it is in many folios in a variety of arrangements. Sound recordings include those by the Kinks, Sarah Vaughan, and a satire by Stan Freeberg. Belafonte's original album, *Calypso,* is on CD reissue (RCA CD 53801).

8. "Maybellene"
Words and Music by Chuck Berry
Copyright © 1955, Arc Music Corporation

During 1954, in Memphis, Sam Phillips recorded the sounds of Elvis Presley, a white man who could sing "black." The next year, in Chicago, the Chess brothers found a black man who could sing "white." Phillips and the Chess brothers were trying the same strategy: find artists who could succeed in both the rhythm and blues and pop fields. Chess Records' Chuck Berry accomplished this feat and helped create rock and roll.

By the mid-1950s, white "covers" of rhythm and blues hits were dominating the pop charts. Prior to rock 'n' roll, radio stations were segregated. Stations aimed toward African American listeners were called "race stations" and played rhythm and blues by black artists. Alan Freed, a Cleveland DJ, recognized that a new hybrid of pop and rhythm and blues, aimed at a young record-buying public with postwar dollars to spend, was emerging. He dubbed this new music "rock 'n' roll."

When twenty-nine-year-old St. Louis native Charles Edward Anderson Berry entered the Chess Records offices in May 1955, he had an introduction from Chess recording star Muddy Waters and a handful of original songs. One of these, "Ida May," was a rewrite of the old country dance song "Ida Red." Leonard Chess scheduled a recording session for May 21, when Berry cut a blues song, "Wee Wee Hours," and "Ida May," retitled "Maybellene," at Chess's request.

The lyrics of "Maybellene" celebrate an inconstant girlfriend and automobiles (a Cadillac Coupe deVille and a V-8 Ford), memories Berry retained from high school. Berry's diction, like his idol

Nat Cole's, was perfect, a necessity for the lyric-laden song. Berry's guitar playing reflected the influence of the country guitarists he heard on the *Grand Ole Opry*, a favorite radio program of his father's.

Sensing the opportunity to capture a mainstream market, Chess sent dubs of the pairing to Alan Freed, who had moved his radio show from Cleveland to New York City. "Maybellene" attracted unprecedented response from Freed's white, teenage audience. The record, Chess 1604, was released to instant success. Freed aired the single constantly on his WINS *Rock 'n' Roll Party* program.

Though the Chess Records label copy credited only Berry as composer of "Maybellene," Berry's first royalty check indicated he had cowriters: Alan Freed and Chicago record distributor Russ Fratto were each receiving one-third. An angry Berry questioned Leonard Chess and was told that the record would sell better if the "cowriters" had a stake in its success. Berry could not dispute Chess's logic, as, over the summer of 1955, "Maybellene" climbed the Billboard pop charts to number 5. Berry, like other artists new to the recording industry, quickly learned that payola (paying for radio airplay) and giving other people songwriter credit were the darker side of the business.

The single sold more than 1 million copies at a time when a hit rhythm and blues record sold less than one-tenth as many copies. None of the middle-of-the-road covers of "Maybellene" sold nearly as well as Berry's; rock 'n' roll had emerged as the dominant popular form when presented by artists with whom white middle-class teens identified. In 1986, Berry sued successfully for sole authorship in the copyright of "Maybellene."

"Maybellene" is unavailable in print. On compact disc, "Maybellene" is available as bluegrass by Jim & Jesse, country by George Jones, and in covers by Berry's contemporaries: Elvis, Ronnie Hawkins, Buddy Knox, and Johnny Rivers. The original recording is on *The Best of Chuck Berry* (MCA CD 11944).

9. "The Flying Saucer"
Written by Bill Buchanan and Richard Goodman
Copyright © 1956, Luniverse Music

In June 1956, a twenty-two-year-old New York University dropout had a brilliant idea. Richard "Dickie" Goodman and his songwriting partner Bill Buchanan, a struggling music publisher, thought they could fashion a four-minute comedic re-creation of Orson Welles's *War of the Worlds* radio broadcast. The "space race" between the United States and the USSR was well underway and it seemed a perfect time to put flying saucers and little green men in popular music; science fiction films had been doing very well at the box office, after all.

Goodman and Buchanan could not afford an office in the Brill Building, known as Manhattan's songwriting mecca. They met, instead, at their "office," Hansen's Drug Store, just down the street from the Brill Building, where they outlined the script for "The Flying Saucer." Buchanan would play the disc jockey who would interrupt his show to announce the news: the flying saucers are real. Then, using the "cut-in," a radio technique in which a snippet of a record is played as if in answer to the disc jockey's comment, Goodman spliced the master tape with a line from the Platters' "Great Pretender."

The songwriters created a fictional character called John Cameron-Cameron, a parody of John Cameron Swayze, the first network anchorman on television. With this model, Buchanan and Goodman (playing the part of John Cameron-Cameron reporting from the street) built a mini drama in which the saucer lands, Cameron-Cameron interviews bystanders who when asked what they will do, reply with a line from Little Richard's "Long Tall Sally" and Fats Domino's "Poor Me." The spaceman's first words are, of course, the nonsense catchphrase from Little Richard's "Tutti Frutti."

Four minutes and seventeen seconds and an enormous number of tape splices later, Buchanan and Goodman had produced their first record. It used techniques that became common decades later in rock and rap: sampling, tape-speed manipulation, and even one pre-Beatles example of backward tape masking.

Unfortunately for the duo, no record company in New York was interested in "The Flying Saucer." In desperation, they took the tape to WINS radio where disc jockey Jack Lacy played it. Following Lacy's show, DJ Alan Freed aired the tape as well. Listeners responded and soon George Goldner of Roulette Records created the "Universe" label for Buchanan and Goodman. Only after the first two thousand discs were pressed did Goldner discover the name was already taken. These first two thousand copies have a handwritten "L" in front of the "Universe."

"The Flying Saucer," issued as Luniverse 101, sold well in New York and attracted the attention of the music publishers and their association's agent Harry Fox. Fox calculated at least nineteen instances of copyright infringement in the record. The record companies whose product was sampled in "The Flying Saucer" did not join the publishers, however. They were busy pressing additional copies of the records sampled. One executive called "The Saucer" the best promotional gimmick ever.

A deal to share a 17-cent royalty among the publishers cleared the record, which had sold more than 1 million copies by the end of August, for jukebox and radio play. Ironically, both NBC and ABC radio networks banned the song, afraid the public might think the invasion from space was real and panic, as it did in 1938 when Welles had created *The War of the Worlds*.

"The Flying Saucer" has never been published in print, but the original sound recording is available on *Billboard Top Rock N' Roll Hits, 1956* (Rhino CD 70599).

10. "Tutti Frutti"
Words and Music by Richard Penniman (also known as Little Richard) and Dorothy La Bostrie (Joe Lubin later rewrote the song and his name was added to the songwriter credits)
Copyright © 1956, Venice Music, Inc.

Little Richard pushed the envelope for outrageous behavior by rock 'n' roll musicians. Born Richard Penniman in Macon, Georgia, in 1932, Little Richard was one of twelve children. During his childhood, he was drawn to the exhilarating services of the Pentecostal and Holiness churches. His need to connect with his faith continued throughout his life and, in fact, interrupted his entertainment career.

Even as a teen, Little Richard did little to hide his homosexuality. His flamboyant style—at times in drag—influenced his onstage demeanor throughout his career. After traveling for several years and perfecting his piano and vocal styles, he settled in New Orleans.

Black entrepreneur Arthur N. Rupe, owner of Specialty Records on the West Coast, signed Little Richard to a recording contract in 1955. Rupe sent producer Robert "Bumps" Blackwell to New Orleans to record Little Richard's first album for Specialty Records.

Bumps Blackwell was disappointed in the first few tunes recorded during the session, begun on September 14, 1955. Blackwell listened to Little Richard improvising on a song during breaks and asked if they could develop it into a song for the album. He also asked, and received, Little Richard's permission to allow Dorothy La Bostrie, a young Creole lyricist in the studio, to "clean up" the lyrics. After a short time, with little time left to record the song, La Bostrie produced the finished product. Even though the lyrics were basically nonsensical, they were perfect for Little Richard's outrageous style of singing. In short time, the song was on the top of the rhythm and blues charts.

Because pop radio stations that catered to predominantly white audiences preferred more mainstream artists, Dot Records decided to record a cover of "Tutti Frutti" using a less outrageous artist. Before Pat Boone, the most clean-cut pop singer of the era, recorded the song, his producer had lyricist Joe Lubin rewrite the song so that it would be more palatable for mass consumption. The musical milktoast version of Little Richard's rock 'n' roll classic that Pat Boone released scored better on the charts.

In 1957, after claiming to have seen God's hand save his airplane from crashing, Little Richard suddenly quit performing in order to become a preacher. He attended Oakwood College in Huntsville, Alabama, and studied the scriptures. True to his promise, Little Richard took his showmanship to the pulpit. In the mid-1960s, he returned to a limited performance schedule, but later focused most of his efforts on preaching.

The fact that a conflicted drag queen turned preacher could be accepted by American teens indicates the radical change in social values that had occurred by the late 1950s. Although Pat Boone's version of this song was more widely accepted by mainstream radio than Little Richard's, it suggests the glacial speed at which society as a whole caught up with teenage trends. This generation gap would evolve into a more divisive standoff as the nation entered the 1960s.

The classic Little Richard version of "Tutti Frutti" is available on *18 Greatest Hits* (Rhino Records, 1985). The Pat Boone rendition can be found on *Jivin' Pat* (Bear Family Records, 1986).

11. "Heartbreak Hotel"
Words and Music by Mae Boren Axton, Tommy Durden, and Elvis Presley
Copyright © 1956, Tree Publishing (Sony/ATV)

The song "Heartbreak Hotel" celebrated a country theme of unrequited love, but it was delivered to the masses by a singer who would eventually earn the title of "King of Rock 'n' Roll." It is unlikely that "Heartbreak Hotel" would have met with the success it did had it not been released by Elvis. It is also doubtful that Elvis was truly a cowriter of this song, because his manager "Colonel" Tom Parker allegedly demanded that Elvis get partial songwriter credit for songs he recorded.

Elvis was born on January 8, 1935, in Tupelo, Mississippi, and began singing with his parents at the local First Assembly of God Church. His first public solo performance was at the Mississippi–Alabama Fair and Dairy Show where he won second prize after singing Country Red Foley's "Old Shep." Elvis was given his first guitar on his eleventh birthday in 1946. Although Elvis and his family felt at home in Tupelo, they moved to Memphis, Tennessee, in 1948. It was rumored that his father had a couple of minor problems with the law—bad checks and moonshine—and the move to Memphis was an attempt to avoid the police.

Although Presley found employment as a truck driver soon after graduating from high school, the music of the west Tennessee region began to mold the future star. The Memphis rhythm and blues and gospel music influenced him, as did the country and western sounds from nearby Nashville. In 1953, he paid the Memphis Recording Service (Sun Records) $4 to record "My Happiness" and "That's When Your Heartache Begins." He gave the acetate masters to his mother as belated birthday gifts.

Sam Phillips, owner of Sun Records, had a gift for scouting emerging talent and trends, but it was a secretary at Sun Records who alerted Phillips to Presley's potential. Phillips signed Elvis to a recording contract and teamed him with a solid instrumental combo of Memphis musicians. After several weeks of rehearsals, they entered the Sun Studios to record two singles. These two singles, and a third recorded later, became regional hits. It was the live performances, however, that generated most of the excitement for the "Hillbilly Cat," a stage name Elvis used at the time.

Elvis released several other country singles that became hits. His combo performed on the *Louisiana Hayride* and *Grand Ole Opry* radio shows in 1954. Although he was quite popular with the Hayride executives, he was told to "stick to driving a truck" by an Opry representative. Through his performances on the Hayride, he met Tom Parker and the two entered into a manager–artist relationship that eventually seemed more like a father–son tie.

Parker, noting that tiny Sun Records in Memphis could not keep up with Elvis's soaring success, brokered a deal in 1955 in which RCA Records bought Elvis's contract from Sun Records for $35,000. Recording in Nashville in 1956, Elvis was teamed with legendary guitarist Chet Atkins and other exceptionally talented studio musicians in the famous RCA Studio B. From the moment his voice was captured on tape in Studio B, Elvis's fame and fortune took wing.

As RCA released his first album, *Elvis Presley*, the King made his first network television appearance on the *Dorsey Brothers Show*. His first single from the album, "Heartbreak Hotel," was an immediate hit. It reached number 1 on the Billboard country, rhythm and blues and pop charts. It stayed in the number 1 position for two weeks and stayed in the top 10 for eight weeks. "Heartbreak Hotel" launched a stream of ten consecutive number 1 hits for Elvis, a truly amazing feat, especially for a relatively new artist. More amazing is his record-setting 150 hit songs throughout his short career.

Producers of films and network television programs quickly recognized the charismatic appeal of Elvis, especially for younger audiences. His second appearance on the *Milton Berle Show* earned him the nickname "Elvis the Pelvis" because of his gyrating hips and what some adults believed were vulgar movements. Ed Sullivan was so concerned about Presley's third appearance on his show that he had the cameras only shoot Elvis from the waist up in order not to offend older viewers. An estimated audience of 54 million watched Elvis that night.

In 1956, the same year that "Heartbreak Hotel" was setting the charts aflame, Presley was on contract with Hal Wallis and Paramount films. That same year, he was lent to Twentieth Century Fox and appeared in *Love Me Tender*, a film with the same title as one of his hit songs. Between 1958 and 1960, Elvis served in the Army, giving him a respite from the entertainment industry. When he returned, he focused his career on films. Regrettably for him, he was consistently cast in overly similar roles for films with scripts that had little artistic merit. He might have had true acting talent, but it was hard to tell as he plodded and sang his way through such teen fodder as *Blue Hawaii, Fun in Acapulco*, and *Viva Las Vegas*. His recording career during the 1960s was relegated to soundtracks as he made three movies a year from 1964 through 1969.

Frustrated with the lack of substantive film roles he was getting, Elvis made his live performance comeback in the 1970s. He continued to be a success in pop, country, and rhythm and blues, but by 1970, he had drifted from his rock 'n' roll roots (by then it was called "rock"). He also stayed in touch with his gospel roots and received a Grammy for Best Sacred Performance for "How Great Thou Art" in 1967 and a Grammy for Best Inspirational Performance for "He Touched Me" in 1972.

As his health began to decline due to weight gain, excessive use of prescription drugs, and fatigue from touring and recording, his behavior became increasingly eccentric. On August 16, 1977, Elvis died at the age of forty-two. Although his personal physician was accused of overprescribing medications that contributed to the King's death, the official cause of death was heart failure.

Despite his early death, Elvis changed much more than the entertainment industry in the United States. Youth found in Elvis not only a spokesperson for their rebelliousness, but also someone who gradually earned the respect of adults as well. The success of Elvis validated the emerging 1950s teen cultural milieu. As the baby boomers matured, his music evolved to serve their needs. Not only did Elvis give teens their own music with which to identify, he proved that much of the disposable income of this generation would be spent on music, fashion, and media of its own choosing. His music also set the stage for other musicians of the future. Without the astonishing success of Elvis—nearly 500 million copies of his records had been sold by the time he died—rock 'n' roll might have been a passing fad.

Sheet music is available in the piano and vocal collection *Elvis Presley: Elvis, Elvis, Elvis Greatest Hits* (Hal Leonard 306610). The original recording by Elvis has been remastered and released on *Elvis: 30 #1 Hits* (RCA Records 68079).

12. "Great Balls of Fire"
Words and Music by Jack Hammer and Otis Blackwell
Copyright © 1957, Hill and Range Songs, Inc.

Although songwriters Hammer and Blackwell helped lay the foundation of the new genre called "rock 'n' roll" by penning some of its earliest and most influential songs, it was two charismatic recording artists—Elvis Presley and Jerry Lee Lewis—who brought their songs to life. "Great Balls of Fire" was one of Lewis's early hits that remained his signature song throughout his dynamic, but sometimes tragic, career.

Jerry Lee Lewis was born in Ferriday, Louisiana, in 1935, the son of Elmo, a carpenter, and Mary Ethel, a preacher. Throughout his career, he struggled with his desire to keep in touch with his strong Pentecostal religious roots while enjoying the "evils" of an entertainer's life. One incident that reflected his conflicting lifestyles happened when he was a student at the Bible Institute in Waxahachie, Texas, in 1953. He was caught playing a hymn in the rhythm and blues piano style, something he had learned in taverns back home, and was expelled from school.

Jerry Lee Lewis was driven to be noticed onstage and offstage. His style of playing piano, unlike the subtler technique of jazz musicians, often included hitting the keyboard with his fists or even bouncing on it with his rump. He set his piano on fire at the end of one performance to, allegedly, keep the next act from getting a better crowd reaction. So, he earned the nickname "Killer."

Lewis's first recording, "Crazy Arms," was a country tune released by Sun Records in 1956, the label that also discovered Elvis Presley. It was a moderate success and Sun released "Whole Lotta Shakin' Goin' On," a song that crossed genre lines and became a hit on country, rhythm and blues, and pop charts, in 1957. Buoyed by his appearance on Steve Allen's television show, his next release,

"Great Balls of Fire," became a tremendous hit, again crossing over to all genres. Ironically, Jerry Lee Lewis, a man who married six times and has struggled with drugs and alcohol at various times during his life, initially declined to record "Great Balls of Fire" because he thought the song was sinful and in poor taste.

After the success of his first four rock 'n' roll singles, many industry insiders expected this exciting young artist's career to soar beyond that of any other artist in history. Like Elvis, Jerry Lee seemed destined to become an international superstar. He began his world tour in England in May 1958. Unfortunately, it was also in England, a nation known for bloodthirsty print journalists and Victorian values, that Jerry Lee Lewis's private life suddenly eclipsed his music.

When a member of the press discovered that Jerry Lee Lewis was touring with his new bride, a young woman who was only thirteen years old, the media—both English and American—began to investigate his personal life. They discovered that he had become involved with Myra, his thirteen-year-old third cousin, before he was legally divorced from his previous wife. He was publicly flogged in the London media and some members of Parliament even suggested that he be deported. As a result of the negative image he had gotten in the media, Jerry Lee was forced to cancel many of his overseas concert dates and return to the United States.

After returning to the United States, Lewis discovered that his newly found infamy had preceded his arrival back home. His records were banned by many radio stations and his reputation was irreparably damaged. Like a rocket shot down as it was leaving the launch pad, Lewis's career never recovered.

He later had moderate success with his version of Ray Charles's "What'd I Say" in 1961, but he was generally relegated to the club and state fair circuits for the remainder of his rock 'n' roll career. In 1970, Jerry Lee Lewis shifted from rock 'n' roll to country, the genre that he sang early in his career. Throughout the 1970s and 1980s, the Killer released numerous successful country records. Nevertheless, even his success in the country genre never approached the stardom that he likely would have reached had it not been for his relationship with his cousin Myra.

Even as he matured, Lewis could not seem to avoid controversy in his personal life. In 1976, he was involved in two shootings, one involving his bass player Norman Owens. He was also arrested for driving while intoxicated during that year.

His second son, Steve Allen Lewis, drowned in a swimming pool accident in 1962 at the age of three. If that weren't enough tragedy for one father, his other son, Jerry Lee Lewis Jr., died in an automobile accident in 1973. After his controversial third wife Myra divorced him, he married Joren Gunn in 1971. In 1982, while Gunn and Jerry Lee were separated, she was found mysteriously drowned in her swimming pool. He married Shawn Stephens in 1983, and two and one-half months later she was found dead of a drug overdose. The media noted the mysterious circumstances surrounding her death and, again, Jerry Lee was in the public eye for the wrong reasons. Although Stephens' family asked the FBI to investigate her death, Lewis was never implicated.

Lewis's problems continued into the 1990s when he had repeated confrontations with the Internal Revenue Service. To pay off his tax debts, he opened his house to tourists. He also released a new album called *Young Blood* on Sire Records in 1995, after a ten-year hiatus from the recording studio.

Jerry Lee Lewis was the subject of the 1989 film *Great Balls of Fire*, in which Dennis Quaid played the role of the Killer. The soundtrack from the film included eight newly recorded versions of his hits. The soundtrack is available on Polydor Records (839516; 1989).

13. "Tonight"
Words by Stephen Sondheim and Music by Leonard Bernstein
Copyright © 1957, Chappell and Company/G. Schirmer

In 1957, a groundbreaking Broadway musical brought together the prodigious talents of composer Leonard Bernstein, lyricist Stephen Sondheim, choreographer Jerome Robbins, and librettist Arthur Laurents. Robbins conceived the show as a modern retelling of the *Romeo and Juliet* story, with the lead characters a Jewish boy and an Irish Catholic girl. It was to be titled *East Side Story*. Fortunately, they shelved the idea for several years before resurrecting it as a story about gang violence between Puerto Rican immigrants (the Sharks) and a group of tough Anglos (the Jets) on the west side of Manhattan. *West Side Story* became Robbins's signature piece and Stephen

Sondheim's first Broadway credit, although as lyricist rather than his preferred role of composer.

The show combined Robbins's athletic choreography and Bernstein's Latin- and jazz-influenced orchestrations in a rough urban setting, all within the context of Laurents's compelling play about racism and street violence. The language was raw with near profanity and ugly ethnic references such as *Spics*, *Micks*, and *Wops*. The performers were mostly young and inexperienced, which proved a good formula for this tale of teenage tough guys, ill-fated romance, and death. Theater people loved the Broadway production, but the mass public was slow to embrace it. However, stunning success came with the 1961 release of a motion picture version and its companion soundtrack album. The film, directed by Robert Wise and Jerome Robbins, won ten academy awards, including Best Picture. The soundtrack album was number 1 on the Billboard album charts for fifty-four weeks, and remained on the chart for 198 weeks total. Its record was unsurpassed at the end of the century.

West Side Story also featured a long string of memorable songs, including the hits "I Feel Pretty," "Somewhere," "Maria," and "Tonight," the latter a duet by two innocent youths from opposite worlds. The film featured Natalie Wood as the Puerto Rican girl Maria (with singing voice dubbed by Marni Nixon, who performed the same service for Deborah Kerr in *The King and I* and Audrey Hepburn in *My Fair Lady*) and Richard Beymer as the Polish American Tony. Recalling Shakespeare's famous balcony scene, Tony comes to the balcony of Maria's tenement and entreats her to see him. They sing, profess their love, and part, only to live out a tragedy that results from the blood rivalry of the two gangs. "Tonight" is reprised as the action builds toward an impending fight, with the two lovers separately singing a sweet song of anticipation, contrasted by gangs singing of violence and retribution. Taking leave from Shakespeare, the musical allows Maria to live while Tony is cut down in a knife fight.

West Side Story is a uniquely American artifact of the mid-twentieth century that remains popular in both the stage and the film versions. "Tonight" is available as sheet music (Hal Leonard 00450046) and in a number of Broadway folios. The original motion picture soundtrack is available in the Sony Broadway Series (CD 48211).

14. "If I Had a Hammer"
Words and Music by Lee Hays and Pete Seeger
Written 1949; copyright © 1958, Ludlow Music

Lee Hays came from a pious family of the rural South, the son of a
Methodist preacher. Pete Seeger came from New York culture and
education, the son of an ethnomusicologist. Born in 1914 and 1919,
respectively, they matured during the Great Depression, an experience that formed deep-rooted political views. Hays was influenced by
radical Presbyterian minister Claude Williams and Myles Horton of
the Highlander Folk School in Tennessee. Seeger kept the company
of Leadbelly and Woody Guthrie, and was an assistant to folklorist
Alan Lomax.

Hays transformed old southern hymns into labor union an-
thems while Seeger played the banjo and collected folk songs. They
eventually met in New York, performed together as the Almanac
Singers and anchored a web of folk artists and left-leaning social re-
formers in Greenwich Village. In 1945, the two formed People's
Songs Inc., which Seeger described as a collector of "union songs
and peace songs, and one-world songs and songs against racism . . .
songs to help change the world" (Willen 1988, 79).

In 1949, as Seeger and Hays sat through a long People's Songs
executive committee meeting, their most successful collaboration
took place. As Hays remembered it, "Pete and I passed manuscript
notes back and forth until I finally nodded at him and agreed we had
the thing down" (Willen 1988, 88). Their handiwork, "The Hammer
Song," was performed by the Weavers, a new folk group formed by
Hays and Seeger that also featured Ronnie Gilbert and Fred Heller-
man. The song also graced the cover of volume 1, number 1 of *Sing
Out Magazine,* which was first issued in May 1950 as a successor to the
People's Songs Bulletin and is still going strong. The Weavers were a surprising success as the 1950s began, performing constantly and top-
ping the charts with hits like "On Top of Old Smokey" and "Tzena,
Tzena," effectively bridging the gap between folk and pop music.
Old friends on the left attacked them for being too commercial, but
they never lost their political edge.

"The Hammer Song" was specifically written to warn about
threats to American liberty as the McCarthy era developed. Those

threats soon became real to Hays, Seeger, and the Weavers when they were investigated by the FBI and the House Un-American Activities Committee, then were blacklisted by the entertainment industry. Seeger was charged with contempt of Congress and sentenced to ten years in prison, though the conviction was later overturned. Ironically, both the Weavers and Seeger, who went on his own in 1952, continued to prosper after an initial setback, in part because of the notoriety of the blacklist.

Despite its serious purpose, "The Hammer Song" never had a great impact during the dark days of the 1950s. Instead, it would become ubiquitous in the folk scene of the early 1960s as arranged by Peter, Paul, and Mary. Now titled "If I Had a Hammer," it rose to number 10 on the Billboard chart for the trio in 1962 and then topped that when the Trini Lopez recording went to number 3 the following year. It was recorded by dozens of other performers. The royalties from the song kept Lee Hays afloat financially after the Weavers disbanded in 1963. He died in 1981 from diabetes and hard living, shortly after a triumphant reunion concert at Carnegie Hall. Seeger would continue his work as musician and activist to the end of the century and beyond.

"If I Had a Hammer" is available in *40 Songs for a Better World* (Hal Leonard 00310096). To hear an early Weavers' performance, try the *Weavers Greatest Hits* (Vanguard CD 15/16).

15. "Tom Dooley"
Traditional, adapted by Dave Guard
Copyright © 1959, Beechwood Music

In 1958, three young men scored a hit with a ballad conceived in the Appalachian Mountains nearly a century before. They sold more than 4 million copies. Its unexpected success launched The Kingston Trio to stardom and jump-started a folk revival that renewed the careers of many older traditional artists and brought commercial success to young folk artists who would become icons of the 1960s, such as Bob Dylan and Joan Baez. The folk revival provided an alternative to the teen-marketed music of rock 'n' roll, forcing the recording industry to acknowledge that acoustically driven music was alive in the nation. The hit song "Tom Dooley" also triggered a complicated copyright case that brought to light the longtime practice of record companies and publishers in claiming copyright for traditional folk material.

It all began when Tom Dula returned from the Civil War to his home in Wilkes County, North Carolina. There he flagrantly consorted with several women in the community of Reedy Branch, including both Laura Foster and Anne Melton, a beautiful married woman with a tolerant husband. On May 25, 1866, Laura Foster bundled her few belongings and left her father's home, expecting to meet Dula and marry, only to disappear. The community searched for Foster and whispered about the possible involvement of Dula and Melton, who were seen in earnest conversation on the day of the disappearance. As fingers began to point, Dula fled to Tennessee, only to be tracked down by two Wilkes County deputies with the help of Colonel James Grayson of Trade, Tennessee. Dula was held until Foster's body was finally found in September. She had been stabbed. He was tried, convicted, and granted an appeal.

The two trials of Tom Dula revealed a web of intrigue that included a third woman, an epidemic of syphilis, and perhaps a pregnancy. Though many believed that Anne Melton was at least involved, and perhaps the perpetrator, Dula took the punishment. They hanged him from a gallows in Statesville, North Carolina—not from the white oak tree named in the ballad—on May 1, 1868.

Because Tom Dula's case was sensational for its place and time, it spawned a number of folk ballads in the local area. They were kept alive by oral tradition until Ralph Peer came to the mountains to record local talent. Fiddler G. B. Grayson (nephew of James Grayson) and guitar player Henry Whitter recorded their version of "Tom Dooley" for the Victor label in 1929. It sold about four thousand copies. In 1938, song collectors Anne and Frank Warner visited Watauga County, North Carolina, where they heard Frank Proffitt sing "Tom Dooley." He had learned it from his father. The Warners taught the song to Alan Lomax, who published it in 1947 with credits to Frank Warner. "Tom Dooley" was recorded by Warner in 1952, then by other folk groups, including the Tarriers and Folksay Trio, and finally by the Kingston Trio. The time was right for trio member Dave Guard's copyrighted, calypso-like adaptation to catch America's ear. Ludlow Music, representing Lomax and Warner, sued, won, and reportedly shared a portion of the royalties with Frank Proffitt.

"Tom Dooley" is found in many folk song collections, including *American Folk Songs* (Hal Leonard 698981). For recordings, one can hear the earliest recording on *The Recordings of Grayson and Whitter* (County CD 3517) or a more contemporary version on *The Essential Doc Watson* (Vanguard CD 45/46).

1960–1969

War in the Streets and Overseas

The decade began with John F. Kennedy taking office as president, a dramatically different personality than his predecessor Dwight Eisenhower. Fidel Castro, who assumed power in Cuba in 1959, was affiliated with the USSR. The same year, Cuban refugees living in Miami, trained by CIA personnel, invaded the Bay of Pigs, Cuba, in a failed attempted to oust Castro. Not only was the Bay of Pigs incident embarrassing for the United States, it angered the Soviets and motivated them to resume nuclear testing. In an appalling show of political divisiveness, the Soviet Union erected the Berlin Wall in 1961. After discovering Soviet missiles on the island of Cuba, Kennedy forced a showdown with the Soviet leaders and Castro and demanded the removal of all missile sites. Although Kennedy's hard-line tactic worked, the Cuban missile crisis reminded Americans of the danger that nuclear missiles, aimed at our shores, posed.

Vietnam had been a French colony prior to World War II, was controlled by Japan during the war, and then returned to French control after the war. Then in 1954, communist forces under the leadership of Ho Chi Minh drove the French from Vietnam. Vietnamese leaders divided the country into communist North Vietnam, under Ho Chi Minh, and South Vietnam, under the dictatorial leadership of president Ngo Dinh Diem. The original plan was to have a national election in 1956 to reunite the country, but Diem scuttled the plan because he feared losing power.

During the first few years of the decade, Kennedy supported the Diem regime and sent sixteen thousand military personnel, called "advisers," to help his cause. But Diem's popularity with the U.S. military and the South Vietnamese people began to decline and he was assassinated in 1963, allegedly with the blessing of U.S. officials.

Kennedy's popularity during his first three years in office was encouraging, but he knew he needed to begin campaigning for re-election in 1964. On November 22, 1963, while riding in a motorcade, Kennedy was assassinated, allegedly by former marine and one-time Soviet resident Lee Harvey Oswald. Two days later, while Oswald was being transported to a different jail, Dallas nightclub owner Jack Ruby shot and killed him while network television stations broadcast the shocking images live to the nation.

Lyndon B. Johnson took office and assumed the role of commander in chief as the U.S. armed forces moved from military advisers to participants in a full-scale war in Vietnam. After U.S. Navy ships were attacked in the Bay of Tonkin in March 1964, Congress gave Johnson power to "take all necessary measures" to protect the increasing number of U.S. forces in Vietnam. By 1965, more than five hundred thousand U.S. military personnel were fighting in Vietnam. As images of the war reached television viewers back home, many people began to question the validity of our involvement in Vietnam's civil war.

The war in Vietnam would continue throughout the decade, becoming the single most divisive issue our nation had faced since the Civil War. The antiwar movement grew with each news report of death tolls in the Asian conflict—the average age of a U.S. soldier killed in the war was twenty-three. A counterculture evolved with a look—long hair, beards, women going braless—as different from the conservative mainstream of America as its liberal beliefs. The 1968 Democratic Convention in Chicago turned into a national disgrace as club-swinging police officers on horseback overreacted to protesters who chanted "The whole world is watching." Ironically, convention delegates inside the convention center were discussing an antiwar plank for the Democratic platform.

Republican Richard M. Nixon was elected president in the 1968 election. Both he and his vice president, Spiro T. Agnew, eventually left office in shame. While in office, Agnew referred to students with antiwar sentiments as "college punks." He also attacked network television and print media journalists, accusing them of biased reporting. While Agnew was losing his battle of public images, Nixon ordered B-52 bombers into Cambodia, which extended the war on communism.

By 1960, 10.5 percent of the population (18.87 million citizens) were African American. Legislation and court decisions during the 1950s laid the groundwork for the 1960s civil rights movement. The Reverend Martin Luther King Jr. preached nonviolent forms of protest such as sit-ins and boycotts. The 1963 civil rights march in Washington, D.C., gave Dr. King a platform for the speech that contained his famous statement "I have a dream." Dr. King, who won the 1964 Nobel Peace Prize, aided in getting the Civil Rights Act and the Voting Rights Act enacted. Four years later, to the horror of the nation, this great leader of the civil rights movement was assassinated in Memphis on April 4, 1968. The same year, his comrade in arms, Robert F. Kennedy, was also assassinated. As if a tribute to these two fallen heroes, the Civil Rights Act was passed in 1968.

Not all African Americans were satisfied with nonviolent forms of protest. Black Muslim leaders Malcolm X and Elijah Mohammed encouraged their followers to reject the help of whites and take up arms when necessary. In 1965, residents of the Watts community in Los Angeles rioted in the streets for six days. By the time the unrest was over, thirty-four persons were dead and 850 were injured. Los Angeles police made three thousand arrests and property owners suffered more than $200 million in damage. Riots erupted over the next two years in other major urban areas including Chicago, New York, Newark, and Detroit. The assassination of Martin Luther King Jr. triggered rioting in more than one hundred cities.

Unlike previous wars that united the nation under an umbrella of patriotism, the war in Vietnam divided the country into two general camps: liberals and conservatives. Songs such as "Alley-Oop" (Hollywood Argyles) and "Itsy Bitsy Teenie Weenie Yellow Polka Dot Bikini" (Brian Hyland) lulled the population into a false sense of security as the decade began. By the end of the decade, songs like "Abraham, Martin and John" (Dion) and "Give Peace a Chance" (John Lennon and Yoko Ono) echoed the traumatic events of the decade.

SONGS

1. "We Shall Overcome"
Words and Music by Zilphia Horton, Frank Hamilton, Guy Carawan, and Pete Seeger
Copyright © 1960, Ludlow Music

African American protesters linked arm in arm, swaying and singing "We Shall Overcome" in the face of southern policemen with clubs, dogs, and even cattle prods, created a powerful image. By the time that image became a regular feature of the evening news in the early 1960s, the song itself had been in service to social change for nearly twenty years. It was quite appropriately drawn from an African American gospel song, that was itself most likely based on an older traditional hymn. The exact chain of creation is still subject to debate, but it is clear that Reverend Charles Tindley's 1903 gospel song "I'll Overcome Some Day" was the foundation for the most essential freedom song of the 1960s.

"I Will Overcome" moved from the church to the streets when it was used in 1946 to motivate striking employees of the American Tobacco Company in Charleston, South Carolina. Striker Lucille Simmons is credited with first singing it as "We Will Overcome," and it evolved further when someone substituted "shall" for "will." Union organizers took the song to the Highlander Folk School in Grundy County, Tennessee, an adult school closely allied with the struggling labor movement in the rural South. At Highlander, Zilphia Horton, wife of Highlander director Myles Horton, learned it and began to pass it along. She taught a version to Pete Seeger, who published it in his mimeographed *People's Songs* in 1947. Seeger taught it to Guy Carawan and Frank Hamilton in California, and Carawan subsequently went to Highlander after Zilphia's death to carry on her work with music. All four were credited with composing the song when its copyright was registered in 1960.

At Highlander, an important cross-fertilization occurred. The school was a radical training center for both union organizers and civil rights activists working to overturn segregation laws in the southern states. Throughout the 1950s black and white activists met at Highlander to learn strategies for social change, including the use of movement songs. "We Shall Overcome" was perfect for the purpose because its simple, repetitive structure allowed verses to be improvised as needed to fit a situation. Highlander was helping to build momentum for the protests, marches, and voter registration drives that would finally compel the passage of the Civil Rights Act of 1964.

In April 1960, Carawan took the song to Raleigh, North Carolina, where civil rights leaders from across the South were taught the protest method of nonviolent sit-ins. Among the trainees were students from black colleges in Nashville who had challenged the segregation of lunch counters in that city and achieved peaceful integration. They became the core of the Student Non-Violent Coordinating Committee (SNCC) that put youth on the front lines in the struggle. The song was soon heard at marches, from jail cells and on stages where SNCC's Freedom Singers performed. They were a shifting assemblage of singers, including Bernice Reagon and her then-husband Cordell Reagon, who traveled the South to support civil rights actions.

The song was indelibly written into the common consciousness on August 28, 1963, when the March on Washington for Jobs and Freedom brought more than one hundred thousand people to the steps of the Lincoln Memorial. There, Dr. Martin Luther King Jr. intoned "I have a dream," and folksinger Joan Baez led the assembly in this powerful song of change.

"We Shall Overcome" is available in sheet music (Hal Leonard 00378854) and on the Smithsonian Folkways *American Roots Collection: The SNCC Freedom Singers, Dorothy Cotton, and Pete Seeger* (SMC 40062). Royalties from the song are assigned to the We Shall Overcome Fund, which continues to support social change in the South.

2. "Shop Around"
Words and Music by Berry Gordy Jr. and Bill "Smokey" Robinson
Copyright © 1961, Jobete Music Company, Inc.

In 1957, Berry Gordy Jr., a Detroit auto-assembly-line worker and fledgling songwriter, heard seventeen-year-old "Smokey" Robinson singing at an audition. Rhythm and blues star Jackie Wilson's manager was not interested in Robinson or his group, the Matadors (soon to be renamed the Miracles), but Gordy thought Robinson's voice was special and the two were soon writing songs together.

By 1959, Gordy had produced and leased several recordings by the Miracles to the Chess, United Artists, and End labels. Unhappy with the quality of the released records and the accounting of royalties, Robinson urged Gordy to take control. With $800 that he borrowed, Gordy started Motown Recording Corporation in the spare room of his apartment.

In 1960, William "Smokey" Robinson Jr., a Detroit native nicknamed for his velvety tenor voice, cowrote and recorded "Shop Around," Motown's first million seller. Robinson and Gordy, eleven years Robinson's senior, formed such an unbeatable team in the music business that, in a few years, Motown Recording Corporation became the most successful black-owned entertainment enterprise in history.

Gordy and Robinson, who became a Motown vice president in 1963, built a company around the slogan "The Sound of Young America." It was a color-blind sound that did much to erase the divide between the races in 1960s America. Acts such as the Temptations, the Supremes, Martha and the Vandellas, Gladys Knight and the Pips, Marvin Gaye, Stevie Wonder, and the Jackson 5 benefited from Motown's regimen of dance lessons, etiquette instruction, and speech classes given to all artists.

Motown's in-house stable of songwriters, in addition to Robinson and Gordy, was impressive to say the least. It included the legendary team of Eddie Holland, Lamont Dozier, and Brian Holland. In addition to outstanding songwriters, Motown provided their artists with great studio musicians and producers. This system paid dividends, as Motown became the only real competition for the "British Invasion" acts that had captured American popular music.

The Stax Records building in Memphis had a sign out front, which read "Soulsville, USA." Motown's read "Hitsville, USA." In 1988, Berry Gordy sold the company that he started with $800 to MCA for $61 million.

"Shop Around" is available in piano/vocal arrangement in various Hal Leonard folios. Sound recordings include the original on *The Best of Smokey Robinson and the Miracles* (Motown CD 153 398) and a cover by the great Stax artists Sam and Dave (Rhino CD 71253).

3. "Surfin' Safari"
Words and Music by Mike Love and Brian Wilson
Copyright © 1962, Guild Music Company

In the very early 1960s, after the rockabilly blast of Elvis and before the ascendance of the Beatles, five kids from a working-class suburb of Los Angeles spontaneously generated a new genre of pop music that fed the country's fascination with the California lifestyle. The Wilson brothers—Carl, Dennis, and Brian—along with their cousin Mike Love and friend Al Jardine, were still teens in 1961 when they decided to form a band. The group was first known as the Pendletones (after the popular wool shirt) and later the Beach Boys. The three brothers had grown up under the musical influence of their father, Murry, a mostly unsuccessful songwriter who nevertheless did have broad tastes and some contacts at record companies. As their manager he arranged dozens of unpaid performances to help them build their instrumental skills and hone their trademark vocal harmonies.

It was drummer Dennis Wilson, the only surfer in the group, who suggested that they latch onto the popularity of surfing for a band identity, taking a cue from teen beach movies that had already created an image of carefree California youth cavorting on the sand. Soon Brian Wilson, the musical foundation for the group, produced "Surfin'," which Murry managed to get released through Candix Records. The single was a surprise regional hit, making it to number 75 on the national charts, but Murry's relationship with Candix Records was muddied by his aggressive and manipulative manner, a characteristic that affected much of the band's early years together.

Murry abandoned Candix for the next project, using an independent studio to record four demos, including "409," which referred to the large engines in "muscle cars" that were popular at the time, and "Surfin' Safari." After rejections from several labels, Murry went to Ken Nelson, an artist and repertoire man at Capitol Records.

Nelson was not interested, but Murry was so persistent that Nelson passed him on to Nikolas Venet, a hot young producer barely out of his teens who had been successful with the Lettermen. Venet recalls hearing "Surfin' Safari" first. "Before eight bars had spun around, I knew it was a hit record. . . . I knew the song was going to change West Coast music" (Gaines 1986, 78).

He was right. The song went to number 14 and was followed by more than fifty other hit singles over the next twenty-five years. The band continued to record up-tempo songs about surfing, cars, and girls, but increasingly mixed them with Brian's wistful ballads. A string of successful albums culminated with *Pet Sounds*, which featured Brian's groundbreaking studio production techniques that preceded, but were eclipsed by the Beatles' landmark album *Sgt. Pepper's Lonely Hearts Club Band*.

The Beach Boys continued to perform through the 1970s without Brian, who suffered a long bout with mental illness. By the end of the century, both Carl and Dennis had passed away but Mike Love and Al Jardine were touring with two different Beach Boy groups while Brian was performing again as a solo artist.

"Surfin' Safari" can be found in *The New Best of the Beach Boys* song folio (Warner Brothers PG9528) and on volume 1 of *The Beach Boys Greatest Hits* (Capitol 21860).

4. "A Hard Rain's a-Gonna Fall"
Words and Music by Bob Dylan
Copyright © 1963, Warner Brothers Music

In 1962, America and Russia risked nuclear annihilation in a confrontation over the issue of Russian arms in Cuba. Nearly two decades had passed since the horrors of Hiroshima and Nagasaki, and the nuclear arms race was at its peak. Headlines declared the escalation in megatons of destructive force in the A-bomb and H-bomb. Islands in the Pacific were leveled by blasts that produced astonishing mushroom clouds—nightmarish icons for the age. Nuclear blasts spread radioactive particles into the atmosphere, around the globe, and the radioactivity became "fallout"—new jargon for the age. A hard rain would fall.

One child of the age was Robert Zimmerman of Hibbing, Minnesota. Born in 1941, he dubbed himself Bob Dylan shortly after finishing high school and then headed out to the coffeehouses with his guitar. Duluth and Minneapolis did not hold him long as Dylan moved on to Greenwich Village, the gathering place for a new generation of folk singers. The ailing Woody Guthrie and Pete Seeger still held sway, but the young people who streamed in during the early 1960s would take folk music in a new direction. At first Bob Dylan seemed just one among many but he would soon distinguish himself with an outpouring of his own songs that would continue to flow for decades.

Dylan's contemporaries in New York differ in their recollections of which song first proved his brilliance as a poet-songwriter, but for many it was "A Hard Rain's a-Gonna Fall." Five long, vision-filled verses foretold of desolation and destruction. The language was beyond anything being sung at the time. Dylan once explained that "every line in it . . . is actually the start of a whole song. But when I wrote it, I thought I wouldn't have enough time alive to write all those songs, so I put all that I could into this one" (Gray 2000, 123). More songs of confrontation followed. "The Times They Are a-Changin'" warned those in power to step aside, while "Masters of War" promised the warmongers that they would themselves be buried.

These were not gentle songs. They grabbed the attention of disaffected teenagers and young adults who wanted resolution for the struggles of the time: civil rights, the cold war, poverty, and more. Dylan's songs served as the soundtrack for a youth protest movement of the 1960s that culminated with violent clashes over the Vietnam War. Yet even as he was idolized for his biting songs of protest, he was moving on to other forms and would continue to do so for the remainder of the century.

"A Hard Rain's a-Gonna Fall" is found with guitar tablature in *Bob Dylan's Greatest Hits* (Music Sales AM87466). For the original recording, try the CD rerelease of *The Freewheelin' Bob Dylan* (Sony–TNK 08786).

5. "For What It's Worth"
Words and Music by Stephen Stills
Copyright © 1966, Ten-East Music/Springalo-Cotillion Music

Los Angeles in 1966 was full of young musicians seeking a foothold for success. The burgeoning city was the nation's media center and home to leading record labels, as well as a lively club scene. Among recent arrivals were Stephen Stills and Richie Furay, who had performed together in an East Coast folk group named the Au Go Go Singers, and Neil Young and Bruce Palmer, young Canadians who had most recently performed with future funk master Rick James in a Motown-style band called the Mynah Birds.

Stills and Young had once crossed paths in Canada and were looking for each other in the metropolis when they were reunited in April 1966 in a now-legendary chance meeting on Sunset Boulevard. They immediately went about the business of creating a band. Stills and Young were both strong lead guitarists, Furay was lead vocalist and played rhythm guitar, and Palmer bass. They lacked a drummer, so they recruited Dewey Martin, another Canadian, who was already an established musician.

Nine days after that fated meeting, the new band, Buffalo Springfield, opened for The Byrds on a short tour, then got a long booking at the Whiskey A Go Go, an important club on the Sunset Strip. By July, they were opening for the Rolling Stones at the Hollywood Bowl. Stills would later recall, "That's when we peaked, and after, then it was down hill" (Einarson 1997, 74). They soon got a recording deal with Atlantic Records. The talents of the five musicians were impressive, but the group dynamics were so volatile that Buffalo Springfield might have been nothing more than a blip on the rock radar if not for a surprise hit.

In November 1966, while the band was playing in San Francisco, there was a clash between police and youths on the Sunset Strip. The fabled Strip had become a magnet for idle teens, long-haired hippies, and drugged-out street people, many of them drawn to the Whiskey, Pandora's Box, and other clubs. The counterculture had become a serious irritant to the businesses, so a 10 P.M. curfew for minors was enacted and then police were called in to enforce it. On November 12, the raid turned violent. The image of cops advancing with nightsticks was disturbing to Stills, and he soon composed a song that warned of the growing division between radicalized youth and mainstream America and foretold greater violence to come. Though less interesting musically than a number of other songs recorded by Buffalo Springfield, "For What It's Worth" struck a nerve and became the band's only charted single.

More success followed, but the band could not survive the conflicts among its members, particularly between Stills and Young. Less than two years after they formed, the ensemble dissolved. However, that brief association influenced much of American popular music in the next decade, helping to create the country–rock California sound of the Eagles and other bands. Buffalo Springfield was inducted into the Rock and Roll Hall of Fame in 1997.

"For What It's Worth" has been used repeatedly in motion pictures to evoke the social strife of the 1960s, most notably in the hugely popular film *Forrest Gump*. That movie spurred both a songbook (Hal Leonard 00312515) and a soundtrack CD (Epic 66329).

6. "The Ballad of the Green Berets"
Words and Music by Staff Sgt. Barry Sadler and Robin Moore Jr.
Copyright © 1966, Eastaboga Music Company

Although the majority of Americans, especially those living in rural communities, supported America's involvement in the Vietnam War, relatively few songs on radio addressed those sentiments. In 1965, Barry McGuire released "Eve of Destruction," a song, like other West Coast protest songs, that angered many conservatives. Feeling a need to respond in song, Barry Sadler and Robin Moore Jr., both members of the Army's elite Special Forces, wrote "Ballad of the Green Berets," a song that became a patriotic anthem. Staff Sgt. Sadler recorded the song and included it on *Ballads of the Green Berets*, an album released on January 1, 1966.

The song, a tribute to U.S. Army Special Forces, was an instant smash. The simple lyrics explain that only three out of every one hundred soldiers who want to wear the Green Beret and silver wings of the Army's Special Forces are accepted. The songwriters' pride in their select branch of the miliary is apparent in every verse.

Sadler's appearance (in uniform) on the *Ed Sullivan Show* promoted him and the song. "The Ballad of the Green Berets" sold 2 million copies in the first two weeks and eventually sold more than 9 million copies. It rose to the number 1 spot on Billboard pop and country charts and became the top song of 1966. Conservatives had indeed embraced this patriotic song. Recognizing the value of

Sadler's instant media visibility, the Army assigned a full-time public relations officer to him.

After Sadler left the Army in 1967, he attempted, unsuccessfully, to use his sole hit song to launch a full-time career in the music industry. While in Nashville, Sadler's clean-cut image came unraveled. He pleaded guilty to voluntary manslaughter after shooting the estranged boyfriend of a woman he was dating. He boasted about his sharpshooting skills, because he shot the victim between the eyes with a single shot in a dark parking lot. His sentence of up to five years in the Tennessee State Penitentiary was reduced to thirty days with two year's probation.

Sadler later moved to Guatemala and purportedly spent his time as an adventurer and author. However, he reportedly also helped train Contra rebels and was fatally shot by two men who stopped his taxi in 1988. Former Staff Sgt. Barry Sadler died on November 5, 1989, in Alvin C. York Medical Center (a veterans' hospital) in Murfreesboro, Tennessee, from brain damage he suffered in the Guatemala attack.

"The Ballad of the Green Berets" is available on *Ballads of the Green Berets* (RCA, 1967).

7. "I Feel Like I'm Fixin' to Die Rag"
Words and Music by Joe McDonald
Copyright © 1967, Tradition Music Company

Country Joe (McDonald) and the Fish was a blatantly counterculture band that became known for their crowd motivating performance at Woodstock. Although McDonald became an antiwar activist later in life, he enlisted in the Navy and served as an air traffic controller in Japan from 1959 to 1962. He spoke out against the war in Vietnam, but throughout his life, he supported the men and women who served in the armed forces. Unlike some antiwar activists who were repulsed by anyone in uniform, McDonald's disagreement was only with military leaders and government officials. His efforts to get northern California cities to honor soldiers who lost their lives in Vietnam continue to this day.

After serving in the Navy, Joe McDonald teamed up with Barry "Fish" Melton and recorded an acoustic version of "I Feel Like I'm

Fixin' to Die Rag." In 1966, they added three more players and released a second recording, this one with an electric sound. Although
it enjoyed an impressive underground following after its local releases, the band did not get any real national notice until they performed at Woodstock.

Woodstock was more than just the live entertainment event of
the decade. It was a public proclamation of the northern California/
Haight Ashbury lifestyle that worked its way across the nation. On Friday, August 15, 1969, 450,000 members of the hippie counterculture
gathered on a muddy field in Bethel, New York, for a four-day music
festival. It turned into the equivalent of a major city where use of
drugs—mostly marijuana and LSD—was ignored and free love was
more than a cliché. And Country Joe and the Fish joined legends of
rock like Janis Joplin, Jimi Hendrix, and the Grateful Dead in career-
establishing performances. In addition to their music, Country Joe
and the Fish created the "Fish Cheer" at Woodstock, an audience-
response chant filled with expletives.

Country Joe and the Fish were not able to maintain the momentum they established at Woodstock. Within a year, they disbanded. Joe McDonald continued to perform concerts, many of
them benefit shows for veterans, over the next thirty years.

This song is available on the original recording of "I Feel Like
I'm Fixin' to Die Rag" (Vanguard 79266; 1967). It is also sung in the
film *Woodstock*.

8. "(Theme from) The Monkees"
Words and Music by Tommy Boyce and Bobby Hart
Copyright © 1966, Screen Gems–EMI Music

By the mid-1960s more than 90 percent of American households
owned a television and the first generation to grow up with television
was in its teens. They knew Dobie Gillis and other characters from sit-
coms better than they knew their neighbors. They also stayed glued
to the tube watching *American Bandstand* and other music shows. In
the process, they viewed an endless string of commercials. The time
was ripe for the disparate forms of the entertainment industry to
merge music and marketing, not to simply promote a megastar but
to create one, or more correctly, four.

In July 1965, producers Bob Rafaelson and Bert Schneider of Screen Gems–Columbia Pictures in Los Angeles placed an ad in *Variety*: "MADNESS!! Auditions. Folk and Roll Musicians Singers for acting roles in new TV series. Running parts for 4 insane boys, age 17–21." Prospects flocked in by the dozens. Among those turned away were Stephen Stills and Paul Williams, but eight lucky young men were chosen. Audience Studies, Inc., a research division of Screen Gems, tested them with an audience aged six to eighteen. Four emerged victorious: Davy Jones, Mickey Dolenz, Peter Tork, and Michael Nesmith would become the Monkees and would be groomed for a weekly television show on NBC. The band was entirely synthetic and shamelessly patterned after the Beatles, and the show would be a knockoff of *Hard Days Night*, the first Beatles film. They were quickly dubbed "The Pre-Fab Four."

The four "amateurs" were not entirely untested, though they were raw enough to be shaped by the producers. Englishman Davy Jones had played in a Broadway production of *Oliver*. Mickey Dolenz had been a child star on television as Circus Boy. Peter Tork had been in Steven Stills's band Buffalo Fish, and Michael Nesmith was serious about his songwriting. All but Jones played guitar, but they were hardly a band. Rafaelson and Schneider worked to turn the four into a cohesive group, but when they failed to gel by May 1966, help was enlisted from record producer Don Kirschner and songwriter and musician Bobby Hart, who along with bandmate Tommy Boyce wrote many of the Monkees' hit songs. It was decided that the Monkees would sing the vocals and fake the instruments, and Hart and his band, the Candy Street Prophets, would play the music.

The stage was set to propel the Monkees into the American consciousness through a feverish campaign that produced, almost simultaneously, a hit single, a live tour, nationwide publicity, the first episodes of the television show, and the Monkees' first LP. It all succeeded. RCA created a label, Colgems, for the Monkees and released their first single "Last Train to Clarksville" by Boyce and Hart on August 16, 1966. The television show premiered September 12, and was an immediate hit. It featured the theme song (also known as "Hey, Hey We're the Monkees!") that also was on the LP released on October 10, from which came a single that went gold on October 14.

More hit singles followed and the television show won an Emmy for Best Comedy in 1967.

Their success could not last and indeed it did not. By the end of 1968 the show was canceled for poor ratings and the Monkees released the last of their six albums (now playing their own music). The band members went their separate ways. But it had been a wild ride and laid the groundwork for MTV and music videos that would come fifteen years later. In 1986 and 2001, the Monkees were again on the road (minus Nesmith) for successful reunion tours.

The Monkees theme song is in *The Baby Boomers Songbook* (Hal Leonard 00310494) and on *The Monkees Anthology* (Rhino CD 75269).

9. "Aquarius" (from the musical *Hair*)
Words by Gerome Ragni and James Rado and Music by
Galt MacDermot
Copyright © 1967, United Artists Music Company, Inc.

The musical *Hair* progressed from a rough off-Broadway show in 1967 to a polished 1,742-performance Broadway smash in 1968. It was billed as a tribal love-rock musical in two acts. *Hair* was an homage to the "make-love-not-war" counterculture of the 1960s.

It was, in every aspect, an antiestablishment statement. The title represented the generation of long-haired hippies who wanted no part of the established military, government, or corporate worlds. Each song seemed to thumb its nose at established norms. Titles such as "Sodomy," "Black Boys/White Boys," "Prisoners in Niggertown," and "Hashish" were clearly intended to shock right-wing conservatives who might venture into the theater to watch this work.

If the song titles and lyric content were not controversial enough, the nudity—both male and female—pushed the envelope of established protocol. Any outcries against the "indecent" nature of *Hair* probably created a mystique surrounding this staged show that motivated ticket sales. Despite concerns expressed by British censors, the musical opened a successful run in London. It later enjoyed tremendous success in other major European cities. *Hair* helped translate the social revolution of the United States to Europe.

The one song that seemed to become a mantra for every flower child but also attained commercial success was "Aquarius." Versions of

"Aquarius" are available on the off-Broadway recording of *Hair* as well as the Broadway cast recording (sung by Ronald Dyson) of 1968. It was included in the 5th Dimension's "Let the Sunshine In" medley single (1969 Grammy winner and number 1 on the pop charts for six weeks) and is available on *Greatest Hits on Earth* (Arista Records, 1972).

10. "Lucy in the Sky with Diamonds"
Words and Music by John Lennon and Paul McCartney
Copyright © 1967, Northern Songs, Ltd./Maclen Music, Inc.

The Beatles were perhaps the most representative band of the 1960s. Fans watched as the band, and their music, evolved in a fish bowl of public scrutiny. In response, the band was a reflection of dramatic social changes occurring throughout the decade. Many critics consider the Beatles to have influenced popular music more than any act in history.

The Beatles were hardly an overnight success. John Lennon and Paul McCartney met in 1957 and began working together while performing with a pub band. By 1960, George Harrison had joined the band and they became a popular act in Hamburg, Germany. On August 23, 1962, the band shocked many fans with the announcement that Ringo Starr would replace Pete Best as drummer. When they returned to their blue-collar hometown of Liverpool, their new manager, Brian Epstein, landed them several performances at the Cavern rock club.

After being rejected by several record labels, including Decca Records, the Beatles signed a recording contract with EMI/Parlorphone Records. In 1962, they recorded their first single, "Love Me Do." Although it only reached number 17 on the pop charts, it was obvious that the Beatles and their producer George Martin had created a distinctly different sound from the other British pop and rock bands. Their next single, "Please Please Me," rose to the top of the charts and got them on local television. Their good looks, charm, and unusual appearance for the times—long hair and suits—made them well suited for television and film.

By 1964, their popularity in England had soared and they ventured across the Atlantic to start what has been called the "British invasion" of pop music. On February 9, 1964, the Beatles appeared on the *Ed Sullivan Show*. Their television appearance, and subsequent live concerts, launched "Beatlemania" in the United States. By April, the Beatles held the top five positions on the singles chart and had fourteen songs on the top 100 chart.

Over the next several years, members of the Beatles began to mature as instrumentalists, singers, and songwriters. Nevertheless, as each of the band's members developed their own lifestyle, those lifestyles affected their music. Differences in attitudes also began to distance them from each other. A permissive attitude toward drugs, especially the psychedelic drug LSD, gradually permeated the Beatles' image. By the time they recorded "Lucy in the Sky with Diamonds," the Beatles (especially Lennon) openly advocated the use of marijuana and LSD.

In 1967, the Beatles released a "concept album," one that veered from the typical formula of albums that were centered around radio-friendly hit songs. The album, *Sgt. Pepper's Lonely Hearts Club Band*, contained "Lucy in the Sky with Diamonds," a song that continues to be controversial. The cover of the album was a montage of many seemingly unrelated images. The songs on the album were, from a production standpoint, much more complex than the typical recordings until that point in history. Instrumentation included orchestral arrangements and exotic sitar sounds of India. Still, what is more important, the lyrics to the songs were more inexplicable than ever before.

Because of the exotic album cover, cryptic lyrics, and innovative production of the album, fans immediately analyzed "Lucy in the Sky with Diamonds" to discover its hidden meaning. Because the acronym for the title spelled LSD, it was assumed the song was about a psychedelic "trip." However, John Lennon, one of the songwriters, insisted that he got the idea for the song from a painting by his young son that was taped to the refrigerator.

Despite Lennon's insistence that the song was nothing more than an impressionistic fantasy song, listeners interpreted the song however they wanted. Conservative critics and radio management executives firmly believed "Lucy in the Sky with Diamonds" was a metaphor for LSD. The BBC banned the song from their stations. Listeners, probably inspired by their drug-induced perceptions, knew that the terms *incredibly high, marmalade skies,* and *kaleidoscope eyes* had to describe an acid trip.

While debate over the hidden meaning of "Lucy in the Sky with Diamonds" will probably continue forever, the contributions of it and the album *Sgt. Pepper's Lonely Heart Club Band* are undisputed. The dominance of AM radio began to wane after FM stations, and not AM stations, played cuts from this album. It was also the first album on which the lyrics were clearly printed on the packaging to emphasize their importance. For the first time in pop music history, songs of extended length began to replace the formulaic three-minute song on radio.

Not only was "Lucy in the Sky with Diamonds" an artistic success, it faired well in the marketplace too. It topped the charts for months and sold more than 8 million copies. The Beatles sang it in their innovative film *Yellow Submarine* in 1968.

Thanks to reissues of Beatles albums by Capitol/EMI Records, "Lucy in the Sky with Diamonds" is available on the CD *Anthology 2: The Beatles* (Capitol CDP-8-34448-2).

11. "(Sittin' on) The Dock of the Bay"
Words and Music by Otis Redding and Steve Cropper
Copyright © 1968, Irving Music, Inc.

Otis Redding, a Georgia native, came to Memphis as driver/road manager for Stax recording artists Johnny Jenkins and the Pinetoppers, an obscure regional act. With a few minutes left over at the end of the session, Redding cut his composition "These Arms of Mine." The record sold eight hundred thousand copies and Stax signed Redding to a long-term contract.

Satellite Records was formed by country fiddler turned banker Jim Stewart, who had noted the success of Sam Phillips's Sun label. Finding little success with initial releases of country, rockabilly, and pop, Stewart borrowed money from his sister, Estelle Axton, and moved the operation, now named Stax, into a rundown movie theater on McLemore Avenue in the heart of a black neighborhood. Stewart soon found a market for "southern soul" by artists like Carla Thomas, Booker T., and Sam and Dave.

Booker T. Jones's group, the MGs, included white guitarist Steve Cropper, who had grown up in Memphis listening to rhythm and blues guitarists as well as rockers Chuck Berry and Bo Diddley.

Cropper soon became indispensable at Stax, playing and engineering sessions and writing songs.

Redding soon fulfilled his promise. A series of rhythm and blues charting singles on Stax's subsidiary label, Volt, led to personal appearances throughout the South. Childhood friend, Phil Walden (who later formed Capricorn Records and managed The Allman Brothers Band) became Redding's manager. Seeing the success Motown was having in the white youth market, yet not wanting to dilute the unique southern soul sound perfected in Memphis, Walden and Redding, with Booker T's MGs as backup band, booked shows at West Coast hippie venues. As a result, Redding was booked at the Monterey Pop Festival in 1967, where he stole the show from many better-known rock acts. This can be seen in the documentary film *Monterey Pop.* Earlier that year, while playing at San Francisco's Fillmore Auditorium and staying on a houseboat across the bay, Redding started writing his most famous song "(Sittin' on) The Dock of the Bay."

On December 7, 1967, Redding was in the studio with Cropper where they fleshed out the song and put it down on tape. Reaction among Redding's peers was uniformly negative. Label president Stewart did not want to release the song. Bassist Donald "Duck" Dunn thought it unredeemable as rhythm and blues. Even Redding's family and friends thought he could do something better. One neighbor thought the whistling at the end was a joke; but through it all, Redding assured everyone that "Dock of the Bay" would be his first number 1 record and southern soul would be as popular as slick Motown music.

Three days later Redding was killed in a small plane accident outside Milwaukee following a performance in Cleveland. He never lived to see his prediction come true.

"(Sittin' on) The Dock of the Bay" is available in dozens of print arrangements for horns, guitar, and piano/vocal from Hal Leonard and Warner Brothers. Over one hundred recorded versions are available including Redding's original on *Otis Redding* (Rhino CD 72692).

12. "Abraham, Martin, and John"
Words and Music by Dick Holler
Copyright © 1968, Regent Music

In 1968, a year after the summer of love, when riots, assassinations, and the never-ending war in Vietnam dragged at the spirit of young America, Dion DiMucci, a former doo-wop singer, recorded, against his better judgment, a poignant ballad, "Abraham, Martin, and John." Written by Dick Holler, a piano-playing bandleader from Baton Rouge, the song, in four stanzas, compares the loss of John and Robert Kennedy and Martin Luther King Jr. with that of Abraham Lincoln. Holler portrays them as like-minded emancipators who died before their time. This simple folk-style song could have easily succumbed to trite sentimentality, but for the performance given by Dion—a performance of a song he did not want to record.

In the mid-1950s, Baton Rouge had an active music scene, with young whites copying the music of Little Richard, Fats Domino, Elvis, and Johnny Ace. Dick Holler led the Rockets, a popular local band that included Jimmy Clanton and Johnny Ramistella (later known as Johnny Rivers). In 1957, they cut some demos at Cosimo Matassa's New Orleans studio where Little Richard, Ray Charles, and many others had recorded. Ace Records owner Johnny Vincent liked Clanton's singing and started him on a solo career that culminated in the hit "Venus in Blue Jeans," in 1962. Holler moved on.

By the mid-1960s, Holler had formed a musical relationship with Phil Gernhard, a friend of the Schwartz brothers who, in 1958, had started Laurie Records as a small, independent label in New York. From the start, the Schwartzes had luck with a street corner harmony group called the Belmonts. Their lead singer, Dion, had solo hits ("The Wanderer," "Runaround Sue") and when he cooled off, Laurie had success with the Chiffons and Gerry and the Pacemakers, a British group.

In 1966, when Gernhard was producing records for Laurie's newest act, the faux-British group The Royal Guardsmen (from Ocala, Florida), Holler came up with "Snoopy vs. the Red Baron," a song, complete with sound effects, based on the Peanuts comic characters. The song was an enormous hit in 1967, and, in 1968, when Holler sent "Abraham, Martin, and John" to Gernhard, he tried to get several Laurie artists to record it. None were interested.

Dion, who had been recording for Columbia, but was between contracts, came by the Laurie offices wanting to record his song "Daddy Rollin' (in Your Arms)." Gernhard agreed only if Dion would record "Abraham" for the flip side. Reluctantly, Dion did the session. In 1969, "Abraham, Martin, and John" went to number 4 on the pop charts and gave Dion a new career. Critics have referred to the song as the best-received protest song of the decade; certainly the best known concerning the assassinations that helped define the 1960s.

"Abraham" is available in over a dozen folios and one piano/vocal sheet from Hal Leonard. Sound recordings include versions by Smokey Robinson and the Miracles, Marvin Gaye, and Harry Belafonte. Dion's recording is on *Songs of Protest* (Rhino CD 70734).

13. "Say It Loud—I'm Black and I'm Proud"
Words and Music by James Brown and Alfred Ellis
Copyright © 1968, Fort Knox Music Company

By 1968, the African American community, influenced by the Black Muslims and the Black Panthers, had endorsed a cultural pride symbolized in the slogan "Black Is Beautiful." Ever sensitive to the spirit of community, singer, dancer, composer, and bandleader James Brown released "Say It Loud—I'm Black and I'm Proud," a song of affirmation, on September 7, 1968, following a summer of civil strife.

Brown grew up in Augusta, Georgia, under the supervision of an aunt who kept a brothel. He shined shoes, worked in a pool hall, and, at the age of sixteen, was sent to Alto Reform School for car theft. He served four years and, after his release in 1952, formed a gospel group. By 1955, the band became the Famous Flames and Brown played drums and sang lead vocals. The group secured a recording contract with Cincinnati's King label, and cut "Please, Please, Please" in 1956. The song went to number 1 on the rhythm and blues charts and the group became known as James Brown and the Famous Flames.

By the 1960s, playing standard rhythm and blues ballads and dance music, Brown was known as the "King of Soul" and the show was billed as the James Brown Revue. As the decade progressed, Brown changed the band's sound. Heavy rhythm, declamatory vocals, and stabbing horn fills as evidenced in "Cold Sweat" (1967) created a new sound that became known as "funk."

On August 7, 1968, in Los Angeles, Brown recorded "Say It Loud—I'm Black and I'm Proud" as a protest against second-class citizenship. With new band members Fred Wesley (trombone), Maceo Parker (saxophone), cowriter Alfred Ellis (saxophone), and Clyde "the Funky Drummer" Stubblefield, Brown defined an Afrocentric style with the introductory "funky" drum solo. Brown employed a chorus of schoolchildren from Los Angeles' Watts district, the scene of the first large race riot of the 1960s, to provide the "response" (the second half of the title) to his "call" (the first half). The first verse also referenced black history with "I've been rebuked and scorned, sure as you're born," a phrase from nineteenth-century spirituals still current in the African American church.

While Stax Records in Memphis and Atlantic Records in New York defined modern soul music with Otis Redding and Aretha Franklin, and Motown in Detroit was creating the "Sound of Young America," James Brown was fashioning new music that spoke to social issues of the day. Stylistically, his music would inform the future success of George Clinton, Sly Stone, and countless disco beats; eventually, it would become the basis for the rhythm of rap.

Print versions of "Say It Loud—I'm Black and I'm Proud" are in various folios by Hal Leonard. The original sound recording of Brown's performance is found in all retrospective collections of his work and in several anthologies including *The 60s* (Mercury CD 538 743).

14. "Okie from Muskogee"
Words and Music by Merle Haggard and Roy Edward Burriss
Copyright © 1969, Tree Publishing Company, Inc.; Sony/ATV Publishing

Merle Haggard's classic "Okie from Muskogee" is as much a piece of journalism for the 1960s as it is a song. His song, and his delivery, became a conservative declaration in a polarized nation. The lyrics are simple and unequivocal. They tell the world that residents of Muskogee, Oklahoma—and every other "red-blooded" American town—do not feel apologetic for their small-town values. Furthermore, at the time, it told the draft-card-burning, long-haired, drug-using liberals that they were not welcome in Muskogee.

Merle Haggard was the perfect torch carrier for conservative rural America. He was born in a converted boxcar in Bakersfield,

California. He was the child of an archetypal Dust Bowl refugee family and his fiddle-playing father worked for the railroad. Young Merle ran away from home at the age of fourteen and began a pattern of run-ins with the law. In 1957, he was convicted of robbing a restaurant and sentenced to fifteen years in San Quentin. After serving two years, he was released on parole . But, while in prison, he joined a country band and learned to play western swing, country blues, and country-folk.

After his release from prison, Haggard began to take his career as a singer, guitarist, and songwriter more seriously. His songs eventually became more introspective, addressing his own troubled past. He obviously connected with country listeners and matured into a true country star. He had emerged as the workingman's singer.

Although "Okie from Muskogee" became a hit song for Haggard, it started as a joke. He has admitted on several occasions that he and some of his musicians were smoking marijuana on the tour bus one night as they drove past a sign that said, "Muskogee." Someone said, "I'll bet they don't smoke pot in Muskogee." Instantly, Haggard and cowriter Roy Edward Burriss knew it would be a great story line for a song.

Although "Okie from Muskogee" began in jest, it became the musical flag to be waived by anyone who had an "America, Love it or Leave it" bumper sticker. Merle Haggard also acknowledged that, although he recognized some of the counterculture's complaints, he just could not accept behavior such as burning the flag. To emphasize his small-town values, or to capitalize on the song's success, he released an answer song, "The Fightin' Side of Me," at the beginning of 1970. Both songs reached number 1 on the country charts and "Okie" scored well on the top 40 charts as well.

"Okie from Muskogee" is available on *Lonesome Fugitive: The Merle Haggard Anthology (1963–1977)* (Razor and Tie Records, 1995).

15. "Brown Sugar"
Words and Music by Mick Jagger and Keith Richards
Copyright © 1971, ABKCO Music, Inc.

Written by the Rolling Stones' lead singer Mick Jagger and guitarist Keith Richards in 1969, this anthem to miscegenation—some reviewers thought it a paean to Mexican heroin—was a symbol of the

horrible end of the 1960s, a decade in which an optimistic generation tried to create a new sense of community.

Near the end of their enormously successful 1969 tour of America, the Rolling Stones, in part to palliate critics who questioned their
ticket pricing and concert promotion ethics, announced a free concert in San Francisco for December 6. Referred to as "Woodstock
West," after the successful New York concert the Stones had not
played at, the free California show was to be filmed by the Maysles
Brothers and was subsequently released as part of the documentary
Gimme Shelter.

December 1, six days before the concert (which still had not secured a location—Golden Gate Park, where the Grateful Dead had
played many times, was not available), found the Stones in Muscle
Shoals, Alabama. Hoping to add some "soul" to their recordings,
they booked producer Rick Hall's Fame studio where so many great
soul hits by Aretha Franklin and Percy Sledge had been recorded.

On December 1, 1969, Jagger and Richards wrote "Brown
Sugar" and "Wild Horses" in the studio. "Brown Sugar" is based on
an unfinished idea Jagger had carried around. It describes the New
Orleans slave market in the Old South and the sexual liberties taken
by the master. That Jagger subsequently had an affair with African
American singer/actress Marsha Hunt (an original cast member of
the musical *Hair*), and that they had a child whose paternity Jagger
denied adds a psychological twist to "Brown Sugar."

Returning to the West Coast, Jagger and company found themselves locked in a difficult position. With the concert announced and
the film crew standing by, the Stones still had no location or infra-
structure in place. The day before the concert, a motor speedway
near Altamont was rented through the efforts of lawyer Melvin Belli
(then working on the defense of the Manson family) who had been
retained by Jagger. Carpenters spent the entire night constructing a
stage, far too few port-a-potties were trucked in, and members of the
Hell's Angels Motorcycle Club were appointed security guards.

The concert was a disaster. The Hell's Angels attacked members
of the audience as well as some of the musicians. (The Jefferson Airplane's Marty Balin was beaten senseless.) The Grateful Dead refused to go on stage and returned to San Francisco. With the film
crew shooting, Jagger took the stage and pleaded the "peace-and-

love" ethic that had distinguished Woodstock the previous August. The violence continued as the Stones played "Street Fighting Man" and other recent hits, and when Jagger launched into "Sympathy for the Devil," the film cameras captured the murder of Meredith Hunter. Finally, this was too much for the Rolling Stones. Playing their newest song, "Brown Sugar," they bid "San Francisco" [*sic*] good-bye and ran to waiting helicopters to escape the melee. The 1960s had, indeed, come to a close.

"Brown Sugar" is included in the Warner Brothers' folio *Rolling Stones Singles Collection—The London Years*. The original recording is part of the *Sticky Fingers* compact disc reissue of the original LP (Virgin CD 39525).

1970–1979

War, Watergate, and Disco

Women, African Americans, and college students became more politically active, and occasionally militant, in the 1970s. The youth-driven counterculture that became more vocal in the 1960s became a major nemesis of the Nixon–Agnew administration. As the U.S. armed forces allegedly crossed the borders into Cambodia in 1970, college students protested on their respective campuses. To the horror of the nation, Ohio national guard soldiers fired on student protesters and killed four students.

The Kent State incident and the escalation of the Vietnam War caused increasing numbers of youths to question their government. Although eighteen-year-olds were given the right to vote in 1971, it took several years for their demographic to become organized enough to make a significant impact on the election process. Increased inflation and an eventual recession added to the distrust college-age students held for authority. This angst was apparent in new forms of music, most notably, punk rock. In addition, escapist drug references in music were no longer subtle.

The underground drug culture of the 1960s became more obvious in the 1970s. Nonprescription drugs were no longer relegated to the hippie counterculture. A 1975 study of high school seniors revealed that 53 percent of the students had tried marijuana. Of those who tried it, 32 percent considered themselves current users (Johnson

1995). Even Spiro T. Agnew, vice president, let his concerns be known when he stated, "we should listen more closely to popular music, because at its best it is worthy of more serious consideration, and at its worst it is blatant drug-culture propaganda" (Safire 1985, 31).

As young adults moved in the direction of discotheque (disco) dancing, cocaine emerged as the boutique drug of choice. Opiates, such as opium and heroin from the Vietnam region, became more readily available. Celebrities were not immune to the destructive power of substance abuse: Janis Joplin, at the age of twenty-seven, died of a heroin overdose; Jimi Hendrix, also at the age of twenty-seven, apparently died from a barbiturate overdose; and Sid Vicious, at the age of twenty-one, died of a heroin overdose.

The National Organization for Women, formed in 1966, became more politically active in the 1970s. Angered by research that showed women were paid only 60 percent of the salaries of their male counterparts, women's rights activists called for equal pay for equal work. The Equal Rights Amendment was approved by Congress in 1972 and was submitted to the states for ratification. The amendment was three states short of the necessary number for ratification and, therefore, died before the 1983 deadline. Although this was a blow to the women's movement, several key court cases lent judicial support. The most contentious case was *Roe v. Wade*, a Supreme Court decision that made abortion legal within the first three months of a pregnancy. The decision split the nation and political parties into two camps. One supported a woman's right to choose an abortion (pro choice) and the other zealously advocated for laws to protect unborn fetuses (pro life).

National census figures for 1970 estimated that 22.5 million African Americans, 11 percent of the population, resided in the United States at this time (U.S. Census Bureau 1973). The Supreme Court upheld busing as a legal means of achieving racial balance in schools. Nevertheless, segregationists, encouraged by former Governor George Wallace of Alabama, resisted most forms of school integration. In an effort to take his views to the White House, Wallace ran for the Democratic presidential nomination. However, while campaigning in Maryland, he was shot in an assassination attempt. Although he lived, his injuries caused his legs to be permanently paralyzed.

African Americans achieved noteworthy political successes during the 1970s. In 1972, Andrew Young (Georgia) and Barbara Jordan (Texas) became the first African Americans from the South elected to the U.S. House of Representatives in this century. Jordan was the first African American female from the South ever elected to the House. Both Jordan and Young were members of the Democratic Party. In 1973, Thomas Bradley was elected mayor of Los Angeles and Maynard Jackson was elected mayor of Atlanta. They were both African American.

Author Alex Haley published *Roots: The Saga of an American Family* in 1976. The story traced his ancestry from Africa through the bondage of slavery in America. His provocative saga motivated many African Americans to research their heritage. *Roots* also helped launch a wave of pride in African and African American culture. Black pride of the 1960s matured into more academic manifestations such as African American studies on college campuses.

The federal government recognized the importance of African Americans during the 1970s. The Association for the Study of Afro-American Life and History proposed that the nation observe the history of African Americans as a part of the 1976 bicentennial. Congress liked the idea and made February Black History Month, which continues to this day. On February 1, 1979, the U.S. Postal Service released a stamp with the image of Harriet Tubman, a heroine who helped keep the Underground Railroad working before the Civil War. Harriet Tubman was the first African American female to appear on a postage stamp in the United States.

There was an increased interest in religion, spiritualism, and introspective self-help studies in the 1970s. Interest in Eastern religions—those outside the Judeo–Christian traditions—might have been fueled by their association with famous musicians such as George Harrison and John Lennon of the Beatles. Six million people were active in transcendental meditation and 5 million identified themselves as practitioners of Yoga. Large numbers of people, dubbed "Jesus freaks," formed a new charismatic Christian movement. Some self-professed spiritual leaders could more accurately be called "cult leaders." One tragic reminder of the power that charismatic leaders can have over followers was the mass suicide by members of the People's Temple, a religious cult in Jonestown, Guyana.

While Pentagon officials repeatedly assured President Nixon that the United States could win the war in Vietnam, the nation's patience and confidence gradually deteriorated. After U.S. troops crossed the border into Cambodia in pursuit of communists, it became increasingly apparent that this was a war unlike others. After it became obvious to White House advisers that the war would not end in this country's favor, Nixon pressed the North Vietnamese for a cease-fire agreement. In 1973, the United States and South Vietnam agreed to a cease-fire plan with North Vietnam and Viet Cong representatives. In 1975, North Vietnamese forces overran South Vietnam and effectively took complete control of the country. This became the first war that the United States had lost. Two films, *The Deer Hunter* and *Coming Home*, communicated the powerful emotional damage done to soldiers who fought in Vietnam.

Soon after Nixon's landslide reelection to a second term—he garnered 521 electoral votes and Senator George McGovern received only 17—his "White House of cards" began to disintegrate. On June 17, 1972, five members of an organization called the Committee to Re-Elect the President burglarized the Democratic headquarters in the Watergate hotel in Washington, D.C. Although the president claimed that he had no knowledge of the break-in, one of the burglars later told Judge John Sirica that a high-level official knew of the plan. Shortly after the burglars were convicted or negotiated guilty pleas, a special Senate investigative committee was charged with determining what Nixon knew and when he knew it.

In March 1974, a federal grand jury indicted Attorney General John Mitchell and six other high-level Nixon aides on charges of obstructing the investigation. All seven were eventually convicted. It was discovered that Nixon had tape-recorded numerous conversations in his office. After first refusing to surrender the tapes to investigators, Nixon eventually provided the tapes. However, some of the tapes had been edited and others were missing. In the summer of 1974, the House Judiciary Committee approved articles of impeachment against Nixon, accusing him of obstructing the investigation. The unprecedented hearings were televised to a stunned nation.

Nixon gave his final television address as president on August 8, 1974. In a brief, but emotionally charged, speech, he resigned. He is the first president to leave office under those circumstances. Adding another stain to this period of political history, Nixon's vice president, Spiro T. Agnew, also resigned from office in 1973, pleading "no contest" to charges of tax evasion in Maryland. Gerald Ford ascended from Republican leader of the House to replace Agnew. Not long after that, Ford became president.

Ford's hopes for reelection were crushed in 1976 when Jimmy Carter, a Democrat from Georgia, won the presidency. Carter inherited economic turbulence, brought on by inflation and oil shortages, that continued throughout the decade. In an effort to bring a divided nation together, Carter pardoned most draft evaders in 1977.

SONGS

1. "What's Going On?"
Words and Music by Al Cleveland, Marvin Gaye, and Renaldo Benson
Copyright © 1970, Jobete Music Company/Stone Agate Music

Marvin Gaye was at the top in 1970. He had been on the charts almost ten years with his distinctive urban soul music, and had brought the Motown label, its biggest hit with "I Heard It through the Grapevine." He was a prolific recording artist and was critically acclaimed as a talented, smooth-voiced, sexy singer. But it was not enough. Gaye's difficult childhood and ambivalence toward religion kept him looking for more, and that search eventually led to his revolutionary, self-produced album and single "What's Going On?"

Marvin Gay (the "e" was added later) was born in 1939 and raised in a poor black neighborhood of Washington, D.C., where he began singing at the age of three in his father's Pentecostal church. The teachings of the small House of God sect would influence him for the remainder of his life, but his relationship to the church was inextricably intertwined with his relationship to his father, Reverend Gay, who beat him throughout his childhood.

By the time Gaye was a teen, his focus was wholly on secular music. At the Howard Theater he watched performers like Sam Cooke and James Brown, dreaming of escape from the life he knew in Washington. Gaye became a doo-wop singer and while touring with The Moonglows found himself in Detroit, where he attracted the eye of the autocratic Motown founder Berry Gordy. Gaye wanted to be a solo act in the Nat King Cole or Frank Sinatra vein, and Motown released several records for the pop market, with little success. But Gordy recognized Gaye's magnetic presence and great musicality, and put it to work in the chart-driven Motown formula. Gaye's first top 10 record came in 1963 with "Pride and Joy," backed by Martha and the Vandellas. For the rest of the 1960s, he alternated solos with songs that used Motown's other acts, including The Supremes, Mary Wells, Smokey Robinson, the Temptations, and, most significantly, Tammi Terrell. Terrell's early death from a brain tumor caused Gaye to close his stage career and to take a break from recording.

In that time of reflection it became clear that Gaye wanted to break from the romantic pop formula to record songs that reflected his views on social issues. The impetus came when his brother Frankie returned home from Vietnam full of stories. Gaye conceived a theme album that would address the nation's troubles: war, pollution, poverty, and injustice. "Mercy, Mercy Me (the Ecology)" questioned environmental destruction. "Inner City Blues (Make Me Wanna Holler)" acknowledged ghetto conditions. But the title song "What's Going On?" grabbed the most attention. Written by friends Renaldo Benson and Al Cleveland, and then embellished by Gaye, it decried the rending divisions in society brought by opposition to the war in Vietnam.

This album was to be Gaye's manifesto, and he worked feverishly—cowriting; coproducing; playing drums, guitar, and keyboards; and overlaying multiple vocals—but when he delivered the finished product at the end of 1970, Gordy did not want to release it. Gaye balked, threatening to quit the label, and was vindicated. The three lead songs were top 10 pop hits and number 1 rhythm and blues hits. The album went gold and stayed on the charts for more than a year. It was acknowledged as groundbreaking both lyrically and sonically, and influenced much of the music that would follow in the 1980s.

"What's Going On?" is available in sheet music (Hal Leonard 00351385). The album *What's Going On?* is available in rerelease (Motown 530883).

2. "Jack Johnson"
Music by Miles Davis
Copyright © 1970, Big Fights Productions

Jack Johnson is the title of a documentary film, made in 1970, which used the music of jazz trumpeter Miles Davis as the soundtrack to the archival photographs, film, and newsreel footage of the first African American heavyweight boxing champion (1908–1915). Rather than use period music for the film, music director Teo Macero used the improvised sounds with which Davis was experimenting. These sounds had recently been named "fusion" by the music press. A combination of modal harmonies and 1960s jazz and rock rhythms, Davis's music had few harmonic or rhythmic subtleties when compared to the bop of the 1950s or the free jazz of the 1960s. Using electronic devices like the wah-wah pedal and echoplex tape delay and with electric keyboards replacing jazz's customary acoustic piano, jazz/rock fusion relied on varying textures to sustain listener interest.

Davis's attempt to merge jazz and rock was unexpected and not well received by jazz lovers. Davis had recorded early on with Charlie Parker. In the 1950s, he defined the "cool" school in his album *Birth of the Cool*. In the late 1950s and into the 1960s, he explored modal melody improvisation in *Sketches of Spain* and other works. With such catholic credentials, Davis's transition from suit-and-tie to tie-dye seemed heresy.

Davis, like Jack Johnson, was an iconoclast; he never cared to do what was expected. Miles Dewey Davis III was born in Alton, Illinois, in 1926. His father was a dental surgeon and Davis was raised in East St. Louis in well-to-do circumstances. He was given a trumpet at the age of thirteen and quickly displayed an enormous talent. He left for New York after graduating from high school where his parents expected him to earn a degree from the prestigious Juilliard School of Music. But Davis dropped out and began working the Harlem clubs with Dizzy Gillespie and Parker. Over the next two decades, Davis cultivated a rebel's image, becoming addicted to heroin along the way.

By 1970, Davis had put together a quintet with Billy Cobham (drums), Herbie Hancock (electric piano and organ), John McLaughlin (guitar), Mike Henderson (bass guitar), and Steve Grossman (soprano saxophone). Profoundly influenced by Jimi Hendrix, with whom he shared stages at rock clubs, Davis featured McLaughlin's rock guitar style and the heavy rhythm of Cobham and ex–Stevie Wonder bassist Henderson. When Columbia Records issued the soundtrack to *Jack Johnson*, Davis wrote in the liner notes: "The music on this album speaks for itself! But dig the guitar and the bass–They are Far-in."

At a time when other African American musicians were looking to Africa for inspiration (James Brown and the funk movement, for example), the contrarian-natured Miles Davis created a sound that replaced jazz elements with those more palatable to mainstream rock audiences. Though he sold more records than ever, he was never comfortable playing for the young whites who bought his records, and in 1975, Davis quit performing. Nominated for Best Documentary at the 1970 Academy Awards, *Jack Johnson* lost to the film *Woodstock*.

The score to *Jack Johnson* was never published in print. The soundtrack recording is available as *A Tribute to Jack Johnson* (Columbia CD 47036).

3. "A Good Hearted Woman"
Words and Music by Waylon Jennings and Willie Nelson
Copyright © 1971, Baron Music Publishing Company/Willie Nelson Music, Inc.

Country music, searching for increased sales, strayed from its traditional sounds during the 1960s. It underwent a major commercial and musical shift in the 1970s. This shift was due, in part, to the aesthetic sense of Willie Nelson and Waylon Jennings.

Waylon Jennings was born on June 15, 1937, in the small town of Littlefield, Texas. A high school dropout, Jennings was a disc jockey as a teenager, first in Littlefield, then in nearby Lubbock. There he befriended Buddy Holly who was making a name for himself as one of the original rock 'n' rollers. By 1958, Jennings was the bass player in Holly's band, the Crickets. On February 2, 1959, Jennings gave up his seat on Holly's chartered plane to J. P. ("Big Bopper") Richardson. The plane crashed in an Iowa cornfield, killing all passengers.

Jennings continued his music career with his band the Waylors and, in 1965, signed a recording contract with RCA in Nashville. His rocking Texas music and gruff voice never quite fit the "countrypoli-tan" Nashville sound developed by producers Chet Atkins and Owen Bradley. By 1972, Jennings was frustrated with Nashville music busi-ness methods and began spending time in Austin, Texas.

Willie Hugh Nelson was born on April 30, 1933, in Abbott, Texas. By the eighth grade he was earning money by playing week-ends at polka dances in nearby Czech communities. In the fall, he picked cotton alongside black families. It was here he first heard the blues.

A talented songwriter, Nelson sold a composition, "Night Life," for $150 to finance his move to Nashville. In Nashville, he continued to write songs, but supported his family as a bass player for Ray Price, who had a number 1 hit with Nelson's "Night Life," for which Nelson never received a penny in royalties.

By the late 1960s, Nelson had written many hits for others and was, at last, receiving royalties; but he was frustrated as an artist. Nashville producers and record companies thought his voice "not commercial" and covered his recordings in strings and background singers. In 1970, Nelson was living in Austin, where he found appreciation for his idiosyncratic musical style. Jennings and Nelson formed a bond based on their Nashville experience and childhood backgrounds, and in 1971, they collaborated on "A Good Hearted Woman," an ode to every musician's dream: a woman who will let her man come and go as he pleased, no expla-nations necessary.

Waylon, who had not given up on the Nashville recording in-dustry, used "A Good Hearted Woman" as the title song of his 1972 RCA album. That year, Jennings, who was, nevertheless, looking for alternatives, signed with Neil Reshen, a New York manager who booked Jennings on shows with the Grateful Dead and other rock bands. The long-haired, bearded Jennings was a sensation with the counterculture, projecting an authenticity not found in the sequin-suited Nashville performers. RCA unwillingly gave Jennings com-plete creative control over his recordings, and in January 1976, the album *Wanted the Outlaws* was released with "A Good Hearted Woman," now a duet by Waylon and Willie, a featured track. The Nashville exiles were vindicated when the album sold over 1 million copies by year's end, the first country LP to ever do so.

"A Good Hearted Woman" is in numerous print folios by Hal Leonard and Warner Brothers. Sound recordings by Willie Nelson and Waylon Jennings, individually, are in various "Best of . . ." issues. The original *Outlaws* duet recording is also on compact disc. A version by country singer George Jones is on *I Am What I Am* (Epic CD 36586).

4. "I Am Woman"
Words by Helen Reddy and Music by Ray Burton
Copyright © 1971, Irving Music Inc./Buggerhugs Music Company

Strength. Power. Womanhood. Those key concepts of "I Am Woman" summed up the message of a vital, aggressive women's liberation movement that swept America in the early 1970s. With its demands for equality of opportunity, the movement changed the social structure of the nation. While women's lib seemed to take the nation by surprise, it had actually been growing for decades, drawing on deep roots in other movements: the suffrage movement; the National Women's Party and its call for an Equal Rights Amendment; the civil rights movement, which became so male dominated that women looked for other avenues; labor unions; woman and child protective organizations; and women's professional associations. All of those interests merged in the 1960s to loudly proclaim a feminist agenda.

The most audible voice was the National Organization for Women (NOW), which was chartered in 1966 with Betty Friedan at its head. Her landmark 1963 book *The Feminine Mystique* became a manifesto for the movement by debunking the myth of the happy homemaker as the typical American woman. In 1970, NOW brought fifty thousand women to march down New York's Fifth Avenue to commemorate the fiftieth anniversary of women's suffrage. As a prelude to that day, Friedan and others smuggled a forty-foot banner up the *Statue of Liberty*, where it declared "Women of the World Unite," echoing the labor call of earlier decades. The nation was on notice that things were going to change.

It was in that politically charged environment that Helen Reddy wrote her feminist ode. Reddy was a diminutive Australian who had begun performing and touring with her show business family at the age of four. By the time she was eighteen her big voice and confident stage presence earned her a regular show on local

Australian television. Her big break came in 1966, when she was twenty-four. She won a major talent contest that awarded her a trip to the United States for an audition at Mercury Records. But Mercury reneged, and Reddy was left on her own in a new country. She worked out of New York, singing anywhere she could, but met with little financial success until she met Jeff Wald, a successful agent, at a party. He soon became both her husband and her manager. His influence and persistence eventually brought an appearance on *The Tonight Show*, and that, in turn, led to a chance with Capitol Records.

Reddy's first Capitol release was "I Don't Know How to Love Him," which was sung by the character Mary Magdalene in Andrew Lloyd Webber's hit show *Jesus Christ Superstar*. The record went to number 13 on the pop singles chart in 1971, prompting Capitol to release an album of the same title. "I Am Woman," which had been put to music by Reddy's fellow Australian Ray Burton, was included but attracted no attention. That is, until director Mike Frankovich used the song in his 1972 comic film about the women's liberation movement, *Stand Up and Be Counted*. Suddenly "Woman" was in demand and Wald persuaded Capitol to put out a single. It sold more than 1 million copies, with 80 percent of those purchased by women.

Reddy herself became notorious in 1973 when she won a Grammy for Best Female Pop Vocalist (winning over Aretha Franklin and Barbra Streisand). Her televised acceptance speech, in which she thanked God "because She makes everything possible," either thrilled or offended most of America. Even so, Reddy claimed "I don't think of myself as a feminist. . . . I'm a singer who has had my woman's consciousness raised" ("Reddy" 1975, 340). Her proud and defiant song helped raise the consciousness of many others.

"I Am Woman" is available as sheet music (Hal Leonard 352284) and on *I Am Woman: The Essential Helen Reddy Collection* (Razor and Tie CD 82180).

5. "American Pie"
Words and Music by Don McLean
Copyright © 1971, Mayday Music

Don McLean, born in 1945, grew up in New Rochelle, a New York City suburb. In his early teens, McLean, a sickly child frequently home from school, fell in love with rock 'n' roll, especially the music of Buddy Holly.

Holly, a skinny, glasses-wearing kid from Texas, proved one did not need to be handsome or tough to be an authentic rocker. McLean could identify with him. When the twenty-two year-old Holly died in a plane crash in February 1959, McLean was deeply affected. For him, it was the day rock 'n' roll died.

In high school, McLean played guitar in rock bands, but in the 1960s he became attracted to folk music. After graduation, he hitchhiked to towns throughout the East and Midwest, playing at coffeehouses. In 1968, as a singer and songwriter, he was hired by the New York State Council on the Arts as its Hudson River troubadour. This brought him in contact with Pete Seeger, who was spearheading the Clearwater Project aimed at cleaning up polluted eastern rivers.

McLean began performing at music festivals, attracting the attention of United Artists Records who recorded his song "American Pie." The song is an eight and one-half minute tour de force of cryptic imagery that follows the evolution of 1950s rock. The first verse and refrain are McLean's eulogy to Holly; the refrain references the last line of Holly's hit "That'll Be the Day." The other five stanzas call up images of the Lovin' Spoonful, James Dean, Marty Robbins, Bob Dylan, Elvis, the Beatles, the Byrds, Janis Joplin, and the Rolling Stones (whose Altamont debacle can be referenced as the day the 1960s died), giving the listener a melancholy history lesson in the decline of an art form.

United Artists "leaked" an advance copy of the single to New York radio station WPLJ-FM on the day the famed Fillmore East rock theater closed. The station played the song as a requiem for the famed venue. The album and single hit the charts in early November 1971, and by the end of the following January, "American Pie" was number 1, with the single showing more than 1 million copies sold. The album eventually sold more than 7 million copies. The irony of a song about the decline of an art form achieving such success was not lost on McLean. For several years, he ceased performing, and has never commented on the meaning of "American Pie."

"American Pie" is in print in numerous folios published by Warner Brothers, who also published the song as a single piano/vocal score. Dozens of sound recordings are available including covers by

Nina Simone, Jim Croce, the King's Singers, and The Brady Bunch. A karaoke recording is also available. McLean's original recording is on the Curb label (CD 77547).

6. "Rocket Man"
Words by Bernie Taupin and Music by Elton John
Copyright © 1972, Dick James Music, Ltd.

In 1972, lyricist Bernie Taupin arrived home after a drive in the country and pieced together words that would be passed along to his collaborator Elton John, who then separately composed the music for "Rocket Man." It was their usual arrangement. The Englishmen had been working together for five years by then, first writing songs for others and then frenetically producing hits for Elton that pushed him quickly to the top of the rock world. The two had developed a system of writing in which Taupin produced the lyrics first, typically in under an hour, and then passed them to Elton, who might spend a half hour coming up with the music. In fact, the two had collaborated by mail before they ever met. In 1967, both had answered an audition notice of Liberty Records, Elton in person and Bernie by mail, and an artist and repertoire executive suggested that they work as cowriters. The executive was not interested in Elton's performance but appreciated his underlying talent. From that shaky beginning grew one of the most productive and successful songwriting teams of the century.

In this case, Bernie had seen a light in the sky—perhaps a shooting star—that made him think about how the extraordinary had become nearly commonplace. He was just twenty-two at the time, yet he had witnessed the space age develop from the first missiles to leave Earth's atmosphere, to the Russian launching of the first satellite, *Sputnik*, in 1957 to the American triumph of placing a man on the moon in July 1969.

A landmark live broadcast from the moon's surface mesmerized the world as Neil Armstrong stepped from the *Eagle* landing module that had taken him from the Apollo rocket *Columbia* to the moon. The image of the space-suited astronaut planting a flag at the Sea of Tranquility became an enduring memory for the nation. By the time the fifth and last landing occurred in April 1972, about the time that

Bernie was composing his words, the world was still impressed but no longer awestruck. His lyrics imagined the loneliness of the rocket man undertaking an arduous but no longer glorious trip. When put to music and performed by Elton John, with his trademark rocking piano and soaring vocals, the song caught the attention of fans on both sides of the ocean. The single went to number 6 on the U.S. pop charts and the album, *Honky Chateau*, went gold.

Elton John himself rocketed from obscurity to superstardom in a few brief months. Born to an English working-class family as Reginald Dwight in Pinner, Middlesex, England, he had demonstrated an early ability to pick out tunes on the piano. By age eleven, he was at the Royal Academy of Music. But he was most fascinated with the piano prowess of Jerry Lee Lewis and Little Richard, so he abandoned formal training at the age of sixteen to work as a freelance musician and songwriter. His career took off in 1970 with a successful self-titled album and a fabled run at the Troubadour in Los Angeles that built his reputation as a brilliant but outrageous performer. His spectacular antics and a flamboyant wardrobe became legendary, but he was much more than just flash. Elton John released at least one charted record every year from 1970 to 2000, with more than one hundred gold and platinum awards overall. Most of the songs were John–Taupin collaborations. At century's end, Elton John was still riding high after winning an Oscar and a Grammy for music in Disney's *Lion King* and touching the world with a plaintive rewrite of "Candle in the Wind" for the funeral of Princess Diana.

"Rocket Man (I Think It's Going to Be a Long, Long Time)" is found in Elton John's *Greatest Hits Updated* (Hal Leonard 308114) and his recorded *Greatest Hits* (Polygram 512532).

7. "Stairway to Heaven"
Words and Music by Jimmy Page and Robert Plant
Copyright © 1972, Superhype Publishing

Guitarist James "Jimmy" Page and vocalist Robert Plant teamed with bassist John Paul Jones (born John Baldwin) and drummer John "Bonzo" Bonham to form Led Zeppelin, the most influential heavy metal band of the century. The band broke from the recording industry tradition of releasing singles directed at top 40 AM radio stations and, instead, found their home on FM album-oriented radio stations. The song "Stairway to Heaven" became a staple of rock music and became their signature song.

Unlike many rock musicians of this period, the Led Zeppelin personnel were exceptional craftsmen on their respective instruments. That, combined with Plant's distinctive high-pitched vocals and consistently well-written songs of Page and Plant, yielded a band that created the template for heavy-metal bands of the future. Their music was a fascinating blend of blues (influenced by Jimi Hendrix, Howlin' Wolf, Albert King, and Willie Dixon), British folk, and heavily amplified 1960s psychedelic rock.

Led Zeppelin signed a recording contract with Atlantic Records in 1968 and began touring in the United States. Their debut album, simply called *Led Zeppelin*, became an immediate success, ascending to the top 10 in the United States. To take advantage of the radio airplay they were receiving, especially on the newly emerging album-oriented FM radio format stations, Zeppelin began touring almost constantly. Despite their unrelenting tour schedule, they were able to create their second album, *Led Zeppelin II*. Like their first eponomously named album, the second work was an immediate success, spending seven weeks at number 1 on the album charts in America.

Their third album was also successful, but it was *Zeppelin IV*, released in 1971, that earned the band enduring acclaim. The song from their fourth album that captured the attention of critics as well as fans was "Stairway to Heaven." Its constant allusions to things of a spiritual nature—stairway to heaven, road you're on, shadows taller than our souls—fueled speculation that Led Zeppelin was a band with supernatural affiliations.

Because of their atypical business practices and unconventional private lives, the band members developed an air of mystique about themselves. They refused to grant interviews or release singles, two things which were unusual for rock musicians who typically pursue promotion that sells records and concert tickets. Plant made no secret of his belief in psychic phenomenon, and Page studied the occult, once living in the home of satanist Aleister Crowley. Whether out of sincere belief in mysticism and the occult, or as a promotional tool, they named their fifth album *Houses of the Holy*. Artwork for the album was four characters from the Runic alphabet. Runes are alphabetic scripts that were developed in the first century and used in northern Europe. This old Germanic script was associated with magical spells until it was outlawed by the church in the sixteenth century.

On September 25, 1980, drummer John Bonham died. He had drunk a large amount of alcohol and was on medication that was prescribed to help him withdraw from his heroin addiction. He fell asleep on his back and, too intoxicated from medication and alcohol to wake, choked to death on his own vomit. After his death, the remaining band members decided to disband. However, Led Zeppelin songs such as "Stairway to Heaven" and "Whole Lotta Love" continue to be played on classic-rock radio stations. Led Zeppelin has sold more than 100 million albums.

Sheet music for "Stairway to Heaven" is available in many guitar folios. It can also be found on *Various Artists Stairways to Heaven* (Atlantic CD, ATL 826 432, 1992), an album that contains twelve different versions of the song, performed in various styles.

8. "I Shot the Sheriff"
Words and Music by Bob Marley
Copyright © 1973, Cayman Music

Jamaican songwriter and musician Bob Marley brought a new genre of music, called "reggae," to the American consciousness. Reggae quickly began to influence many genre of music for the remainder of the century. More than just music, Marley brought the concept of Rastifarianism to the states. (Rastifarianism was founded in the belief that Emperor Haile Selassie of Ethiopia, who died in 1974, was a spiritual, as well as political, leader.) Bob Marley also taught music listeners the terms *Jah* (the all-loving, all-knowing God), *dreadlocks* (representative hairstyle), *ganja* (marijuana used for meditation and in religious ceremonies), and *spliff* (slang for a large marijuana cigarette).

After working with several different bands, Marley found success with a band called Bob Marley and the Wailers, comprised of himself, Bunny Wailer, and Peter Tosh. They signed a recording contract in 1972 with Island Records, founded by Chris Blackwell, the son of wealthy plantation owners in Jamaica. Their first collaboration with Chris Blackwell yielded *Catch a Fire*, an album conceived and produced to capture the huge rock audience in the United Kingdom and the United States. The band toured in support of the album and quickly became the band that critics and established rock stars loved.

Their second album, *Burnin'*, contained their strongest material to date, including "I Shot the Sheriff," written by Marley. The song was originally titled "I Shot the Police," but Marley and his record label decided to change it, probably to avoid antagonizing Jamaican authorities. This and two other "black-power" songs—"Burnin'" and "Get Up, Stand Up"—helped establish Bob Marley and the Wailers as a social and political activist group in the United States as well as Jamaica. Surprisingly, though, Peter Tosh and Bunny Wailer left the band by the time their third album was released.

Bob Marley, like most Rasta songwriters, used lyrics as a way of presenting his feelings about social problems. "I Shot the Sheriff" sounds like a cowboy plot set in Jamaica, but its message is much more complex than a shootout between the singer and the authorities. Marley explained on several occasions that "I Shot the Sheriff" was a metaphor for killing evil and injustice of the majority. The most important lyric message in the song was that the sheriff, for some reason, hated the character singing the song. It goes on to explain that the sheriff wanted to kill the singer's seed before it grows. Clearly, the song is not about violence, but the social power structure that minorities fight in Jamaica and the United States.

After Jamaica won independence from England in 1962, Rastafarianism became a popular religion. The roots of the Rastafarian movement lie in the Book of Revelations. Although there is no official doctrine nor church hierarchy, most Rastafarians believe in a divine line of descendants from King David to Haile Selassie of Ethiopia. Although Haile Selassie died in 1974, he remains in the hearts of believers. There are many branches of Rastafarianism, but all believe that the spiritual home for all descendants of the Negro race is Africa. Furthermore, each is destined to return to the motherland someday. This note of Afrocentrism resonated loudly in America where the black power movement was gaining political strength.

Eric Clapton included "I Shot the Sheriff" on his July 1974 release entitled *461 Ocean Boulevard*. It spent five weeks in the top 10 and ultimately reached the number 1 position. Clapton's guitar virtuosity, along with a well-conceived arrangement, made this a remarkable cover of Marley's classic song.

Bob Marley never strayed from his mission of using music to promulgate his theosophical message. He was awarded the United Nations Peace Medal on behalf of 500 million Africans in 1978 for his humanitarian activities on their behalf. His highest honor came when he performed as the featured artist for the Zimbabwe Independence Celebration in 1980. He died on May 11, 1981, at the age of thirty-six, from melanoma.

"I Shot the Sheriff" is available on *Legend* (Island Records, BMW1) a fourteen-song collection of Marley's greatest hits.

9. "Mothership Connection (Star Child)"
Words and Music by George Clinton, William Collins, and Bernard Worrell
Copyright © 1975, Bridgeport Music

As the 1970s progressed, funk music, as first defined by James Brown, mutated from a rhythm and blues–based sound to a psychedelic/ heavy-rhythm hybrid. George Clinton and his bands, Parliament, Funkadelic, and, later, P-Funk, were its prime instigators.

"Mothership Connection" is an anthem to Clinton's cosmic mysticism that was influenced by the worldview of jazzman Sun Ra, the psychedelica of Haight-Ashbury, and the rhythms of James Brown. Played on electronic keyboards (by Bernie Worrell), wah-wah electric guitar, electric bass guitar (by William "Bootsy" Collins), horns (by Maceo Parker and Fred Wesley), and a host of percussionists, "Mothership" is chanted by Clinton (the Starchild) to all cosmic life-forms. Telling them about the good times on Earth, Clinton references Easter Island and the Bermuda Triangle while background singers quote the Negro spiritual "Swing Down Chariot, and Let Me Ride."

George Edward Clinton was born in Kannapolis, North Carolina, in 1941. Working as a hairdresser in Plainfield, New Jersey, he formed a vocal group, The Parliaments, in 1955. The group auditioned for Motown Records in the mid-1960s, but was passed over. In 1967, The Parliaments had some success on the independent Detroit label Revilot. By 1969, when Bernie Worrell joined The Parliaments' backing band, Clinton had the core musicians that he named Funkadelic.

Bernard Worrell was born in 1945 in Long Branch, New Jersey. A child prodigy, he gave his first piano concert at the age of four. At the age of eleven, he met Clinton at the Plainfield barbershop and developed an interest in popular music. After attending the Juilliard School and the New England Conservatory of Music, he earned his living playing piano for rhythm and blues artists, until he was called by Clinton to help transmute the rhythm and blues harmonies of The Parliaments into the LSD-tinged funk of Funkadelic.

The third writer of "Mothership," Bootsy Collins was born in Cincinnati in 1951. As a teenager, Bootsy and his brother Catfish (Phelps) Collins were playing on sessions at King recording studio in Cincinnati. When King artist James Brown needed replacement musicians in 1969, the Collins brothers were hired. In 1971, Bootsy left Brown to join Clinton because Collins was tired of wearing a suit and tie on the bandstand. Clinton's "wilder-is-better" ethic appealed to the adventurous bass player. A little later, Collins helped Clinton recruit Maceo Parker and Fred Wesley, the heart of James Brown's famed horn section, the JB Horns.

At times, during the 1970s, Clinton's crew of musicians would number over forty. Spin-off acts were the norm: Bootsy's Rubber Band, The Brides of Funkenstein, Parlet, Zapp, Sweat Band, Godmoma, Wesley's Horny Horns; they all shared musicians, tours, record labels, and management. It is no surprise that a tangle of financial conflicts, lawsuits, countersuits, and threats led to the collapse of Clinton's "Mothership" in 1980. In its ten prime years, the P-Funk complex showed the black community a science-fiction worldview that included technology, mysticism, freedom, and love.

"Mothership Connection (Star Child)" is in the folio *The Best of George Clinton* (JPMC Books 1507). The original recording is on *Mothership Connection* (Casablanca CD 824 502).

10. "The Rock That Doesn't Roll"
Words and Music by Larry Norman
Copyright © 1976, Beechwood Music Corporation/JC Love
Publishing Company

Larry Norman, born April 8, 1947, in Corpus Christi, Texas, is credited as one of the founders of "Jesus rock," a controversial expression of Christianity that evolved in the 1970s and manifested its most popular expression in Bob Dylan's "Slow Train Coming" album of 1979. He grew up in San Francisco's tough Fillmore district where he was abused by neighborhood kids. An impoverished upbringing left Norman with an unfulfilled need for familial and communal love. Music provided an escape.

By the age of twenty-one, Norman was lead singer in a band, People, in San Jose, California. The pop-rock sextet, led by guitarist Geoff Levine, released a single on Capitol Records, "I Love You (but the Words Won't Come)." It sold well, reaching number 14 on the Billboard charts. Norman, a committed Christian, wanted to title the follow-up album *We Need a Whole Lot More of Jesus and a Lot Less Rock and Roll*, and put the Savior's image on the cover. Capitol vetoed the idea, and the day the album was released (entitled, simply, *I Love You*), Norman left the band.

By 1970, the "turn on, tune in, drop out" message of the mid-1960s was no longer relevant to some of America's youth. Spiritual seekers were sitting at the feet of Indian yogis, Bahai teachers, and charismatic Christian evangelists. Barefoot, long-haired youth in southern California were dubbed "the Jesus people" by the press. Shunned by mainstream churches, these young folk, many of them musicians, found acceptance at Calvary Chapel in Costa Mesa. The church formed a youth music/outreach ministry, Maranatha! Music, which released its first album in 1971. Maranatha! eventually became one of the most successful contemporary Christian music companies.

In such an environment, it was impossible for a talented visionary like Larry Norman to go unnoticed. Using rock forms and instruments, he wrote songs—"Why Should the Devil Have All the Good Music," "The Outlaw," and many others—that spoke to disillusioned youth, portraying Jesus as sympathetic to their community. Norman was denounced by mainstream Protestants, Jimmy Swaggart in particular.

By 1976, Norman had recorded several albums for Capitol and MGM/Verve and was the musical leader of the Jesus rock movement. When MGM refused to release the third album of a trilogy that depicted the past, present, and future of Norman's spiritual vision, he formed his own label, Solid Rock Records, to distribute *In Another Land*.

"The Rock That Doesn't Roll" from that album became an enduring metaphor for a loving, caring Jesus.

"The Rock That Doesn't Roll" is not available in print. Norman's original is on the album *In Another Land* (Word Records CD 701 200 1380).

11. "Coal Miner's Daughter"
Words and Music by Loretta Lynn
Copyright © 1969, Sure Fire Music Company, Inc.

As the 1960s became the 1970s, psychedelic rock music, the drug culture, and war demonstrations dominated the media, but there were always other voices telling different stories. Some belonged to the leading country singers of the day, who countered the counterculture by singing traditional country ballads or defiant songs like Merle Haggard's "Okie from Muskogee." Perhaps the most compelling belonged to a winsome young woman who sang of the trials of married women and the hard life of the rural poor.

When Loretta Webb was born in 1935, one of eight children in a miner's family, times were hard everywhere, but the poverty of Butcher Holler in the east Kentucky coal country was perennial. Loretta left school after fourth grade, was married when she was thirteen to Oliver "Mooney" Lynn, left her family for Washington State, and had four children before she was eighteen. "So when I sing those country songs about women struggling, you could say I've been there. . . . I know what it's like to be pregnant and nervous and poor" (Lynn 1976, x). Those early experiences would give Loretta's singing a raw honesty that reached the hearts of country music fans, and propelled her to stardom.

Loretta always sang around the house, prompting Mooney to buy a guitar from Sears and Roebuck. She taught herself to play. Mooney believed she had talent and pushed her to sing at local bars with country bands. A talent contest at a county fair led to a television appearance with Buck Owens, then to a recording session. In 1960, the Zero label released "I'm a Honky Tonk Girl," one of her own compositions. Loretta and Mooney were relentless promoters, pushing it to number 14 on Billboard's hot country singles chart, a stunning achievement for a new artist on a minor label. She was on her way, and she headed

straight to Nashville. There were still very few successful female country stars in 1960, but by year's end she had appeared on the Grand Ole
Opry and landed a deal with Decca Records. Her strong, expressive
voice brought comparisons to Kitty Wells and Patsy Cline. Cline became both friend and mentor until her death in 1963.

Success came fast for the girl with the big voice and a coal-
country accent. She put twenty-four songs on the charts in the 1960s,
including three number 1 hits: "Don't Come Home a Drinkin'," "Fist
City," and "Woman of the World." These and other songs from that
decade dealt with infidelity and marital conflict, but by 1969 she
wanted to tell of her early life. Despite the hard times, Loretta trea-
sured her childhood: "It's funny how most of the things I remember
are about being poor. . . . In some ways, that was the best part of my
life, learning to survive" (1976, xiii). From her musings came twelve
verses of "Coal Miner's Daughter." The song was pared to six for the
recorded version. Like Dolly Parton's "Coat of Many Colors" from
the same period, Loretta's song about pride in her roots and an abid-
ing love for her family struck a chord with the fans, who sent it up
the charts.

By 1976, Loretta was already a successful, wealthy and respected
performer when her autobiography *Loretta Lynn: Coal Miner's Daughter*, spent two months on the *New York Times* bestseller list. In 1980,
the country star's fame was taken to a new level when Sissy Spacek
portrayed Loretta in the hit motion picture based on the book, and
took home the Oscar for Best Actress.

"Coal Miner's Daughter" is available in volume 5 of the *Country
Music Hall of Fame* song folio (Hal Leonard 00313062), with a
recorded version on *Loretta Lynn* (MCA 10083), also part of the
Country Music Hall of Fame series.

12. "Sheena Is a Punk Rocker"
Words and Music by Douglas Colvin, John Cummins, Thomas
Erdely, and Jeffrey Hyman
Copyright © 1977, Bleu Disque Music Company, Inc./
Taco Tunes, Inc.

The Ramones helped create a genre of music called "punk rock"
and, unlike other early punk artists, remained relatively unchanged

until they disbanded in 1995. Their music was minimalistic and was intentionally unpolished. Their first performances, which were only ten- to fifteen-minutes long, amounted to a string of two-minute or less songs. Their song lyrics were sarcastic and an homage to what they perceived to be banality of pop culture.

The band was formed in 1974 when three young men from Forest Hills in the borough of Queens in New York purchased instruments and learned to play them well enough to perform their visceral songs. From the inception of the ensemble, the band members chose to create a parody image, based on 1950s stereotypes of rebellious youths. Building on the image of James Dean and other entertainment idols of the 1950s, the band members wore torn blue jeans and leather jackets.

Each founding member adopted the surname Ramone in a tongue-in-cheek attempt to create a band of brothers. They allegedly heard Paul McCartney make the comment "We [the Beatles] could have as easily called ourselves the Ramones" (Sullivan 1996). Joey Ramone (Jeffrey Hyman) became their drummer and vocalist and Johnny Ramone (John Cummings) assumed the role of guitarist. Dee Dee Ramone (Douglas Colvin) was the band's bass player, and Tommy Ramone (Tom Erdelyi) acted as the band's manager.

Shortly after their first performance, Tommy Ramone became the band's drummer and Joey focused on singing. The band began to perform at CBGB's, a club in the Bowery section of New York City that became famous for punk and other nonmainstream music. Ironically, the club's acronym originally stood for country, bluegrass, and blues. After they developed a cult following at CBGB's, the Ramones became one of the first punk rock bands to get signed to a recording contract. In 1976, they released *Ramones*, their first album on Sire Records. Staying true to their anticommercialism beliefs, they recorded the album for $6,000—substantially less than the typical pop or rock album of that period.

Although their first album only reached 111 on the U.S. charts, it helped them land a European tour. Because of the growing punk counterculture in the United Kingdom, the Ramones performed before crowds of young people who were familiar with their music. In 1977, they released *The Ramones Leave Home*, their second album. Although it was not very successful in the United States, the album did well in the United Kingdom, reaching number 48 on the album charts. The band's greatest success, however, came with the song "Sheena Is a Punk Rocker," a single that became a top-forty hit in the United Kingdom. The song was subsequently included on their third album, *Rocket to Russia.*

The Ramones' music intentionally mocked the overproduced and self-indulgent music of the mid-1970s. "Sheena Is a Punk Rocker," like other songs the Ramones created, relied on a simple statement presented in terse repetitive lyrics. This song paints a picture of the stereotypical pop-head California surfers headed for the disco, but Sheena breaks away from the crowd to become a New York punk rocker.

The Ramones ridiculed pot-smoking hippies, but the band members had substance abuse problems. The band had several turnovers in personnel. One such change was due to Marky Ramone leaving the band for several years to battle alcoholism. Dee Dee Ramone never shrouded the fact that he was a heroin addict. Joey Ramone died of lymphatic cancer on April 16, 2001, at the age of forty-nine.

The Ramones will always be known as the prototypical punk rock band. Their influence on other punk bands, as well as more modern grunge and hardcore bands, is noteworthy. They have been acknowledged by hardcore rock band Green Day; as a matter of fact, Green Day band members have children named Joey and Romona. The Ramones were inducted into the Rock and Roll Hall of Fame in 2002.

The Ramones recorded their final album, appropriately titled *Adios,* in 1995. "Sheena Is a Punk Rocker" is available on the CD *All the Stuff & More, vol. 2* (Sire Records, 1990).

13. "Stayin' Alive"
Words and Music by Barry Gibb, Maurice Gibb, and Robin Gibb
Copyright © 1977, Gibb Brothers Music

The Bee Gees (an acronym for Brothers Gibb) are synonymous with the disco dance craze of the 1970s. The disco scene was about more than dancing. Disco clubs were also the gathering places for young people needing a place to display their late-night personae. The fashions, like the self-absorbed persons wearing them, were markedly different than the organic hippies of the 1960s and early 1970s. The disco look included stylish polyester vests, fashionably flared double-knit pants, and platform heels for both males and females. The summer of love was replaced by the evening of swirling mirror balls, strobe lights, and tight-fitting polyester outfits.

The disco dance phenomenon likely originated in gay dance clubs in the early half of the decade and then moved into straight clubs. By 1975, dance contests had become an established ritual in New York. That same year, Nik Cohn, a contributing editor for *New York*, wrote an article called "Tribal Rights of the New Saturday Night" in which he described the emerging disco mileau. Robert Stigwood, manager of the Bee Gees and producer of *Jesus Christ Superstar*, read the article and thought that it might be the basis of a film. Stigwood, who had just signed a deal to produce three films staring John Travolta, contacted Cohn and they struck a deal. The film was called *Saturday Night Fever*, starring Travolta, and it became a box office smash.

Stigwood asked the Bee Gees to write music for the film and they accepted the offer. The music they wrote became more than a financial success; it emerged as music that was the aural identity of the disco era. The double-album soundtrack was even more successful than the movie. It went on to sell over 30 million copies, making it one of the top-selling albums in history. "Stayin' Alive," along with John Travolta's white-suited, pointing-to-the-sky pose, remains a disco era logo.

"Stayin' Alive" entered Billboard at number 10 on January 21, 1978, and rose to the top position after two weeks. It then retained the top chart position for four weeks. It was pushed out of first place by "Love Is Thicker Than Water," by Andy Gibb, younger brother of the Bee Gees. Three weeks later, "Night Fever," another Bee Gees song from the movie took the number 2 position on the charts. *Fever mania* became the new catchword, along with *disco mania.*

The Bee Gees were inducted into the Rock and Roll Hall of Fame in 1997. The original Bee Gees version of "Stayin' Alive" was released on *Saturday Night Fever* (RSO Records, 1977). For the full effect, hear it in the film.

14. "Tie a Yellow Ribbon Round the Old Oak Tree"
Words and Music by L. Russell Brown and Irwin Levine
Copyright © 1972, Levine and Brown Music, Inc.

Two threads of American popular culture were woven together to create an enormously successful commercial song hit, which then became the basis of a poignant national moment. The first thread was an unattributed story from the 1950s of a convict returning home after his release. He has asked his wife to place a white handkerchief in an apple tree near the train tracks if he was welcome home. If he did not see it, he would ride on. He found the tree festooned with white. The story circulated among Christian youth groups in the 1960s and author Pete Hammill's 1971 short story set it among college students headed for spring break in Florida.

The second thread is a song with roots in the American minstrel stage. "'Round Her Neck She Wore a Yellow Ribbon" was a modest hit in the early 1950s after it was featured in a John Wayne movie set during the Civil War, and was subsequently a favorite on *Sing Along with Mitch*, a television show of the 1960s. The song was copyrighted in 1917, but it derived from a comic dialect song printed in 1838, "All Round My Hat."

These two unrelated elements influenced Russell Brown and Irwin Levine when they wrote "Tie a Yellow Ribbon Round the Old Oak Tree." The song tells of a returning prisoner who is looking for a sign of forgiveness, or else he will just stay on the bus and move on. When sued by Hammill over the song's content, the writers argued successfully that they had used the earlier folk version of the story as a starting point, but because they needed the lyrics to read differently, the white handkerchief became a yellow ribbon and the apple tree became an oak. The songwriters did not credit the earlier song about a yellow ribbon, but almost certainly had heard it in the previous decade.

The song was a hit for Tony Orlando (Michael Anthony Orlando Cassavitas) and Dawn (vocalists Telma Hopkins and Joyce Vincent). The group had scored its first hit, "Candida," before they even met. Orlando had added a lead vocal to a demo by two anonymous session singers, and it became a surprise hit in 1970. The trio then scrambled to create a performing entity to capitalize on the song's popularity. The following year "Knock Three Times," written by Brown and Levine, was a number 1 hit. Then, in 1973, they bested themselves with "Tie a Yellow Ribbon," which sold 3 million records in three weeks. It faded from the charts but clearly stayed in the national consciousness.

In 1975, Gail Magruder, wife of Jeb Stuart Magruder, referenced the popular song when she used yellow ribbons to welcome the convicted Watergate conspirator home from prison. The popular tradition really took hold five years later, when Penne Laingen, wife of Bruce Laingen, charge d'affaires of the U.S. Embassy in Iran, invited the press to watch her tie a yellow ribbon around her own oak tree as a symbol that she wanted him home. Fifty-two Americans, including Laingen and his entire embassy staff, had been taken hostage by Iranian revolutionaries on November 4, 1979, and were held for fourteen tortuous months. Americans rushed to adopt the symbol. Trees across the country were decorated, and stayed that way until the hostages were brought safely home in January 1981, just as Ronald Reagan was inaugurated to his first term. Ten short years later yellow ribbons again lined the nation's roadways as Desert Storm got underway and American soldiers shipped out for war with Iraq in the Persian Gulf.

"Tie a Yellow Ribbon Round the Old Oak Tree" is available as sheet music (Warner Brothers 2869TSMX) and on Tony Orlando and Dawn's *Definitive Collection* (Arista 19036.)

15. "Rapper's Delight"
Rap Lyrics by B. Edwards, Grandmaster Caz, and N. Rodgers
Copyright © 1979, Sylvia Robinson

As the disco dance craze became an obsession with many New York teenagers and young adults, clubs capitalized on the income potential. Cover charges escalated at the uptown clubs, forcing many young people to find less expensive places to dance. Inventive inner-city youths, particularly in Harlem and the Bronx, created their own entertainment environments on the streets. The art form to emerge from this urban street scene came to be called "rap."

Three early innovators of rap, Afrika Bambaataa, Grandmaster Flash, and Kool Herc, are now referred to as "old-school" rappers.

Bambaataa is credited with first using the term *hip-hop* to describe jam sessions. The term slowly came to be associated with an urban, youth-oriented cultural milieu that includes graffiti art, break dancing, and rap music. Rap artist Kool Herc (born Clive Campbell) moved from Jamaica to the Bronx in 1967. The influence of reggae on his rap style is noteworthy.

Old-school rap was a strictly local phenomenon until two music entrepreneurs created a label and multiple-artist rap act that led the way for rap's commercial development. Sylvia Robinson, who had modest success as a recording artist in the 1950s, and her husband Joe operated a struggling label called All Platinum. After noting that rap performers were moving their shows from the street corners of the Bronx and Harlem to uptown clubs, gymnasiums, and private parties, the Robinsons decided to start a new label, called Sugar Hill Records, and release what appears to be the first rap single.

Sylvia Robinson recruited three rappers—Master Gee, Wonder Mike, and Big Bank Hank—and named the group the Sugar Hill Gang. The trio created a song, "Rapper's Delight," based on the instrumental break from "Good Times" by Chic. Sugar Hill Records cleverly released the song on the twelve-inch vinyl, a configuration preferred by club DJs. They distributed "Rapper's Delight" through small and midsize retail record stores. They also promoted the record to roller rinks, discos, dance clubs, and any other venues at which their young, predominantly African American audiences might hear it.

Their marketing strategy paid off and "Rapper's Delight" became the first rap song to appear on the Billboard hot 100 chart, reaching number 36. In addition, it sold over 2 million copies. Although "Rapper's Delight" is often considered little more than light entertainment intended to support dancing, it changed the recording industry forever. The commercial success of this song alerted major labels to the existence of a new genre. Moreover, it signaled the sales potential of rap, a genre previously ignored by the industry.

"Rapper's Delight" is available on *Best of the Sugarhill Gang* (Rhino Records, 1996). It has also been recorded by several other rap artists as a "salute" to the old-school gang.

1980–1989

MTV and Reaganomics

After the turbulence of the 1960s and 1970s, the nation seemed eager to find a more conservative father figure to occupy the White House. As the decade began, sixty-nine-year-old former Hollywood actor Ronald Reagan easily won the presidency in 1980, giving the country its oldest elected president up until that time.

The fastest growing areas of the country—the southeast, southwest, and west—began to flex their political muscle through increased representation in Congress. Many businesses in the Sunbelt states lobbied politicians for less federal regulation of commerce that relied on natural resources such as logging, mining, oil rights, and the environment in general. This came to be called the "Sagebrush Rebellion," and fit perfectly with the Reagan agenda.

The Sunbelt states also shared a concern for the growing number of immigrants settling within their borders. The primary concern that states like Florida, Texas, Arizona, and California had with increasing numbers of immigrants was the strain the new citizens placed on state social programs and educational systems. Between 1940 and 1980, the number of Latinos in the United States increased from less than 2 million to more than 14 million (U.S. Census Bureau 2002). During the 1970s and 1980s, the flood of Latino immigrants impacted certain regions, particularly Cubans and South Americans settling in Florida and Mexicans moving to Texas, Arizona, and California.

Ronald Reagan presented the country, and Congress, his vision for a new economic system as soon as he took office. His plan was conceptually very simple. He proposed cutting taxes, especially on businesses and wealthy investors, in order to stimulate the economy. His system, which was quickly dubbed "Reaganomics," theorized that wealthy people would use their additional money from tax savings for investments in businesses. Companies, in turn, would expand production and hire more workers. Reagan was confident that this, the trickle-down process, would gradually spread prosperity from the wealthiest to the poorest citizens.

Although there was sound logic in the trickle-down theory, it depended on cutting government spending as well as cutting taxes. Unfortunately for the economy, neither Congress nor President Reagan was successful in cutting spending. The lack of spending cuts in general, and a dramatic increase in defense spending in particular, led to an increased national debt. The national debt was $712 billion when Reagan took office, but it had soared to $2 trillion by the time he left office in 1990 (Congressional Budget Office 2003).

Reaganomics looked promising on paper, but in practice, the economy became quite volatile. The prime interest rate rose to 21 percent in 1981. In 1982, 9 million Americans were out of work (Cannon 2000). On October 19, 1987, the stock market fell 508 points, double the size of the 1929 stock market crash that triggered the Great Depression. Clearly, Reaganomics worked better in theory than in practice.

This was a decade of renewed social awareness. More than 550,000 people assembled in New York City's Central Park to demand an end to nuclear weapons. It was the largest protest rally in U.S. history. Musicians moved beyond merely writing songs about issues close to their hearts; they donated their time to raise awareness of, and money for, social causes, such as AIDS, world hunger, apartheid, U.S. farmers, and victims of natural disasters. Song lyrics also addressed current social problems such as domestic violence, poverty, and AIDS, which was first discovered in 1981.

Not everyone was happy, though, with the state of the music industry. A group called the Parents Music Resource Center (PMRC) was created in 1985 by Tipper Gore, wife of then-Senator Al Gore Jr., to make the industry more responsible regarding the lyrics of music that children listened to. The group was successful in getting a Senate Commerce Committee formed to hold hearings on the subject of lyrics. The PMRC tried unsuccessfully to force record labels to stop releasing songs with lyrics that included sex, violence, drug and alcohol abuse, and the occult. However, the PMRC was successful in convincing the Recording Industry Association of America to create a voluntary system of warning labels for recordings.

Of all the influences that impacted the music of the 1980s, none was as influential as MTV, a cable television format that debuted in the summer of 1981. Because MTV focused on visual images, a performer's physical attributes—weight, dance skills, and overall attractiveness—seemed to eclipse the music. A youthful look, packaged in well-choreographed productions, became so important to promotion-hungry label executives that older established artists were often overlooked. The expression *video-friendly artist* entered the lexicon of the recording industry.

SONGS

1. "Video Killed the Radio Star"
Words and Music by Trevor Horn, Geoffrey Downes, and Bruce Woolley
Copyright © 1979, Carbert Music
First song aired on MTV, 1981

Trevor Horn was born in Hertfordshire, England, on July 15, 1949. His father, a dairy engineer by trade, was also a talented bass player in local bands. Following in his footsteps, Trevor played bass in school bands. At the age of nineteen, he quit college and became a professional musician. Being an excellent sight reader of bass parts, he found work as a session player in British recording studios.

After years of playing on others' recordings, Horn built his own studio and began recording original songs that he could pitch to established artists. Among the first songs was "Video Killed the Radio Star," written with Bruce Woolley, a longtime friend. Inspired by a science-fiction story by J. G. Ballard, "The Sound Sweep," the song, like the story, portrays a future when pictures have replaced sound as the primary human emotional center.

Horn and Woolley recorded the song with electronic keyboardist Geoff Downes. They decided to release the song under the group name the Buggles, the most disgusting name Horn could think of. The song was not a big hit, charting at number 40 for one week at the end of 1979.

In the early 1980s, cable television was proving its money-making potential. Ted Turner's CNN was up and running well, and American Express and Warner Brothers had merged and formed an all-kids cable network, Nickelodeon. Amex–Warner vice president John Lack committed $20 million to develop an all-music channel. Hiring former Monkee Michael Nesmith, Lack commissioned thirteen episodes of *Pop Clips* for Nickelodeon. The music videos were based on European models that had been popular for several years.

Hosted by comedians, *Pop Clips* featured zany animation and sight gags. They looked little like what later became MTV's basic style. The thirteen episodes of *Pop Clips* were rerun for six months. On March 3, 1981, John Lack announced that MTV's debut as a cable network would commence on August 1, 1981. Bob Pittman, a former DJ, was hired to secure promotional music videos from the record companies to program the channel. Pittman had a tough time. Most record companies were willing to sell the cablecast rights to their music videos, but very few saw the promotional value in MTV. As the deadline approached, Pittman found only Warner Brothers totally cooperative with the new venture. Turning to Europe, where videos had proven to be effective promotional tools for the record companies, Pittman acquired videos of touring American acts and European artists known in the United States.

On August 1, 1981, the MTV staff gathered in a restaurant in Fort Lee, New Jersey—MTV was not carried on any of the cable systems in New York—to watch the premiere of an extremely important event in American cultural history. The only press coverage was by the *Los Angeles Times*' Robert Hilburn. At 12:01 A.M., the screen lit up with black-and-white footage of Neil Armstrong's lunar mission. However, the flag Armstrong planted on the moon displayed the MTV logo. The first clip played on MTV was the Buggles' prophetic "Video Killed the Radio Star."

The song is available in print in the folio *The Wedding Singer Soundtrack Selections* from Warner Brothers Publishing. The original recording by the Buggles is on *The Age of Plastic* CD (Island Records 842 849).

2. "Karma Chameleon"
Words and Music by George O'Dowd, Jon Moss, Roy Hay, Mickey Craig, and Phil Pickett
Copyright © 1983, Virgin Music, Warner–Tamerlane Music

In January 1984, the cover of *Newsweek* featured Annie Lennox of the Eurythmics and Boy George of Culture Club, two androgynous British stars of the new wave style that succeeded punk music. New wave was, at the time, considered an alternative to the dominant pop genre. Most pop music that was successful in the marketplace just prior to new wave was recognizable by its reliance on formulaic studio production techniques and predictable lyrics.

At the time, Culture Club was riding high on the top-selling album *Colour by Numbers*, and its irresistible hit song "Karma Chameleon." Their way had been paved by 1970s glam rockers like David Bowie and Marc Bolan, but Boy George took the glitter and posturing to new heights. In a decade marked both by a swelling gay pride movement and the tragedy of AIDS, Boy George challenged Americans to accept his unconventional sexual identity.

Boy George began life in 1961 as George O'Dowd and grew into a misfit youngster in his working-class suburb of London. At the age of sixteen, he abandoned school in favor of the trendy London club scene. While working days at fashion boutiques he refined the theatrical, sexually ambiguous look that attracted the attention of Malcolm McLaren, manipulative genius behind Sid Vicious and the Sex Pistols. McLaren was building a new band, Bow Wow Wow, and needed a boy singer as foil to his fourteen-year-old lead singer Annabella Lwin. George's rich and enticing voice was an unexpected bonus.

The increasingly quirky George, now known as Boy George, did not last long with McLaren, but soon joined a diverse (white, black, Protestant, Catholic, Jewish) group of musicians that evolved into Culture Club, combining elements of reggae, rhythm and blues, Latin music, and pure pop. After a few hardscrabble years, the band was picked up by Virgin Records for a first album, *Kissing to Be Clever,* from which came the catchy single "Do You Really Want to Hurt Me?" It was a quick hit on both sides of the Atlantic. A tour of the United States followed and everywhere the womanly young man went there was speculation about his exaggerated cross-dressing style, to such an extent that the music of Culture Club was sometimes lost in the media buzz.

The American tour was followed with *Colour by Numbers,* which featured a cover photo of coquettish George in vivid makeup with long braids tied by a floppy scarf and a Hasidic fedora. The single, "Karma Chameleon," was an instant hit, topping charts worldwide. Culture Club operated as a songwriting collective, with all members credited for each song, but George recalled that the smash hit single "was a really old tune that I had which Roy [Hay] wouldn't work out because he hated it so much" (Cohen 1984, 109). The light but hypnotic song reflected his distrust of people who changed their colors (that is, were not loyal) and acknowledged reggae music with a reference to colors of the Rastafarian flag: red, gold, and green. The song was so indelible once heard, and so in demand, the band grew sick of it and disliked performing it even years later on their reunion tour.

Unfortunately, Boy George did not thrive on fame and the resulting lack of privacy. His affair with band member Jon Moss was played out in the tabloids, followed by news of his heroin addiction. Soon, each band member went his own way, but not before winning the 1984 Grammy for Best New Artist. At the ceremonies Boy George blew a kiss and thanked America because "you know a good drag queen when you see one" (Boy George and Bright 1995, 226).

"Karma Chameleon" is available on the CD release of *Colour by Numbers* (Virgin 86180) and in print in *Great Songs of the 1980s* (Hal Leonard 02502125a0).

3. "Desapariciones"
Words and Music by Ruben Blades
Copyright © 1984, Ruben Blades Music

Ruben Blades Jr. was born on July 16, 1948, in Panama City, Panama. His mother was an actress and singer, but it was his grandmother, Emma, who instilled in young Ruben the social conscience that would be displayed in his music decades later.

Through his adolescent years in Panama, Blades was captivated by American culture, especially rock and doo-wop music. In the early 1960s, Blades, a singer in his brother's pop band, stopped singing in English after the American administrators of the Canal Zone refused to fly the Panamanian flag, sparking a riot that killed twenty-one and wounded almost five hundred.

Blades earned a law degree from the University of Panama. In 1974, he moved to New York to restart his music career. He worked as a vocalist with Ray Barretto's salsa band, a popular Latin dance orchestra. In 1976, he began singing and writing songs for the Willie Colon Combo. These songs established Blades's reputation as a social commentator.

Latin music forms have a long history within American popular music prior to Blades arrival. Dance-oriented, they include tango (World War I era), mambo (1940s), and cha-cha (1950s). Blades's innovation was to bring a social and political viewpoint to the culturally hybrid dance music known in New York as "salsa."

By 1980, Blades's songs were having such an impact in the Latin communities in America that "Tiburon" ("the Shark"), a song comparing Central American interventionists (contras) to the titled predator, was banned from radio in Miami. In 1983, Blades signed a recording contract with Electra Records as a solo artist. His first Electra album, *Buscando America* (Searching for America), contained the song "Desapariciones" (Disappearances). Set in a minor key to a lockstep beat with a funeral-parlor-organ accompaniment, "Desapariciones," in six chilling stanzas, tells of a vanished husband, son, sister, mother—everyday people who cannot be found in the hospitals or at the police station. The last stanza asks where they go, and answers: in the water or the fields.

Blades's major-label recordings drew rave reviews from mainstream critics. English translations of the lyrics were printed in the album liner notes, making Blades's message accessible to non-Latins. *Buscando America* sold over three hundred thousand copies, a remarkable number for a Spanish-language album.

Not content with only a music career, Blades has acted in films such as *Waiting for Salazar* and *The Milagro Beanfield War*. He has been a political columnist for a Panamanian newspaper and formed an independent political party in Panama. "Desapariciones" is out of print.

4. "Find a Way"
Words and Music by Amy Grant and Michael W. Smith
Copyright © 1985, Meadowgreen Music

In 1981, Michael Whitaker Smith, a twenty-three-year-old West Virginia native, signed a publishing contract with Nashville's Meadowgreen Music. Known primarily as a publisher of Christian songs, Meadowgreen was hoping to have pop success with songs sung by a professed Christian, Vanderbilt University coed Amy Grant.

Grant is the daughter and granddaughter of surgeons and grew up in the exclusive Belle Meade section of Nashville. She began singing and writing songs while a student at Harpeth Hall, a private girls school. During her last years at Harpeth Hall, Grant began singing at a Christian coffeehouse in Nashville. She was not aware of the Christian-rock music of the 1970s, but her compositions reflected the concerns of her upper-class peers.

She became a recording star when a tape of her songs, made as a present for her parents in 1977, was heard by an executive of Word Records, a gospel label. The ensuing release did well, and by the early 1980s, she was touring with a band that included keyboardist Michael Smith.

Word signed a distribution contract with powerhouse A&M Records when it became apparent that Grant's appeal extended well beyond committed Christians. Indeed, her musical message soft-pedaled gospel's usual evangelism to the point of complete ambiguity. At its most explicit, in her earlier songs, her message seemed to be that it is OK to be a Christian and dress well; a comfort to her primarily adolescent fans. Her cheerleader-like good looks were a marketing dream for A&M.

The year 1985 brought Grant's most ambitious attempt to succeed in the pop market. Writing songs with Christian music's most progressive talents—Gary Chapman, Brown Bannister, and Michael W. Smith—Grant assembled an album, *Unguarded*, that contained "Find a Way," a song that only mentions God in the coda, almost as an afterthought. The bulk of the lyric is made up of a mantra about love finding its way, undoubtedly an affirming message for a lovesick teen. The transition from Christian (albeit Christian-lite) to pop was complete.

The album and single did very well. *Unguarded* became the first (nominally) Christian album to sell 1 million copies, and "Find a Way" spent sixteen weeks on Billboard's pop charts. This success opened the door to pop for other Christian artists, eventually creating a talent pool large enough to be marketed as "contemporary Christian."

Amy Grant, coming from a different direction, completed the circle started by the 1970s Jesus freaks who moved to Christianity as part of a spiritual quest, bringing their religious views to the hostile genre of rock. Grant grafted her easygoing brand of Christian belief onto the pop music of the 1980s, which welcomed her with ringing cash registers.

"Find a Way" is in the *Best of Amy Grant* song folio (Hal Leonard 00702099). The *Unguarded* album is available from RCA (CD B000002WOF).

5. "Material Girl"
Words and Music by Peter Brown and Robert Rans
Copyright © 1984, Minong Music

Madonna: dancer, choreographer, sultry chanteuse, fashion idol, sex goddess, film actress, Broadway star, record executive, movie producer, art patron, AIDS activist, and promiscuous provocateur. The labels are endless for one of the most interesting popular culture figures of the twentieth century. With her distinctive gap-toothed smile, prominent mole, and deep compelling eyes, she became arguably the most photographed woman of the century (surpassing even her own role model, Marilyn Monroe) while her brassy public persona was the subject of relentless analysis by the media. And then there were her fans, especially the budding pubescent girls who so eagerly aped her dress and attitude that they spawned the pop culture cliché *wannabe.*

Madonna Ciccone doggedly chose her own track after leaving her suburban home in Bay City, Michigan, for the lights of New York City. She envisioned herself a dancer and her talent and drive won a spot in Alvin Ailey's third company and then Pearl Lang's troupe. But dancing alone did not bring enough fame and excitement. She found the latter during nights trawling New York's dance club scene, where she established a stylish notoriety and made contacts that led to jobs singing backup for post-punk and disco bands. Her fame would soon follow.

But "backup" anything was not Madonna's style. So in 1981, at the age of twenty-three, she formed her own band with herself as lead singer. From that point, success came very quickly for the driven performer. Several of her band's demo tapes caught the attention of executives at Sire Records. A couple of successful singles led to the 1983 self-titled first album, which spawned "Lucky Star," the first of fifteen consecutive top 5 hits.

As the songs were climbing the charts, Madonna was making her first movie, *Desperately Seeking Susan*, after beating out a string of established actresses for the title role in the low-budget feminist film. One of the producers would recall, "She had a sense of self, of supreme confidence. She seemed more secure about whom she was than anyone I'd seen" (Andersen 1991, 123). Madonna herself, in the same period, noted, "If I weren't as talented as I am ambitious, I would be a gross monstrosity" (Andersen 1991, 76).

Then came a second album, *Like a Virgin*. The cover featured Madonna in a wedding dress with a sexy bustier and the "boy-toy" belt that was briefly a trademark. The controversial title track was an immediate hit, especially on MTV, which until then had been dominated by Michael Jackson and other male performers. It was followed by "Material Girl," Madonna's vamp on the memorable Marilyn Monroe film *Gentlemen Prefer Blondes* and its lead song "Diamonds Are a Girl's Best Friend." For some, the song symbolized the consumer-driven, glitzy 1980s. At the same time Madonna's rise to the top, and her insistence on controlling every aspect of her career, began to win respect. Soon the woman dismissed as a shameless but insignificant exhibitionist was having scholarly papers written about her role as "postmodern feminist heroine" (Kaplan 1987). By 1992, Madonna would grace the cover of *Forbes*, with the caption: "America's Smartest Businesswoman?"

"Material Girl" is available on Madonna's *The Immaculate Collection* (Warner Brothers CD 26440) and in print in *Golden Decade of the 1980s* (Warner Brothers VF 1770).

6. "Miami Vice Theme"
Music by Jan Hammer
Copyright © 1985, Universal City Studios, Inc.

In the autumn of 1984, a cop show, airing on Friday nights on NBC, captured the fancy of millions of American television viewers. By the time it went off the air near the end of the decade, *Miami Vice* was a worldwide hit. Contributing to this popularity was a soundtrack so varied and unique that many fans turned on their television sets to "listen" to the show. The music backgrounds or "cues" might sound like voodoo drums or Thai temple bells layered with rock guitars and whispering voices. In fact, it was none of these; each week the entire soundtrack was the product of one man and his synthesizers at work in his home studio.

Jan Hammer was born on April 17, 1948, in Prague, Czechoslovakia, to a jazz-singer mother and physician father. By the age of four, Jan was playing piano, and his first public performance came at the age of twelve. In high school he formed a jazz trio with his brothers and the ensemble won first prize at the 1966 International Music Competition. For the next two years, Jan studied composition and piano in Prague.

In 1968, the Soviets invaded Czechoslovakia and Hammer fled to the United States where he enrolled at Boston's Berklee School of Music. He played in clubs at night and, in 1970, was asked to back singer Sarah Vaughan on a thirteen-month tour. Eventually settling in New York, Hammer formed the Mahavishnu Orchestra with avant-garde guitarist John McLaughlin. It was with this band that Hammer discovered and explored the capabilities of synthesized sound.

A digital synthesizer is a microprocessor that can generate sound and modify prerecorded sounds using specially designed computer programs. When synthesizers and computers evolved in sophistication, a modern personal workstation, based on Musical-Instrument-Digital-Interface (MIDI) technology emerged. In the mid-1970s, such instruments were just beginning to develop from tools of experimental classical composers into true instruments. Only a few professional performing musicians were brave enough to play them in public. Hammer, unlike the musicians who would create New Age music, used the synthesizer to aggressively emulate rock sounds—guitars, drums, and horns—as well as sounds from other national cultures. Hammer's technical expertise set the framework for future innovations in the music backgrounds, called "beats" and "loops," to be exploited by hip-hop and rap artists in the coming decades.

While television producer Michael Mann was making the pilot episode of *Miami Vice*, he met Hammer at a mutual friend's house where he heard a sample of Hammer's synthesizer compositions. Mann had already decided on an unusual "look" for the show—the cops wore designer suits and drove Ferraris past the pastel-painted Miami Beach hotels—and he wanted a distinctive sound to fit with the tone. The show, with Hammer's unique music, helped make Miami, like New York, Chicago, and Los Angeles, a trendy new "cop-show" location.

Hammer was hired and over the next four years he composed, played, and recorded seventy-seven soundtracks for the show. In the first year, it was clear that the show was a hit, and MCA Records released a soundtrack album. The first selection, "Miami Vice Theme," rose to number 1 on the pop charts in October 1985, and stayed there eleven weeks. No television theme music had done as well since 1959's *Music from Peter Gunn* by Henry Mancini.

"Miami Vice Theme" is in print in various Hal Leonard folios of the "great-TV-show" type. The original soundtrack album is available from MCA Records (MCA CD 6150).

7. "River Run"
Music by Glen Velez, Paul Halley, Eugene Friesen, Oscar Castro-Neves, and Paul Winter
Copyright © 1985, Bright Angel Music, Living Earth Music

Canyon, an album released in 1985, is a synthesis of jazz, New Age, and environmental esthetics in music. Layering ambient recordings made in the Grand Canyon with improvised music played by the Paul Winter Consort at sessions in the Cathedral of St. John the Divine in New York, the track titled "River Run" illustrated Winter's philosophy that music and nature are forms of worship; a philosophy in keeping with values first espoused in popular culture by the New Age (Aquarian) movement.

Paul Winter was born in Altoona, Pennsylvania, on August 31, 1939. His grandfather was a bandsman during the Civil War, and his father was a piano tuner and music store owner. Winter began playing clarinet and piano as a child, but switched to alto saxophone as a teen.

While attending Northwestern University in Chicago, he formed a jazz group with other students, and, in 1961, the Paul Winter Sextet won the Intercollegiate Jazz Festival. Columbia Records executive John Hammond signed the group to a contract, but Winter soon tired of standard jazz. In 1967, he made his first attempt at forming a consort of musicians who could fuse European, African, and South American sounds in an improvisational manner. In 1972, however, Winter disbanded this group, dissatisfied with its direction.

Winter gradually became involved with Greenpeace, an activist environmental organization, and other socially conscious causes. He played his soprano saxophone to wolves in the wild and to whales from aboard Greenpeace ships. It became clear to Winter that the "songs" of the whales, wolves, and birds could be a starting point for a new school of musical composition. In 1977, he formed the Paul Winter Consort to manifest his vision. Three years later, in 1980, they released *Callings*, which combined recordings of thirteen sea mammals with the Consort's collective improvisation.

Winter was named artist-in-residence at New York's Cathedral of St. John the Divine in 1980, and each year since he has played a "Winter Consort Winter Solstice Whole Earth Christmas Celebration" concert there. The music, improvised inside the largest Gothic cathedral in the world, is designed to create in the listener the universal spirit of the solstice.

In 1981, and again in 1983, Winter, acting on a long-held desire, rafted 279 miles of the Colorado River into the Grand Canyon. Carrying portable audio recorders and various musical instruments, Winter and a group of guides and musicians played in various locations in the Grand Canyon. On October 22, 1981, at the start of the first expedition, guide Sam West blew a conch shell at mile 40. The recording of the conch sound serves as the opening of "River Run." During the 1983 trip, improvisations by Winter recorded at mile 120 (Blacktail Canyon) became the main musical theme of "River Run."

These location recordings, plus recordings of canyon wrens and other wildlife, were combined with recordings made by the full Consort at St. John the Divine in 1985. The resulting seven-minute composition, "River Run," represents Winter's vision of translating the spirit of the Earth into sound.

"River Run" is unavailable in print. The original Consort album *Canyon* is available on Living Music Records (CD 81505).

8. "We Are the World"
Words and Music by Michael Jackson and Lionel Richie Jr.
Copyright © 1985, Mijac Music/Brockman Enterprises, Inc.

In November 1984, an Irish singer/songwriter, Bob Geldof, turned on his television and saw pictures of famine-plagued Ethiopians. Geldof, a thirty-one-year-old former laborer and leader of the Boomtown Rats, a moderately successful Irish rock band, was shaken by the images. With no resources at hand, Geldof created Band Aid, a who's who of British rock musicians recording gratis. The resultant record, *Do They Know It's Christmas*, raised over $10 million before the end of the year.

A few days before Christmas 1984, Harry Belafonte telephoned Ken Kragen, the manager of singer Lionel Richie. Belafonte wanted Kragen's help in producing a benefit concert featuring African American musicians who were not doing enough, in Belafonte's view, to help the starving Africans. Geldof had shamed the Americans.

Kragen, a former concert promoter, remembered the 1971 financial fiasco that was George Harrison's Concert for Bangladesh. Kragen suggested instead an "American Band Aid." The first thing they needed was a song.

Lionel Richie grew up on the campus of Tuskegee University in Alabama. His grandfather had worked with the school's founder, Booker T. Washington. Richie was trained in classical piano and exposed to ballet and opera at the school. He formed a musical group with five other Tuskegee students, and, in the early 1970s, his group, called the Commodores, opened some shows for Motown's Jackson 5. A recording contract followed, and by 1975, Richie's songwriting and smooth vocals put the Commodore's "Three Times a Lady" at the top of the charts.

Kragen knew he had a seasoned songwriter in Lionel Richie, and Richie was enthusiastic about the project. Kragen enlisted producer Quincy Jones to supervise the recording session, while Richie tried to contact his friend Stevie Wonder to cowrite the needed song.

Many days slipped by with no progress by the songwriters. Meanwhile, Kragen enlisted two dozen of the biggest names in popular music as singers. They were to be in Los Angeles on January 28, 1985, for the American Music Awards telecast. Paul Simon, Diana Ross, Ray Charles, Smokey Robinson, Bob Dylan, Willie Nelson, Bruce Springsteen, Cyndi Lauper, Tina Turner, Bette Midler, the Jacksons (Randy, LaToya, Marlin, Tito, and Jackie—Michael had left the group for a solo career) all, and more, were willing to donate their services to USA for Africa, as the project had been named.

By the middle of January, still songless, Kragen and Jones were nervous. Jones called on Michael Jackson to get the ball rolling. Having produced Jackson's 1982 mega hit "Thriller," Jones knew Michael could work under pressure. The next day Jackson played a melody for Jones and Kragen. It was a soaring anthem with a lovely bridge where many of the star singers could have a solo line or two. Richie and Jackson spent the next week crafting the lyrics. A week before the session, they had a demonstration tape made and sent copies to the performers.

The evening of the recording session, Bob Geldof arrived from Ethiopia. He went to the studio and told the performers about the needs of their African brothers and sisters. Many of the singers were moved to tears. Geldof also commented, jokingly, that he had never seen more millionaires in one room. "We Are the World" was released on March 23, 1985, and, by May, had sold 8 million copies. It is the most successful nongovernmental fund-raiser in history.

"We Are the World" is available as piano/vocal sheet music from Warner Brothers Publishing. The sound recording, with other songs donated by individual USA for Africa performers, is on the CD *We Are the World* (Mercury 824 822).

9. "Living in the Promiseland"
Words and Music by David Lynn Jones
Copyright © 1985, Mighty Nice Music/Skunk Deville Music

David Lynn Jones was born on January 15, 1950, in Bexar, Arkansas, where his father was the postmaster of the small town. His grandfather lived there and the Joneses had deep roots in the Arkansas soil. By the mid-1970s, Jones was singing and writing songs that were being noticed beyond Arkansas. Charlie Daniels, the Nashville "long-haired country boy," and Bob Johnston, producer of Bob Dylan's "Nashville Skyline" sessions, helped spread the word of Jones's talent.

In 1980, the news of the Mariel Boatlift caught Jones's attention. The mass migration of Cuban refugees to Florida in flimsy watercraft hit the headlines when it was reported that Cuba's President Fidel Castro had emptied his country's prisons, mixing criminals with the economically desperate. (The Florida governor and President Carter's public political dispute over the desirability of the illegal immigrants helped sink Carter's presidency.)

Jones reflected on America's history and image as a refuge and wrote most of "Living in the Promiseland" in one sitting. He put it away unfinished, but in 1984, Jones finished "Promiseland" in five minutes during a recording session. His new publisher had requested tape copies of all of his songs, finished and unfinished, and one of the session musicians reminded Jones of the song. Jones had forgotten it, but a tape of his material found its way to Bee Spears, Willie Nelson's bass player. Nelson heard and liked the song.

Nelson, along with Neil Young and John Mellencamp, produced Farm Aid in September 1985, a benefit concert for America's farmers. Patterned after Bob Geldof's Live Aid concert, an African famine relief benefit, Farm Aid presented many name acts from the rock, pop, and country fields. Jones sang "Promiseland." The following week, Nelson recorded the song at his Texas studio.

Nelson's recording of the song was released by Columbia Records the following March. By June it was number 1 on the country charts, and went on to sell over 1 million copies. In July 1986, Nelson sang "Promiseland" at the centennial celebration of the *Statue of Liberty*. The stately anthem to immigrant dreams has been used at public ceremonies many times since.

In 1987, Jones recorded his album *Hard Times on Easy Street* for Mercury Records. His version of "Living in the Promiseland" is included. In Jones' reading, the song is a bittersweet, ambiguous hymn reflecting the hope and selfishness in immigrant expectations and the promise and selfishness of our American society.

Farm Aid became a successful annual event and Farm Aid XV was held in September 2002. Appropriate to his connection with

Farm Aid, Jones remains close to his agricultural roots and lives in Arkansas in the house his grandfather owned.

"Living in the Promiseland" is not available in a songbook or song folio, but Willie Nelson's recording is on his CD *Sixteen Biggest Hits* (Columbia 69322). A cover by Joe Cocker is on *Joe Cocker Live* (Capitol CD 93416). David Lynn Jones's recording is out of print.

10. "Walk This Way"
Words and Music by Steven Tyler and Joe Perry
Copyright © 1975, DAKSEL Music

The rap band Run-D.M.C. is considered by some to be the first act to make hardcore rap popular. But, more important than that, they were the first rap act to penetrate the heavy-metal market by using both rap and metal genres in their music. In addition to creating some of the most innovative rap music in our history, their marketing savvy was exceptional.

Joseph Simmons was a young man from the New York borough of Hollis, Queens, who adopted the moniker Run for his stage name. While still in high school, Run met Darryl McDaniel and the two formed the band Run-D.M.C. from their combined nicknames. Soon after the two rappers graduated from high school, they invited Jason Mizell to join them. The trio was managed by Russell Simmons, the brother of Joseph.

After two albums that were modestly successful, Run-D.M.C. hired Russell Simmons and Rick Rubin to coproduce their third album, *Raising Hell*. Russell Simmons, who would later form the tremendously successful rap label Def Jam Records, knew the value of expanding the base of fans for Run-D.M.C. beyond urban African American youths. He also knew that the band Aerosmith was, at the time, one of the top heavy-metal bands in the world. His marketing concept was simple: position Run-D.M.C. with Aerosmith and "hook" their fans.

The production duo of Simmons and Rubin selected an Aerosmith song, "Walk This Way," from the mid-1970s. To make their rap-meets-metal production concept more unusual, they persuaded Aerosmith vocalist Steven Tyler and guitarist Joe Perry to perform on the recording. The resulting song had a sound more refreshing than either act could have created alone and it became the most impressive song from the Run-D.M.C. July 1986 release *Raising Hell.* The Run-D.M.C. version of "Walk This Way" was the first rap video to get MTV airplay. It was also the first rap album (not just single) to go platinum. The final indication that the song had truly crossed genre lines was its position of number 4 on the pop charts in addition to number 1 on the rhythm and blues charts. The crossover appeal of this particular rap album likely helped sales of *Licensed to Ill,* another album released in 1986 by a new all-white rap act, the Beastie Boys.

Although Run-D.M.C. helped eliminate racial lines separating young music consumers much the same way that early rock 'n' roll did, they also bore the brunt of criticism for violence that was gradually becoming associated with rap music. During their "Raising Hell Tour," the media noted that street violence and muggings in New York City had followed a Madison Square Garden performance in the summer of 1986. The violence associated with this and other rap tours caused per capita insurance costs paid by concert promoters to increase at alarming rates. It also generated a great deal of discussion within the music industry about the growing level of violence associated with rap. Run-D.M.C., however, pointed out to police officials that it was gang members, not fans, who were responsible for the postconcert violence. The band asked police, "Why aren't you controlling gangs instead of criticizing us?"

The Run-D.M.C. version of "Walk This Way" is available on the CD *Raising Hell* (Profile Records PRF 16408, 1986).

11. "Homeless"
Words and Music by Paul Simon and Joseph Shabalala
Copyright © 1986, Paul Simon Music

Paul Simon was already a well-known performer and writer, having been half of Simon & Garfunkel ("Sounds of Silence," "Bridge over Troubled Water," and "Mrs. Robinson," from the film *The Graduate*), when, in 1984, a friend gave him a cassette labeled, simply, "Gumboots." The sounds on this tape captivated Simon, but it was several months before he discovered that the music was South African *umbaqanga* (township jive).

Joseph Shabalala, a black man born in Ladysmith, South Africa, moved to coastal Durban as a teenager and worked in a factory. At night, he sang in a local pop group, the Highlanders. In the mid-1960s, he returned to Ladysmith and formed Black Mambazo, an a cappella singing group. Ladysmith Black Mambazo became the premier South African vocal group, and, beginning in 1971, recording artists as well.

South Africa's apartheid government, under President P. W. Botha, was under United Nations (U.N.) sanction for its treatment of blacks. Artists, including musicians, from other countries, were restricted from performing there. Ignoring the political situation, Simon journeyed to Johannesburg in 1985 to meet some of the musicians he had heard on "Gumboots."

Simon was unable to resist the music he heard in South Africa, and renting a recording studio in Johannesburg, he began recording. Concerned with the moral issues, Simon consulted with American friends Quincy Jones and Harry Belafonte as well as with exiled South African musicians Miriam Makeba and Hugh Masekela; all thought his recording project could benefit black South African music.

Paying the African musicians triple scale, as he would New York union musicians, Simon recorded the musical backing tracks before writing the lyrics. He took the tapes to New York for editing and then put his vocals on the songs. The album was called *Graceland*.

One exception to this method was the song "Homeless." Shabalala, who had been careful to present Black Mambazo as apolitical (they had family living in the townships and, therefore, at the mercy of the government's security forces), sang in Zulu about the homeless and the dead. Recorded without instrumental accompaniment, the second half of the song is sung in English by Simon. Shabalala would never publicly comment on the meaning behind the lyrics.

Despite the symbolism of a white New Yorker and black South Africans uniting to produce heartfelt music, *Graceland* and Simon were publicly criticized by U.N. functionaries and some members of the African National Congress. The liberal music press accused him of "ripping off" South African blacks to further his career. The U.N. threatened to put him on a blacklist of musicians who had performed in South Africa.

Simon, normally reclusive, made his case publicly. He went, he said, to South Africa out of love for music, not knowing if commercially viable recordings were possible. All money spent went to black South Africans, not the racist government. Simon was disgusted with those on both sides who were using *Graceland* as a political tool.

Simon received support in his views from Bishop Desmond Tutu and Reverend Allan Boesak of the United Democratic Front. The public gave its support by buying 5 million copies of the album, which won multiple Grammy awards. But, perhaps most telling, is the Zulu nickname given Simon by Shabalala which, rendered in English, is "he who opens doors."

"Homeless" is in print in the *Graceland* folio from Music Sales Publishers, and as a sound recording on *Graceland* (Warner Brothers CD 46430).

12. "Where the Streets Have No Name"
Words and Music by Adam Clayton, David Evans, Paul David Hewson, and Laurence Mullen
Copyright © 1987, Universal Polygram International Publishing, Inc.

Few artists represented the emotions of a generation and decade better than U2 did in the 1980s. The band matured into what might be called the "consciousness of the decade." Their music was spiritual without being preachy. Their songs reflected a concern for contemporary issues, but also presented an aura of optimism. Although other artists sang about social issues, members of U2 were in the foreground of fund-raising for numerous causes such as Greenpeace, Ethiopian Famine Relief, Artists Against Apartheid, and Amnesty International. The band, and its music, will be remembered for helping bring global issues to the forefront in addition to entertaining millions of listeners.

The decade was one of the most disastrous in environmental history. In 1980, President Carter was forced to order the relocation of seven hundred families from the Love Canal area of Niagara Falls, New York. The toxic waste left by the Hooker Chemical Company made the area uninhabitable and caused the federal government to get into the toxic waste cleanup business. Congress created the "Superfund" to help the Environmental Protection Agency pay for cleanup of toxic waste sites in the United States. In 1984, a methyl-icocyanide leak at a Union Carbide Company fertilizer plant in Bhopal, India, caused the deaths of two thousand people. Later, another eight thousand would die of chronic effects caused by the Bhopal disaster. As of 1994, the International Medical Commission of Bhopal estimated that fifty thousand people remained partially or totally disabled as a result of the chemical spill (see the United States Chemical Safety and Hazard Investigation Board under the Web sites section in the Bibliography).

A nuclear reactor exploded in Chernobyl, Ukraine, in 1986 killing thirty-four people almost instantly. Subsequent deaths from the aftereffects of radiation reached forty-two hundred. After scientists from around the world warned of global warming, the United States and twenty-three other countries signed an agreement in 1987 to phase out ozone-depleting chemicals. As the decade came to a close in 1989, the *Exxon Valdez* oil tanker ran aground in Prince William Sound, Alaska. The *Valdez* spilled 11 million gallons of crude oil, devastating the natural environment of the region. These and other environmental issues troubled members of U2.

The band U2 was "born" in 1976 when a high school student named Larry Mullen Jr. placed a note on a bulletin board: "Drummer seeks musicians to form a band." He got responses from Paul Hewson, an aspiring guitarist who was not a great instrumentalist, so the other band mates asked him to sing. Later, when the band saw an advertisement for a hearing aid retailer that read "Bono Vox" (Latin for good voice), Hewson won the moniker "Bono." The two were joined in the band by Adam Clayton on bass, David Evans (nicknamed "The Edge") on guitar and keyboards, and Dick Evans on guitar. Dick Evans, the older brother of The Edge, left the band after less than a year.

The band's form of socially conscious rock was immediately popular in Ireland, but it took a long time for the band to become successful in England and the United States. In 1987, producers Daniel Benoit and Brian Eno helped U2 create *The Joshua Tree*, an album consumed with biblical references. The song "Where the Streets Have No Name" was one of the songs that mixed emotions of disillusionment with those of hope.

The title for the song allegedly came from a disagreement in a small Nicaraguan town that pitted local citizens against government officials. The local population was upset with the local government's decision to create street names in Managua, Nicaragua, where streets had traditionally been described in folklike terminology rather than with modern street names. The Managua dissonance was a symbol of modern government that does not represent the needs of the citizens whom they are charged to protect.

The lyrics of "Where the Streets Have No Name" allude to poison rain and a dust cloud that hides the sunshine. Each stanza seems to challenge the listener to become angry about environmental problems, but, at the same time, accept that there is hope for the future. The lyrics are deceptively simple, but each subsequent listening reveals subtle nuances of meaning that were missed earlier.

The album, released by Island Records in 1987, entered the charts at number 1 in the United Kingdom and was certified platinum after only forty-eight hours, making it the fastest selling album in the history of the United Kingdom. It soon reached the top of U.S. charts and remained at number 1 for nine weeks.

The band filmed a music video for the song "Where the Streets Have No Name" from the rooftop of a building in downtown Los Angeles. The video for the song won a Grammy for Best Music Video and *The Joshua Tree* won a Grammy for Best Rock Performance by a Group or Duo.

The song "Where the Streets Have No Name" is available on the album *The Joshua Tree* (Island Records, 1987, 422-842-298-2U.S.).

13. "Luka"
Words and Music by Suzanne Vega
Copyright © 1987, Suzanne Vega Music/Warner Brothers, Inc.

Suzanne Vega was born in Santa Monica, California, but her family moved to New York City when she was two years old. After receiving a B.A. in anthropology from Barnard College, she began to combine her interests in songwriting, singing, and human behavior. She began performing her neofolk music in Greenwich Village coffeehouses to more cerebral audiences than her pop and rock counterparts. She was quickly discovered by an artist and repertoire executive and signed a contract with A&M Records in 1984.

She completed recording *Suzanne Vega*, her first album for A&M Records, in 1985. It garnered a great deal of praise from critics, but it was not what the industry calls a "hit" album. A&M Records released her second album, *Solitude Standing*, in 1987. One song on the album, "Luka," spoke directly to the issue of child abuse. When the song became a surprise hit, Vega reminded broadcasters and label executives that Americans were interested in social issues of the 1980s just as they had been in the 1960s.

This song helped bring the horror of domestic violence to the attention of the nation. A House Select Committee on Children, Youth and Families, chaired by George Miller, representative from California, had studied the problems of child welfare and domestic violence for several years. In 1986, Miller's committee revealed that between 1981 and 1985, the number of neglected or abused children rose 54.9 percent. Between 1983 and 1985, sexual abuse of children rose 57.4 percent (Rovner 1987). The information collected by the Select Committee helped both the House and the Senate develop nonpartisan reform of the child welfare system.

Suzanne Vega crafted an extremely listenable song about domestic violence and, therefore, was responsible for millions of radio listeners and record buyers learning about a serious social issue. Her gentle-voiced vocal style and nonpreachy attitude lent support to her delivery method. The song "Luka" might best be described as a three-minute sociology lesson that entertains as much as it informs.

"Luka" can be found on Suzanne Vega's *Solitude Standing* (A&M Records CD 215-136, 1987).

14. "Girl You Know It's True"
Words and Music by Bill Pettaway Jr., Sean Spencer, Kevin Lyles, Rodney Hollaman, and Ky Adeyemo
Copyright © 1989, MCA/Two Pieters

By 1989, the image of a recording artist became a primary factor in their success. German producer Frank Farian was well aware of that fact when he invited Rob Pilatus and Fabrice Morvan, two handsome break-dancers, to a recording studio in Frankfurt to discuss a deal wherein they would dance on one of his videos. As the conversation progressed, Farian realized the potential the duo had as recording artists who could dance in their own videos. He played the young men a song that he described as a demo and asked them if they could sing it. As quickly as they answered yes, Farian invited the duo into a scheme of deception that deceived the public and many industry insiders.

Farian used singers Charles Shaw, John Davis, and Brad Howe on the album and let the two attractive dancers perform in videos and onstage under the name Milli Vanilli. They used a technique, called "lip syncing," to deceive concert audiences. Although Pilatus and Morvan sang every note of the songs as they were dancing, their voices were not channeled through the speaker system at concerts. Instead, the live-sound engineers fed prerecorded tracks through the system.

The most deceptive part of the overall scheme was that Farian allegedly never told the record label that Pilatus and Morvan did not sing a note on the album nor in live performances (it is not unusual for performers to lip-sync on videos). The plan worked and Milli Vanilli became a worldwide success, due in large part to their entertaining videos and exciting concerts.

The first Milli Vanilli hit, "Girl You Know It's True," entered the charts on January 7, 1989. The album it was on, *All or Nothing*, continued to garner hit single slots on the charts, three of which peaked at number 1, and spent an astonishing seventy-eight weeks on the top pop albums chart and held the number 1 slot for eight nonconsecutive weeks. After consuming a tremendous amount of video and radio airplay, Milli Vanilli was a household name. Arista Records, home to the duo, eventually sold 10 million copies of the debut album. But the best recognition of their success was winning the Grammy for Best New Artist.

Not everyone thought as highly of the album as did consumers. In 1989, *Rolling Stone* magazine voted Milli Vanilli the worst band of the year and *All or Nothing* the worst album. Rumors began to circulate that Pilatus and Morvan were not the true singers on their recordings. One of the real singers revealed to the media that he had sung the lead vocal on one of the recordings, but later recanted his statement. But critics eventually began to wonder if the dancers were lip-syncing at concerts the same way they did when shooting their videos.

The band slid down the ladder of success as quickly as they had climbed it. On November 14, 1990, Farian held a press conference at which he admitted that Pilatus and Morvan did not sing on their own album. Five days later, Michael Greene, executive director of the National Academy of Recording Arts and Sciences, announced that his organization would ask Milli Vanilli to return their Grammy Award.

The toll of being publicly humiliated and ridiculed in the press took its toll on Rob Pilatus. In 1991, he attempted suicide. In 1996, he was convicted on eight counts of assault and battery and ordered into a substance abuse program. Regrettably, his problems with substance abuse continued. He was found dead in a Frankfurt, Germany, hotel in 1998 and his death was attributed to consumption of both drugs and alcohol.

Although recording industry executives were quick to condemn Milli Vanilli and their producer for deception, they have done little to reverse the trend of artists who allegedly lip-sync in concerts. The pressure for artists to promote their recordings through music video programs such as BET, MTV, VH1, and CMT continues to affect the types of artists that labels sign to recording contracts.

The song "Girl You Know It's True" can be found on the original album *All or Nothing* (Arista 8592).

15. "Break It on Down" (from *As Nasty As They Wanna Be*)
Words and Music by Luther Campbell, David Hobbs, Mark Ross, and Chris Wongwon
Copyright © 1989, Skyywalker Records; 1996, Little Joe Records

Luke Skyywalker, born Luther Campbell, formed the rap band 2 Live Crew and helped establish a subgenre of rap. His name will likely be associated with the history of music forever, but for reasons other than his talent in the studio and onstage. Luther Campbell, his record company Skyywalker Records, and his band 2 Live Crew will be remembered for the legal battles that carried them to the Supreme Court.

As rap music moved from its New York roots across the continent, a style called "Miami bass" emerged in southern Florida. The subgenre is best known for its fast dance tempos and exaggerated heavy bass sounds. The booming bass of Miami bass CDs quickly became popular with youths, eager to show off their car stereo systems.

Miami bass met with resistance from adults as quickly as it was born. City officials hurried to pass local noise ordinances to discourage the loud thumping bass sounds emerging from vehicles cruising Florida streets. Because the music was ripe for dancing, and later influenced a genre called "techno," Miami bass has always felt like party music. As one might expect, the lyrics began to reflect the "anything goes" atmosphere of beachside dances during spring break or street parties.

The party lyrics of Miami bass often sounded misogynistic and blatantly sexual. The sexual allusions and foul language of Miami bass were pushed to extremes when 2 Live Crew released *As Nasty As They Wanna Be* in 1986. The album was rereleased in 1989 by Skyywalker Records. The titles and lyrics of some songs on the album sound like comedic attempts to shock listeners. The song "Break It on Down" is one of the cleanest, but most honest, songs on the album. The rappers explain, in blunt language, that listeners who don't like their lyrics should leave the area. As the band found out, legal authorities did not like what they were saying, nor did they take their advice and leave.

In 1989, Mick Navarro, sheriff of Broward County, Florida, began to collect evidence to prove his assertion that *As Nasty As They Wanna Be* was obscene. He bought a copy of the CD and had the lyrics transcribed. He then took the typed lyrics and an affidavit to a state judge who declared the lyrics obscene. Furthermore, he determined that the sale of the CD was a criminal offense. Thus began the first case in which songwriters were arrested on charges of creating obscene lyrics.

The controversy progressed to the U.S. District Court for the Southern District of Florida, Fort Lauderdale Division. On June 6, 1990, the court decided that members of 2 Live Crew had indeed created obscene material and released it on their album. The district court relied on a previous Supreme Court decision that defined obscenity as something that a typical person, using community standards, would find is designed to stir sexual arousal, depict sex in a patently offensive manner, or if the work lacks artistic, literary, political, or scientific value. After applying the test established by the Supreme Court, the district court found that *As Nasty As They Wanna Be* was obscene.

Testifying for 2 Live Crew, Henry Louis Gates Jr., a professor of English at Duke University, explained that the music in question was similar to "signifying," a verbal form of complimenting or insulting someone that dates to the days of slavery. Furthermore, it is a way of releasing anger or tension, not a literal insult to females or others. Defense attorneys also alluded to the racial bias of the police when they revealed that there were two adult bookstores within one block of the police station that had not been subjected to the same treatment as the band had for selling allegedly obscene material.

Upon appeal to the U.S. Court of Appeals for the Eleventh Circuit, 2 Live Crew prevailed. The court determined that the lower court incorrectly applied the test for determining obscenity. The court also believed that the recording was, by itself, not sufficient to determine if the work had (or lacked) serious artistic, scientific, literary, or political value.

If this legal battle were not enough for one artist's career, Luther Campbell was sued by Lucasfilms, Inc., owned by the award-winning filmmaker George Lucas. Attorneys for Lucasfilms alleged that Luther Campbell diminished the value of the name Luke Skyywalker, a character in the film *Star Wars*, because of the controversy surrounding the band 2 Live Crew. Although Lucasfilms initially asked for $300 million in this trademark infringement case, it was settled out of court for an undisclosed amount.

Although Luther Campbell and 2 Live Crew no doubt breathed a sigh of relief after their trademark and First Amendment struggles, they had a third legal issue that again ended in the Supreme Court. In 1989, 2 Live Crew created a parody of "Pretty Woman," a song written by Roy Orbison and William Dees. The parody was titled "Ugly Woman" and it offended Acuff–Rose, the publisher of the original song. Acuff–Rose filed a copyright infringement lawsuit, but a federal district court in Nashville ruled in favor of 2 Live Crew. Acuff–Rose appealed the decision to the Sixth Circuit Court of Appeals in Cincinnati, which reversed the lower court decision. 2 Live Crew, in turn, appealed the case to the U.S. Supreme Court. The Supreme Court ruled in favor of 2 Live Crew and described their right to create a parody under the fair-use exemption of U.S. copyright laws.

Although 2 Live Crew can be credited with helping popularize Miami bass, they will probably be better known as the band that is cited more often in legal history than music history.

"Break It on Down" is available on *As Nasty As They Wanna Be* by 2 Live Crew (Little Joe Records, catalog number 107; UPC 22471010722).

1990–2000

The End of the
Second Millennium

The last decade of the century was also the last decade of the second millennium. Somewhat symbolically, it was a decade of contrasts: incremental social gains at the same time that many types of violence increased; an end to the Cold War and an escalation of conflict in the Middle East; and a president who helped establish a strong economy but ended his term in office with shame and controversy.

As the administration of George Herbert Walker Bush came to an end, the economy was in appalling shape for a major world power. In 1991, unemployment had reached 6.1 percent, the new budget was $1,446 billion, and, most distressing, the federal budget deficit was $280.9 billion. A year later, the projected deficit had rapidly increased to $352 billion.

Public displeasure with the economy helped make the 1992 presidential election a hotly contested one. H. Ross Perot, a billionaire from Texas, ran as an independent candidate and received the largest percentage of votes any third-party candidate has ever garnered. William Jefferson Clinton, the handsome former governor of Arkansas, was elected president with only 43 percent of the vote. Bill Clinton and his vice president, former Tennessee Senator Albert Gore, brought their dreams of liberal social programs to the White House.

The economy improved throughout the Clinton years. By 1999, the economy was stronger than it had been in many years, but controversies surrounding financial dealings of the first lady and the president continued throughout the entire Clinton administration. Over the next several years, investigations of the Clintons' financial connections to a questionable business enterprise called "Whitewater" generated numerous investigations and hearings. Even during formal impeachment hearings, however, Clinton's already high job approval rating continued to climb. A CNN/*USA Today* poll released on December 12, 1998, indicated that Clinton was the most admired man in America. Pope John Paul II was second. But it is likely that Bill Clinton will be remembered more for his affair with his twenty-one-year-old intern Monica Lewinsky than his success in rebuilding the nation's economy.

In 1990, Saddam Hussein, leader of Iraq, marshaled troops and invaded Kuwait. In preparation for war in the region, and to help protect our interests in Middle East oil, George Bush, president at the time, sent U.S. troops to Saudi Arabia. The United States, backed by the United Nations, set a January 15, 1991, deadline for Iraqi troops to withdraw from Kuwait. After Saddam Hussein ignored threats, the United States launched several hours of air strikes before sending ground troops into Iraq. The dramatic nighttime air strikes were broadcast live to an amazed audience back in the United States. After alleged violations of the 1991 Gulf War Peace Agreement, Clinton ordered U.S. troops into a second brief war—this time three days—against Iraq in 1998.

While the United States faced new enemies in the Middle East, their old nemesis, the USSR, began to crumble. In 1991, Mikhail Gorbachev resigned as leader of the USSR. As the former Soviet Union began to separate into independent countries, the Cold War came to an end.

This was also a decade that will be remembered for several vicious acts of violence in the United States. Terrorists set off a bomb at the World Trade Center in New York in 1993 that killed six people. (The World Trade Center would become the site of a second, more devastating, act of terrorism on September 11, 2001.) Two terrorists, angry at the federal government, bombed the Alfred P. Murrah building in Oklahoma City in 1995. Their act killed 168 people, including 19 children who were in a day care center housed in the building. Ted Kaczynski, referred to as the "Unabomber," had mailed sixteen bombs over an eighteen-year period. His terrorist acts killed three people and injured twenty-three before the reclusive Kacyznski was captured in 1997.

Celebration of the 1996 Centennial Olympics in Atlanta was disrupted when a bomb exploded in Centennial Park injuring many people. As the decade drew to a close, two high school students, Eric Harris and Dylan Klebold, shot and killed twelve students, a teacher and themselves on April 20, 1999, at Columbine High School in Littleton, Colorado. These, and other acts of violence, reminded the people of the United States that warfare takes many forms. Although the nation had become accustomed to domestic tranquility, a hard lesson was learned during this decade that violence is no stranger to America.

As the 1990s began, Nelson Mandela was freed in South Africa after being held in prison for twenty-seven years. His freedom served as a metaphor for progress in several areas of civil rights in the United States. Janet Reno was appointed to the post of attorney general, the first female to hold that position. Clinton implemented a controversial policy called "Don't Ask, Don't Tell," thereby allowing gays and lesbians to serve in the military for the first time. And to encourage African American males to become better fathers and community leaders, Louis Farrakhan began an annual event called the "Million Man March" on October 16, 1995, in Washington, D.C.

A computer network called the "Internet," developed in 1969 to help university researchers transfer information to one another, emerged into a worldwide web that helped transform the U.S. economy into a truly global one. The term *E-mail* became a part of everyday language and surfing the 'Net became a national pastime, just like baseball. But as the computerized world looked forward to celebrating the new millennium, computer scientists discovered a serious problem. In the early days of computing, programmers tended to abbreviate the year with two digits in order to save computer memory. The typical computerized forms had 19__, with only two spaces for the year. As the year 2000 (2K) approached, all computer-controlled devices and systems needed to be converted. The dilemma was called the "Y2K bug" and computer technicians scrambled to make computers Y2K compliant. Governments around the world spent billions of dollars to prepare for Y2K; authors wrote books on how to prepare for new millennium crises; and many people prepared for a disruption of municipal services by stockpiling food, water, and fuel. Fortunately, as the illuminated globe descended on Times Square in New York, utilities still worked and Dick Clark's New Year's Eve telecast welcomed in the new millennium without any Y2K gremlins.

SONGS

1. "From a Distance"
Words and Music by Julie Gold
Copyright © 1991, Julie Gold's Music/Irving Music, Inc.

On January 17, 1991, after excruciating months of buildup, a coalition of forces led by the United States began a devastating attack on Iraq and its forces in northern Kuwait, the scene of a recent Iraqi invasion. Operation Desert Shield had become Operation Desert Storm, later known as the Gulf War. Americans were transfixed by minute-by-minute coverage of the destruction as "smart bombs" rained down, and marveled at the awesome power of their military. Broadcast news organizations created special logos and sets for their coverage and competed for the most compelling stories. The nation had been introduced to televised warfare in Vietnam, but that was a slogging war in jungles and rice paddies, while this was a high-tech, seemingly surgical operation. The war was over in less than two months with only 148 American deaths.

Two immensely popular songs emerged as part of the national response to the war. Lee Greenwood's "God Bless the USA" was standard flag-waving patriotic fare. More subtle was "From a Distance," a gospel-tinged song recorded by Bette Midler shortly before the troops were mobilized. Nancy Griffith had done a low-key acoustic version that was a favorite among her fans, but it was Midler's version that would become the most requested song on Armed Forces Radio while the troops were in the desert, and would bring consolation to their families at home, where it was the top request for radio dedications.

Julie Gold was still a secretary at HBO when she wrote "From a Distance." She had written many songs by then, but this one was special. In the winter of 1986, her parents had shipped her piano to New York for her thirtieth birthday. For nine years she had been making do with inexpensive electronic keyboards. The movers warned her not to play the piano until it had come to room temperature, she recalled, "then 12 hours later, when I finally played it, I wrote 'From a Distance.' It took a very short time, but I believe I had been writing that song for my entire life" (Business Wire 1991).

Music critic Stephen Holden knew the song and suggested it to Midler, who made it the first single on her album *Some People's Lives*. Her faith in the song paid off when it went to number 1 on the adult contemporary chart and number 2 on the pop chart, while the album achieved double-platinum sales figures. At the time, Midler was still enjoying the success of "Wind beneath My Wings" and its parent movie *Beaches*. That song had won the Grammy as Song of the Year for 1989, and "Distance" would do the same for 1990.

The curious thing about "From a Distance" was that listeners could find a variety of messages in its extensive lyrics. A repeated refrain reminding us that a higher power watches over us was interpreted by many to mean that God was protecting America's soldiers, which surely was the reason that families of soldiers became so attached to the song. But other lyrics that described war as uncomprehensible and questioned its purpose were perceived to be essentially antiwar in nature. For either group, Midler's strong, soaring voice, and the highly evocative lyrics combined to deliver an emotional punch.

"From a Distance" is available on Midler's *Divine Collection* (Atlantic CD 82497). It is available in several choral arrangements, as well as a basic piano vocal (Hal Leonard 02504161).

2. "Cop Killer"
Words and Music by Tracy Marrow and Ernest Cunnigan
Copyright © 1992, Rhyme Syndicate Music/Ernkeesea Music,
c/o Polygram International Publishing

Rap artist Ice-T (born Tracy Marrow) is often associated with the subgenre of rap called "gangsta rap." His 1987 debut album *Rhyme Pays* helped establish a Los Angeles presence in the world of rap. Lyrics of early Ice-T rap songs tended to elaborate on gang violence, sex, and drugs in the inner city, using his rhyming skills to describe urban life with journalistic accuracy. As he matured as an artist, he ventured into social and political themes for his raps.

In the summer of 1991, Ice-T and Body Count, the heavy-metal band that backed him, joined *Lollapalooza*, a multiact tour. At each show, Ice-T performed "Cop Killer," a song that was obviously intended to show disdain for members of law enforcement. After the tour ended in the fall, Body Count began work on a self-titled album. Before that album was completed, Ice-T revised the lyrics of "Cop Killer" to include a reference to Rodney King, the victim of what many Americans felt was police brutality.

On March 3, 1991, a bystander with a videotape recorder captured footage of four Los Angeles Police Department officers kicking and hitting Rodney King. The owner of the videotape attempted to give it to the police, thinking that officials would investigate the possibility of police abuse. However, he was ignored by the person with whom he spoke. He then took the videotape to a Los Angeles television station and an edited version of the tape was soon airing on every television station in the nation.

The album *Body Count* was released in late March 1992. It entered the Billboard pop album chart at number 32 on April 18. Although it was difficult for Sire/Warner Brothers to market the album—it was not really heavy metal or rap and radio stations would not broadcast it because it contained profanity—it remained on the charts until the end of June. But "Cop Killer" incited a firestorm of anger directed at the band and its label Sire/Warner Brothers.

On June 11, 1992, local and statewide law enforcement associations in Texas held a press conference at which spokespersons announced their campaign to pressure Warner Brothers into removing "Cop Killer" from all future albums. Within days, organizations representing police in California and New York joined the campaign against Warner Brothers. Soon, politicians, including President Bush, made public statements criticizing the record label for releasing "Cop Killer." Bowing to pressure, hundreds of stores across the nation pulled *Body Count* from their shelves. On July 28, Ice-T held his own press conference and told the media that he had decided to remove "Cop Killer" from all future copies of the album.

On April 29, 1992, an all-white jury acquitted three of the police officers who had beaten Rodney King. The jury's decision came at the worst time for residents of South Central Los Angeles. Two weeks after the Rodney King beating, a fifteen-year-old girl was shot in the back of the head by a Korean store owner who mistakenly thought that she was stealing. The store owner was, in some people's minds, not punished because he was convicted of manslaughter, but set free on probation.

During this same time, unemployment in the South Central Los Angeles area was extremely high and many African American residents resented immigrants, especially Latinos and Asians. By the time the jury found three officers not guilty in the Rodney King incident, South Central Los Angeles was like dry kindling ready to burst into flames, and the news of the acquittals ignited the tense inner city. Hundreds of residents rioted, causing the deaths of fifty-four people and injuring more than two thousand others. More than eight hundred buildings in South Central Los Angeles were burned and damage was estimated at $900 million.

Some critics of Ice-T believe that "Cop Killer" contributed to the atmosphere of tension that resulted in the riots. Others theorize that Ice-T was merely a journalist who saw the tension before the general population did.

"Cop Killer" is on the original *Body Count* album (Sire/Warner) but it is out of print. The lyrics are available on several Web sites.

3. "We Shall Be Free"
Words and Music by Garth Brooks and Stephanie Davis
Copyright © 1992, Major Bob Music/No Fences Music

"We Shall Be Free" may seem an odd choice to represent Garth Brooks's dominant presence in American music during the 1990s, but it demonstrated the new social consciousness that had migrated into country music, a genre that had often been dominated by "drinkin' and cheatin'" types of songs. When the song was released in 1992, it stalled out at number 12 on the country chart, when almost every other Brooks single to that point had gone to number 1. Just five years into his career, he already had a pattern of CD sales and concert attendance that gave him unprecedented power as an artist on Nashville's Music Row.

It seemed that everything Brooks did was huge. He drew more than two hundred thousand fans to a free concert in Central Park. He staged television specials with astonishing special effects. In 2000, he became the first solo artist in any genre to be certified for sales of 100 million albums. He had enough pull with parent label EMI to depose Scott Hendricks, the chief executive officer of Capitol Nashville, and to dictate the release date of his albums over label objections.

Garth Brooks came to Nashville from Oklahoma in 1987, after following his mother's advice to finish college first, and brought with him a strong voice, roaring ambition, prodigious energy, and a keen business sense. The following year he was signed by Capitol, which released his first album in 1989 with an immediate number 1 hit, "If Tomorrow Never Comes." His choice of "We Shall Be Free" as the first track on his fifth album, *The Chase*, demonstrated his willingness to take on issues and risk making his core country audience uncomfortable. Brooks was motivated to write the song (with help from Nashville tunesmith Stephanie Davis) after hearing a statement made by Rodney King. In the midst of the riots in South Central Los Angeles, King uttered his famous plea for reason, asking plaintively, "Can we all get along?"

For "We Shall Be Free," a hopeful, gospel-like song, Brooks used a soaring choir behind lyrics that covered the waterfront: advocating clean air and water, rights for homosexuals, relief from poverty, religious freedom, and a perfect state in which race is no longer a factor in society. Brooks was clearly signaling his intent to alter the course of country music and, hopefully, raise a new social awareness in traditional country music listeners. Putting the move in context, one critic noted that "it was only four years ago that Hank Williams Jr. delighted cave dwellers with his 'If The South Woulda Won'" (Morris 1992, 40). "We Shall Be Free" is available in choral arrangement through Hal Leonard (08200092) and on Brooks's album *The Chase* (Capitol CD 30121).

4. "(The) River of Dreams"
Words and Music by William "Billy" Joel
Copyright © 1993, Impulsive Music

Billy Joel's lyrics, like those of Bruce Springsteen, described concerns of working-class people, including memories of growing up, family issues, and the "old neighborhood." In addition to his songs, his personal life reflected the dreams of a blue-collar hero—someone who fought for his rights, no matter how powerful the foe. His first wave of fans, dubbed "baby boomers," remained loyal as they matured. And as boomers taught their children and grandchildren to appreciate the music of Billy Joel, his fan base continued to grow throughout the last three decades of the century.

Joel quit high school a few weeks before graduation so that he could pursue his passion for music. In 1967, he joined the Echoes, an ensemble that emulated bands of the British Invasion, such as the Beatles. He soon left that band and joined the Hassels, another short-lived rock band. His next attempt at success was a duo called Attila, but it too failed miserably. Joel then turned to writing reviews of rock music and composing advertising music.

In 1971, Billy Joel entered into a production and record label deal that proved to be the first of many sour business relationships in his career. He did not realize that the contract he signed with Family Productions bound him for life to its parent company Ripp. After Family Productions/Ripp released Joel's first album, *Cold Spring Harbor*, the label and production company encountered financial problems. Their unstable business footing made it impossible to release a second album, yet Joel remained bound to his legal agreement.

Joel adopted the pseudonym Bill Miller and began a six-month engagement as a pianist/singer in a hotel lounge. It was during this period that he discovered ideas for some of his most meaningful songs, such as "Piano Man." He then began to travel, performing shows around the country.

When a Columbia Records (later Columbia/Sony Music) executive heard Joel's live recording of "Captain Jack" on a Philadelphia radio station in 1973, he offered Joel a recording contract. To sign Joel, however, Columbia had to buy him out of his agreement with Family Productions. Although many of Joel's business relationships ended in the courtroom, his affiliation with Columbia/Sony Music remained firm for the remainder of the century and into the next millennium.

Joel's career became increasingly successful with each album he released, but sour business relationships continued to plague his life. He began one of the industry's most contentious and extended legal battles in 1989 when he charged his former manager and brother-in-law Frank Weber with fraud, breach of fiduciary duty and federal racketeering statute violations.

After prevailing in his suit against Weber, Joel became determined to continue on his Quixotic quest for restitution from others who he felt had violated his trust. He filed lawsuits against an accounting firm who he alleged helped Weber, Weber's attorney Frank Conforti, and his former attorney Alan Grubman. In an attempt to calm Joel's legal storms, Columbia/Sony Music agreed to pay him $3 million to settle his dispute with Grubman.

Obviously, as Billy Joel matured, so did his audience. Millions of baby boomers, persons born during the post–World War II baby boom between 1946 and the early 1960s, had watched their children grow and their careers develop. By the early 1990s, boomers were, because of their stage in life, more able to purchase records and concert tickets than younger adults. Joel's fan base, represented by this powerful demographic cohort, helped make his concert tours some of the most successful in the history of live entertainment.

As many adults do when they enter their forties, Joel began to reflect on his life. He also pondered the universal question of what happens after we die. In 1993, he wrote "(The) River of Dreams," a deceptively simple song that revealed his concern for this topic. In the song, Joel alludes to someone who is not overly religious, but thinks about the afterlife. The lyrics also emphasize a search, like that of Siddhartha, for something we think eludes us. "(The) River of Dreams" appeared to be Joel's attempt to articulate his need, like the boomers who fell in love with this song, to find some meaning and resolution to years of struggles to establish a career. It apparently touched a nerve in his fans: the album on which it was included, *River of Dreams*, was released August 10, 1993, and sold over 3 million copies by the end of the year. By the end of the decade, the album had sold 5 million copies. "(The) River of Dreams" helped define Joel as the spokesperson of baby boomers.

The recording of "(The) River of Dreams" is available on the Billy Joel album *River of Dreams* (Columbia Records Col TNK 67347) and sheet music is available in *Billy Joel Greatest Hits, Vol. III* (Hal Leonard 306191).

5. "Streets of Philadelphia"
Words and Music by Bruce Springsteen
Copyright © 1993, Bruce Springsteen

In 1981, health scientists began reporting a wasting disease that gradually eroded its victim's health, usually resulting in death. It was named Acquired Immune Deficiency Syndrome, or AIDS, and it killed by breaking down the body's ability to fight off other opportunistic diseases, such as pneumonia, tuberculosis, and certain cancers. Because it was both sexually transmitted and blood borne, it spread quickly among promiscuous gay men and drug addicts. For a time it seemed the "normal" heterosexual world would not be affected, but that confidence was misplaced. By 1993, AIDS had infected 340,000 Americans and killed nearly two-thirds of them. It most often struck down people in the prime of life and was the leading cause of death among young men aged twenty-five to forty-four.

It did not take long for the disease to become a subject for plays, stories, and a couple of minor movies, but it was Jonathan Demme who first attempted a major film. He was enjoying the success of *Silence of the Lambs* and looking for another powerful story to direct. He chose one about a high-powered young, gay lawyer (Tom Hanks) who contracted AIDS and was then dismissed from his firm after the disease was recognized.

The somewhat predictable courtroom fight for justice drove home both the reality of discrimination against homosexuals and the distaste of the healthy for the sick. Only after *Philadelphia* had been shot did Demme go looking for a few songs. He turned to Bruce Springsteen, an unmistakably heterosexual male who was famous both as a rebellious rocker and a social activist. Springsteen agreed to give it a try and quickly turned out a song alone in his home studio, which he sent off as a demo tape to get Demme's reaction.

Demme loved the song, used it exactly as it arrived, playing it over opening images of bustling daily life in the City of Brotherly Love while its lyrics intoned, "Oh brother are you going to leave me wasting away on the streets of Philadelphia?" The same skeletal version was later released as a single from the soundtrack album.

The song was not classic Springsteen, full of macho guitar or personal bravado. Instead, its brooding delivery mourned loss and acknowledged fear, mirroring the mood of a country that now understood it would be dealing with the epidemic for decades to come. For "The Boss," the song came at a time when he needed new direction after nearly twenty years on the rock charts.

"Streets of Philadelphia" garnered four Grammy's and an Oscar for Best Original Song, ironically beating out Neil Young's "Philadelphia," which had closed the film. In accepting his Oscar, Springsteen said, "You do your best work and you hope that . . . some piece of it spills over into the real world" (Sandford 1999, 348).

"Streets of Philadelphia" is available in print in *Bruce Springsteen: Greatest Hits* (Warner Brothers PF 9541) and on the *Philadelphia* soundtrack (Sony CD 57624).

6. "One of Us"
Words and Music by Eric Bazilian
Copyright © 1995, Human Boy Music

As the twentieth century began to wane, the line between religious and popular music, which began blurring in the 1930s, was erased with the release of a song written by an agnostic, Jewish-born, Quaker-raised, rock and roller from Philadelphia. Eric Bazilian was born in Philadelphia in 1953. His mother had played the piano professionally, and Eric played the instrument in the family home. In 1972, at the University of Pennsylvania, Bazilian met Rob Hyman with whom he would form the band the Hooters several years later.

The Hooters achieved modest success, but Bazilian found his stride when, in 1983, a former classmate turned record producer, Rick Chertoff, hired Eric and Rob to arrange and play on recordings of one of his artists, Cyndi Lauper. They helped Lauper create the songs "She's So Unusual," "Time after Time," and "Girls Just Want to Have Fun," all of which became big hits for her.

Ten years later, producer Chertoff, on Rob Hyman's recommendation, signed Kentucky-born (July 8, 1962) singer Joan Osborne to his label. Again, Bazilian and Hyman were called to the studio to cowrite, arrange, and play on her album *Relish*. The sessions were progressing and Chertoff and the others were enthusiastic about Osborne's big, bluesy voice and the songs being written for it. Then, as Bazilian told *Musician* magazine, "One night my wife and I had just seen *The Making of Sgt. Pepper*, and she was intrigued by the multitrack recording process. She wanted me to record something for her on my four-track Portastudio" (1996, 16). With nothing in particular in mind, Bazilian recorded a guitar riff, bass and drum parts, and an electric piano part. Upon hearing the instrumental track, Bazilian's wife, Sara, asked him to "sing it." Again, with nothing in mind, Bazilian punched the record button and "heard a voice. . . . It was going 'If God has a name. . . .' I thought, Okay, I'll go with that. . . . The verses all came out in one take, totally stream of consciousness" (ibid.).

The next day, Bazilian took his tape to the studio to play for Chertoff as entertainment only. The producer asked Osborne if she could sing it, and she thought she could. Chertoff coaxed an innocent, girlish performance from the artist and they recorded the song that afternoon.

"One of Us" poses questions about the nature of divinity. If humans are made in God's image, what if God really was like us. As Bazilian told *Musician*, "I've always wondered: If I saw a miracle, would that mean I would have to believe all of it, the whole story about Jesus and the saints and prophets?" (ibid.).

Released as a single by Mercury Records two weeks before Christmas 1995, "One of Us" shot up the charts and was nominated for a Grammy as Song of the Year. Agnostics heard irony in the song; evangelicals heard a call back to the original message of the Jesus who associated with common folk; the record-buying public heard a catchy pop melody.

"One of Us" is in various Warner Brothers' folios including *1997 Top of the Charts*. The original recording is on the Joan Osborne album *Relish* (Blue Gorilla/Mercury CD 526 699).

7. "Only God Can Judge Me"
Word and Music by Tupac Amaru Shakur
Copyright © 1996, Death Row Records/Interscope

Tupac Amaru Shakur raps about his own demise, as a physician attends to his bullet wounds, in his recording of "Only God Can Judge

Me." The act Rappin 4-Tay, support artists on the recording, rap about finding vengeance on the street, because courts are no help. These lyrics were an eerie prophecy, because a few months after the song was released, Tupac Shakur died of gunshot wounds from an unknown assailant. Despite many theories about the possible assassin, police have never charged anyone with the slaying.

Tupac was the son of Alice Faye Williams, a political activist in the Black Panther Party, who later changed her name to Afeni Shakur. Tupac Amaru, named after an Inca Indian chief, was born on June 16, 1971, in New York City. Even as a child, Tupac was surrounded by role models who fell from grace with the law.

His mother, while eight months pregnant with Tupac, stood trial with twenty other members of the Black Panther Party on charges of conspiracy to blow up several buildings in New York City. She was acquitted of the charges and soon gave birth to a young man who could conceivably have done anything in the world of music, due to his natural talent. Afeni Shakur gave birth to a daughter, Sekyiwa, when Tupac was two. A few months before her birth, Sekyiwa's father, Mutulu, was sentenced to sixty years in prison for robbing an armored car.

Although Tupac might have emerged from his stressful environment through his success in the music industry, he chose instead to wed his music alter ego, 2PAC, to the violent thug persona of gangsta rap. He entered the world of rap music as a dancer in the band Digital Underground. His first solo album, *2pacalypse NOW*, was a commercial success and it garnered good reviews. Tupac was clearly established as rap star with just one album.

His subsequent albums were successful and his charisma and good looks caught the attention of Hollywood casting agents. He appeared in several films, including *Juice*, *Poetic Justice*, and *Above the Rim*. The street-hardened character he played in film and on the concert stage spilled over to real life when he assaulted the Hughes brothers, directors of the film *Menace II Society*, for firing him.

Media reports of Tupac's behavior were soon more about his brushes with the law than his music. He was charged with shooting two off-duty police officers in Atlanta in 1993. That same year, he was charged with sexually assaulting a woman at a hotel in New York. While on his way to a recording studio in New York in 1994,

Tupac was robbed and shot five times. While serving a prison sentence in 1995 for his sexual assault conviction, his label released *Me against the World*, an album title that described his attitude at the time. The album entered the pop charts at number 1 and generated a top 10 single position for the song "Dear Mamma." Less than a year later, Shakur released *All Eyez on Me*, a two-CD set that contained the song "Only God Can Judge Me." The double album reached number 1 on both the Billboard 200 and the rhythm and blues/hip-hop albums charts.

The gangsta life he rapped about in his music became tragic reality on Saturday, September 8, 1996, when the car that Tupac Shakur and Marion "Suge" Knight, chairman of Death Row Records, were riding in became the target of gunfire. Knight survived the attack, but Tupac died. Like a mystic describing the future, Tupac told us in the song "Only God Can Judge Me" that he would die a violent death, perhaps by those he called friends.

"Only God Can Judge Me" is available on *All Eyez on Me* (Death Row Records/Interscope, 314-524204-2).

8. "Change the World"
Words and Music by Tommy Sims, Gordon Kennedy, and
Wayne Kirkpatrick
Copyright © 1996, BMG Songs, Inc./Universal MCA Music
Publishing/Universal Polygram International Publishing, Inc.

Like many many events of the decade, "Change the World" was the result of several chance occurrences. The positive and uplifting tone of both the song and the film that promoted it were, however, quite representative of the late 1990s mood in America: life is good.

Nashville songwriters Tommy Sims, Gordon Kennedy, and Wayne Kirkpatrick had strong roots in contemporary Christian music, a genre that had emerged as popular music with a positive message by the late 1990s. Although the three successful songwriters knew one another, they had never written as a three-person team before.

Sims brought the basic idea for the song, along with a basic melody and title, to Kennedy and Kirkpatrick and asked if they would like to collaborate on the song. Kirkpatrick took Sims's music and wrote lyrics for the chorus and most of the second verse. He then passed the song to Kennedy, who wrote the remaining lyrics and some additional music. Finally, they returned the song to Sims, its originator, and he produced a demo recording.

This odd chain-letter manner of writing a song, although unorthodox, worked. Tony Brown, president of MCA Records Nashville, heard the demo and asked to use it on the next album for Wynnona Judd, a country artist with a rhythm and blues influence. "Change the World" appeared on Wynnona's *Revelations* album.

A short time later, Kathy Nelson, a music coordinator for Disney's film division, was looking for songs to use in *Phenomenon*, a film that would star John Travolta. She met with Tony Brown and, after listening to several songs, heard "Change the World." She did not, however, want a country version of the song. Instead, she wanted a smooth rhythm and blues/pop sound.

The hottest producer of pop rhythm and blues at the time was Babyface (born Kenneth Edmonds). Babyface was the most sought after singer, producer, and musician in the 1990s. Nelson wanted him to produce the song using Eric Clapton as singer and guitarist. The combination of Babyface's contemporary production techniques, Clapton's listenable blue-eyed soul, and a spirit-lifting song worked miraculously well. Ironically, this blend of artist, producer, and song would in all likelihood never have happened if the song were under the direction of a typical record label artist and repertoire team.

The Miramax film *Phenomenon*, released July 3, 1996, had an extremely strong cast including John Travolta, Forest Whitaker, and Robert Duvall. It was definitely a feel-good movie for the time period. The primary character, played by Travolta, mysteriously begins to develop remarkable gifts, such as telekinetic powers and accelerated learning skills. As the character develops his special talents, he becomes increasingly compassionate and optimistic. And as others are affected by his excitement for life, he dreams of changing the world for the better.

The single "Change the World" was released on July 25, 1996, and reached gold sales status on September 12, 1996. It won Grammy Awards for Song of the Year and Record of the Year.

The recording is available as a seven-inch single (Reprise 7-17621). The sheet music is available through Hal Leonard (00351364).

9. "Stomp"
Words and Music by Kirk Franklin and George Clinton Jr., Garry
Shider, and Walter Morrison
Copyright © 1997; Lilly Mack Music/Copyright Control

By the 1990s, African American religious music had changed from
the gospel style of Thomas Dorsey to a sophisticated choral style.
Black churches, with their congregations, moved up the economic
ladder, affording the churches the means to hire well-trained choir directors for choirs of one hundred voices or more. The magnificent
sound of such groups found favor among religious music aficionados.

"Oh Happy Day," a hit recording of 1969 by the Edwin
Hawkins Singers, opened the door to mainstream acceptance of
the choral sound in gospel. Through the following decades, larger
and larger choirs were common, leading to massed choirs of hundreds of voices, a phenomenon reminiscent of the early work of
Homer Rodeheaver.

Kirk Franklin, a Texan born in 1970 to unmarried teenage parents and raised by a great-aunt, began singing in the choir of Fort
Worth's Mt. Rose Baptist Church. By the age of eleven, Franklin was
the minister of music, but in his teen years he was hedonistic, running with gang members, fighting, and smoking marijuana. The ac-
cidental death of a close friend from gunshot wounds, and the
unplanned pregnancy of his girlfriend, led seventeen-year-old
Franklin back to the church with a deep resolve to find purpose in
his life. Milton Biggham, an executive with Savoy Records, a leading
gospel label, became Franklin's mentor, persuading him to join the
Dallas–Ft. Worth Mass Choir.

After recording two albums with the choir, Franklin left to pursue a solo career. His album *Kirk Franklin and the Family*, on the small
Gospo-Centric label, became the surprise hit of 1993, crossing over
from the gospel chart to the rhythm and blues and contemporary
Christian charts. It became the first gospel album to sell 1 million
copies in America.

This was the prelude for Franklin's 1997 album *God's Property*
from Kirk Franklin's Nu Nation ensemble. Using the fifty-two voices
of God's Property, a Dallas youth choir, combined with a sample of
George Clinton's Funkadelic hit "One Nation under a Groove,"

overlaid with a rap by Cheryl James ("Salt" of "Salt 'N' Peppa"),
Franklin created "Stomp," the album's opening track. Designed to
appeal to the hip-hop generation, "Stomp" does not dilute the
Christian message to gain crossover appeal, as did many contemporary Christian songs of the 1990s. The lyric portrays Jesus' love as
narcotic-like and energizing.

Facing the same criticism from conservative black churchgoers
that Tom Dorsey had received sixty years earlier, Franklin told *U.S.
News and World Report* that "there's nothing sinful about the beat.
When I've got their attention, I hit them with the holy dope. I'm a
holy dope dealer" (Geier 1997).

"Stomp" was the first gospel song to be put in heavy rotation on
MTV. It crossed to number 1 on the rhythm and blues chart and
number 3 on the pop chart. The album sold over 2 million copies.

"Stomp" is available in a vocal/piano arrangement from the
Jane Peterer Music Corporation in New York City. The sound record-
ing is part of *God's Property* from Kirk Franklin's Nu Nation (B-Rite
Music CD 90093).

10. "Quit Playing Games (with My Heart)"
Words and Music by Max Martin and Herbert Crichlow
Copyright © 1997, Zomba Music/Creative Science Music/Megasongs

During the 1990s, teen pop music was a strong and proliferating
force, featuring boy bands, girl groups, and solo acts who delivered
light and frothy, danceable music. The almost-wholesome young performers were attractively packaged to appeal to the lucrative youth
market. Surprisingly, much of the creative energy behind America's
top-grossing pop acts actually derived from Sweden, which trailed
only the United States and the United Kingdom in the exportation
of popular music during the decade. Among those who made the
trip to Stockholm were Christina Aguilera, 'N Sync, Celine Dion,
Britney Spears, and the biggest of the boy bands, the Backstreet Boys.

The Backstreet Boys emerged from sunny Orlando, Florida,
where natives A. J. McLean and Howie Dorough met New Yorker Nick
Carter through auditions for television and commercials. The three
began singing together before meeting Kentuckian Kevin Richardson, who had come to Florida to work at Disney's sprawling kingdom,

and Richardson's cousin Brian Littrell. They all shared an enthusiasm for a cappella singing, rhythm and blues and soul music. As the group began to solidify, they chose the name Backstreet Boys in reference to Orlando's Backstreet Flea Market, a popular hangout.

The Backstreet Boys typify the experience of many top young pop acts in that they were shaped by—in some opinions manipulated by—experienced managers and producers who made most of the commercial and artistic decisions. It began with local entrepreneur Lou Pearlman, who helped the singers develop their showmanship and get a first record out.

The Backstreet Boys were the first of a stable of pop icons that Pearlman developed. His next group, 'N Sync, was practically a clone. As he explained, "It was starting to work with Backstreet, . . . so I knew it would work with 'N Sync because you have Pepsi and you have Coke, you have McDonald's and you have Burger King. And if I didn't do it, somebody else would" (Carlson 1999). Pearlman then enlisted Donna and Johnny Wright of Wright Stuff Management. Johnny Wright had honed his skills working as road manager for the leading 1980s heartthrob boy band, New Kids on the Block.

The Wrights, in turn, got the Backstreet Boys noticed by Dave McPherson at Jive Records. Jive signed them in 1994 and sent them off to Sweden to work with Denniz Pop (real name Dag Volle) and his partner, songwriter Max Martin. The team of Pop and Martin worked at the Cheiron studios, where the role of the producer was pushed to new limits. As one journalist noted, "They write the songs, play the instruments, engineer and mix the recordings and teach the artist the material" (Boucher 2000).

The result was the 1996 album *Backstreet Boys*, which hit big in Europe, sold more than 11 million copies worldwide, was certified in thirty countries, and spawned an eighteen-month global tour. But the Backstreet Boys barely caused a ripple in the United States, where the album was not even released until 1997. Finally, a single, "Quit Playing Games (with My Heart)," cowritten by Max Martin, caught on and began to get relentless airplay in the Backstreet Boys' home country. That drum-heavy number rose quickly to number 2 on the pop chart, and would prove to be the group's biggest hit.

With such overwhelming success, the Backstreet Boys faced familiar problems. Soon after their second album, *Backstreets Back,* was released, the boys sued Pearlman over money matters (though they kept him as manager), and had to take a breather while one member entered rehab. They regrouped for the 1999 album *Millennium,* which debuted at the number 1 position on the album chart and included the hit single "I Want It That Way" (also by Max Martin). The Backstreet Boys went into the new millennium still a band, but with individual members intent on solo efforts. Meanwhile, Lou Pearlman stayed busy with O-Town, another boy band that he "manufactured," à la the Monkees, for the short-lived television series *Making the Band.*

"Quit Playing Games" can be found in both the eponymous *Backstreet Boys* song folio (Warner Brothers 5608831) and the *Backstreet Boys* CD (Jive 41589).

11. "My Heart Will Go On (Love Theme from *Titanic*)"
Words and Music by James Horner and Will Jennings
Copyright © 1997, Famous Music Corporation

In 1912, the "unsinkable" luxury liner *Titanic* went down in the North Atlantic with more than fifteen hundred aboard, including many famous and wealthy people. The tragedy fascinated the public, spawning months of journalistic coverage, popular songs, first-person accounts, and fictional retellings. Over time, it became woven into our cultural fabric. Interest was refreshed in 1985 when a salvage team found the wreckage of the great ship two miles beneath the ocean surface. They began to photograph the remains and retrieve artifacts, many of which were included in a traveling exhibition that drew millions. To flesh out the historical record, there came a final round of interviews with the last survivors of the fateful night when the *Titanic* sank.

The idea of an aged survivor recalling her days on the ship, and a lost love, was the concept behind an ambitious motion picture undertaken by Canadian director James Cameron. He was known for successful action thrillers like his *Terminator* series and *Aliens,* which helped to secure the extraordinary sum of $250 million that was spent on this epic period piece. The film *Titanic* revolves around the story of a poor but reasonably honest third-class immigrant (Leonardo DiCaprio) and a beautiful, free-spirited first-class girl

(Kate Winslet) whose family had recently lost its fortune. He perishes, as did most of the real-life lower-class passengers, while she survives. Starring in a supporting role was the ship itself, meticulously researched and re-created, along with the exceptional visual effects of its sinking. While not uniformly praised by critics, the film was such a runaway hit that it ultimately grossed more than $1 billion at box offices worldwide, breaking all records. Released late in 1997, the film won eleven Oscars the following spring, matching the record set by *Ben Hur* in 1959.

Two of the awards were for Best Original Dramatic Score and Best Original Song. Behind both was composer James Horner, already a veteran of dozens of films, who worked on *Titanic* for more than six months. Initially, the film was to have only orchestral music, but as the production neared completion, Horner thought a love song was needed. He composed a tune based on one of the film's central themes, then turned to Nashville songwriter Will Jennings for lyrics. The result was an affecting pledge to the power of remembered love, but Horner had no idea if Cameron would be interested. To increase the likelihood of acceptance by the director, he needed a persuasive performance.

His choice was a singer who had begun her career at the age of twelve, in 1980, as "La P'tit Quebecois," a little Quebec girl with a big voice. When she became eighteen and independent, Celine Dion learned English, married her manager, and set her sights high. By 1997, she was a proven performer with a string of hits, including her recent chart topper "Because You Loved Me." She was performing in Las Vegas when Horner arranged to meet her and husband/manager Rene Angelil. Both were taken with the song and, after viewing an early cut of the movie, Dion offered to make a professional demo in Sony's New York studios.

Horner kept the tape for weeks, waiting for the right opportunity to present it to Cameron. When he finally did, the director was pleased, and used it as first recorded. The musical theme for the song was heard intermittently throughout the three-hour movie, climaxed by its powerful vocal performance as the credits rolled.

When the song was released as a record to radio stations weeks before the movie opened, it generated only lukewarm interest. After the film's strong release, however, it shot up the charts. It was also the featured cut on both the soundtrack album and Celine Dion's *Let's Talk about Love*. The two albums held the number 1 and 2 positions on the album chart for six weeks and together sold more than 50 million units, clearly boosting Dion to megastar status.

"My Heart Will Go On" is available in many print arrangements through Hal Leonard (HL 00313120) and on the *Titanic* soundtrack album (Sony CD 62313).

12. "Scarecrow"
Words and Music by Melissa Etheridge
Copyright © 1999; MLE Music (ASCAP)
All rights reserved. Used by permission.

Melissa Lou Etheridge was born in Leavenworth, Kansas, in 1961. Her father, a schoolteacher, and mother, a homemaker, gave Melissa a typical midwestern upbringing. Her father gave her a guitar when she was eight, and she wrote her first song at ten. In high school she formed a band and began playing around Leavenworth. In her teen years, Etheridge realized she was gay, but dated boys as camouflage. After a year at Boston's Berklee College of Music, she moved to Los Angeles to pursue a music career.

In 1983, Etheridge played a demonstration tape of some of her songs for a friend whose husband was an artists' manager. He took an interest in Etheridge and began bringing record executives to her performances at Los Angeles area clubs. When Chris Blackwell, owner of Island Records, heard her, he signed her to a recording contract immediately.

Her initial album, *Melissa Etheridge*, won critical acclaim and a Grammy Award nomination for Best Female Rock Performance in 1988. She received repeat Grammy nominations in 1989 and 1990. Etheridge was hailed in the popular press as the female Bruce Springsteen.

By 1993, she had released three albums of original songs, which sold well. Her sexual preferences were not at issue in her music, as her songs of lost love and rejection were addressed to a sexually neutral "you." That year, Etheridge declared her homosexuality. Invited to sing at the Clinton Presidential Inauguration's Triangle Ball, she used the occasion to make public her lesbian lifestyle.

Her value to the gay–lesbian community was in her mainstream, nonconfrontational popularity. Etheridge was relieved when her audience, a cross section of straight and gay, male and female rock fans, continued to respond to the music she presented.

In October 1998, an event occurred that Etheridge could not refuse to address in her music. University of Wyoming student Matthew Shepard was tortured and murdered by two local youths. Shepard was overtly gay. His killers did not know him, but beat and set him on fire, leaving him to die pinned to a fence.

Etheridge wrote "Scarecrow" in a fury. She had been asked to write a song for the U.S. Women's Soccer team in November 1998, but was unable to. She could only think about the Shepard hate crime. A few days later, "Scarecrow" was finished. This disturbing song, in five stanzas, indicts our nation for "thinly veiled intolerance, bigotry and hate." Comparing Matthew Shepard to "The Shepherd Young and Mild," Etheridge sings, "for love they crucified you."

"Scarecrow" was included on 1999's *Breakdown* compilation. It was also released as one side of a special-issue seven-inch single. Since 1999, the song has become an anthem for antihate crime activists.

A guitar/vocal arrangement of "Scarecrow" was included in the Warner Brothers' folio *Breakdown*, but is out of print. The recording is available on the compact disc *Breakdown* (Island CD ISL 546 518).

13. "Rival"
Words and Music by Stone Gossard
Copyright 1999, Write Treatage Music

Pearl Jam is a hard-rock band that quickly became accustomed to controversy and success. After Andrew Wood, vocalist for the band Mother Love Bone, died of a heroin overdose, two of the remaining musicians—bassist Jeff Ament and guitarist Stone Gossard—formed a new band and named it Pearl Jam. Eddie Vedder joined Pearl Jam as vocalist, Mike McCready was added to play lead guitar, and Dave Krusen became the band's drummer.

Pearl Jam's debut album *Ten* was completed in 1991. The band's sound was a blend of classic rock from the 1960s and 1970s combined with hard-edged Seattle grunge. Several songs from the album became favorites of MTV and radio programmers. Almost instantly, Pearl Jam was a success.

But in an effort to shed themselves of the rock star persona, the band decided to resist traditional marketing techniques for their second album *Vs.* Pearl Jam did not allow their record label to release any singles from the album to radio stations. They also refused to create videos for distribution to MTV. Despite the band's resistance to these conventional promotional tools for radio and MTV airplay, their sophomore album sold well. Remarkably, the band that did not want stardom sold more than 15 million copies of their first two albums.

The band continued its antiestablishment behavior and continued to thumb their noses at customary music industry practice. On one occasion, lead singer Eddie Vedder arrived at a photo session wearing a mask. Pearl Jam became a household name, even with people who had never heard their music, when they refused to allow industry giant TicketMaster to sell tickets for their concerts. Although they were forced to cancel numerous concert dates, they focused national attention on business practices of the live entertainment industry.

During the fall of 1999, Pearl Jam began to work on a new album called *Binaural.* Guitarist and songwriter Stone Gossard wrote three songs for the album, including "Rival." It started as a song about competition and paranoia. Gossard thought about the way major countries have the power to bully less-developed nations. But before he completed the song, a shocking mass murder changed his approach to the song.

At 11:35 on Tuesday morning, April 20, 1999, eighteen-year-old Eric Harris and seventeen-year-old Dylan Klebold entered Columbine High School in Littleton, Colorado, carrying automatic weapons. Harris and Klebold opened fire and continued their shooting rampage for almost an hour. They reportedly smiled and occasionally laughed as they murdered twelve students and one teacher. They eventually committed suicide before the day's tragedy ended.

Stone Gossard reflected on the Columbine shootings and wove his reaction into the fabric of the song. The Pearl Jam recording of "Rival" begins with Gossard's dog growling. The lyrics are not easily interpreted, but they provide an eerie warning that the nation has not seen the last of this type of bloodshed—murders committed by "loners" who extract revenge from those who ostracize them from social groups. Its lyrics also make one wonder if medical practitioners and parents should accept some responsibility for the lost children who commit these adult crimes.

"Rival" is available on the Pearl Jam album *Binaural* (Epic Records 63665).

14. "Stan"
Words and Music by Marshall Mathers, Dido Armstrong, and Paul Herman
Copyright © 2000, Eight Mile Style/Ensign Music Corporation/ WB Music Corporation

In 1997, a twenty-three-year-old Detroit kid stormed the world of "freestyle" rap, a demanding, improvised African American form of rhyming commentary and storytelling. The young man, Marshall Mathers, was the Wake Up Show Freestyle Performer of the Year in Los Angeles, home of many of the hip-hop community's most famous performers. Mathers, who is white, received the respect of African American rappers. Dr. Dre (Andre Young), a founding member of the seminal rap group N.W.A., signed Mathers, known professionally as Eminem, to a record contract.

Marshall Mathers III was born on October 17, 1974, in Kansas City, Missouri. His teenage mother and father separated months after his birth, and Marshall was raised by his welfare mom in the 8 Mile section of Detroit, a tense neighborhood of poor whites and blacks. His uncle, Ronnie (Nelson), only three years Marshall's senior, took an interest in the boy. It was Nelson who introduced Mathers to the art of rappers LL Cool J and 2 Live Crew. Mathers dropped out of high school and supported himself with odd jobs while honing the rhyming skills that would eventually lead to his association with Dr. Dre and the album *The Slim Shady LP*, which was 1998's surprise best-seller.

Slim Shady was Eminem's neurotic alter ego; a character who rapped out Mathers's anger toward his mother, his fantasy of wife murder, his mistrust of middle-class mores, and his loathing of homosexuals. In 1999, while Eminem was touring as Slim Shady, Dido, a British pop singer (born Florian Armstrong on December 25,

1971, in London), released her album *No Angel.* The song "Thank You" was used on the soundtrack of the film *Sliding Doors.* Eminem heard the song and secured Dido's license to use a sadly reflective verse of "Thank You" as a chorus in a track he was preparing for his next album.

"Stan" is a masterpiece of storytelling. In less than one hundred lines, Mathers, in the persona of a deranged fan, explores the relationship between the published word and responsibility. When an artist uses irony to produce work of personal meaning, is the artist culpable if a fan acts out the work? Stan, the deranged fan, in a series of letters to Slim Shady, details his knowledge of Shady's personal life and reenacts the wife murder portrayed in "97 Bonnie and Clyde" from The Slim Shady LP.

Eminem has been dubbed a misogynist and homophobe, yet when "Stan" was performed on the 2000 *Grammy Awards Show,* Mathers asked the openly bisexual Elton John to sing Dido's part. Eminem was sending a message to the world: words are complex tools—don't assume the surface message is the only message.

Music is the most fluid of the arts, and throughout the twentieth century, music has flowed among races and social and political groups. Regardless of the source, eventually the form becomes the property of all.

"Stan" is unavailable in print. The sound recording is included in *The Marshall Mathers* LP (Interscope CD 90632).

15. "I Am a Man of Constant Sorrow"
Traditional/arrangement by Carter Stanley
In the public domain
Arranged and recorded for film in 2000

A few days before Christmas 2000, a film opened in which the music of an earlier America played the featured role. The film *O Brother, Where Art Thou?* is the story of a trio of escaped convicts in Mississippi in 1937, and their efforts to avoid recapture. The plot centers on the inadvertent "hit" recording they make of the folk song "I Am a Man of Constant Sorrow."

The opening line—"I am a man of constant sorrow. I've seen trouble all my days"—is a variant of the nineteenth-century hymn

"Christ Suffering": "He was a man of constant sorrow. He went a mourner all his days." The songwriter who first "secularized" the lyric is unknown, but in 1913 a blind Kentucky street singer, Dick Burnett (1883–1977), printed and sold copies of the song, titled "Farewell Song," on the streets of his native Monticello, Kentucky.

Burnett was caught up in the hillbilly recording craze of the 1920s, making records for the Columbia label in 1926. Oddly, he never recorded "Farewell Song," one of his most popular live performance pieces. Burnett was friends with the Arthur family of Monticello, and one of the Arthur boys, Emry, recorded for the Vocalion label in January 1928. The eighth, and last, song of the session was Burnett's "Farewell Song," now titled "I Am a Man of Constant Sorrow."

The record, when released later that year, sold modestly well, but the song disappeared from the music industry. However, it must have continued to be sung in eastern Kentucky, West Virginia, and North Carolina, because Library of Congress song collectors recorded the song in the 1930s. Also, a labor activist and native of a Knox County, Kentucky, coal camp, Sarah Ogan Gunning, rewrote the song, titled "Girl of Constant Sorrow," as a miners' anthem when she moved to New York in 1935, the year John L. Lewis's United Mine Workers formed the Committee of Industrial Organizations.

"I Am a Man of Constant Sorrow" resurfaced in commercial music in 1950 when the Stanley Brothers, a bluegrass group from Virginia following in Bill Monroe's footsteps, recorded the song for Columbia Records. They had learned the song from their father who sang a cappella in the tradition of the rural Primitive Baptist denomination.

On March 19, 1962, Columbia Records released the first recordings of Bob Dylan. Halfway through the LP's first side is Dylan's interpretation entitled "Man of Constant Sorrow." Dylan's recording owes much to the Stanley Brothers, but it was Dylan who placed the song firmly in the folk music canon.

When film producers Joel and Ethan Coen were writing the script for *O Brother, Where Art Thou?*, they knew music would be an important element. When the music supervisor began sending them tapes of vintage songs, however, the Coens decided to reverse filmmaking's usual approach and shoot the film after the music was selected and recorded. The Coens picked "Constant Sorrow" as the emotional centerpiece of the film. *O Brother* was a successful movie, and the soundtrack featuring "I Am a Man of Constant Sorrow," sold over 6 million copies.

From 1910 Appalachia to turn-of-the-century Hollywood, the song has had a most peculiar journey through American music history.

"I Am a Man of Constant Sorrow" is in sheet music in a piano/vocal arrangement from Hal Leonard Publishing (0352483). The song is on the soundtrack recording *O Brother, Where Art Thou?* (Mercury Records CD 170-069).

Bibliography

WORKS CITED AND CONSULTED

Abbott, Lynn, and Doug Seroff. 2001. "Brown Skin (Who You Really For?)"
 The Jazz Archivist. Vol. 15. New Orleans: Hogan Jazz Archive.

Andersen, Christopher P. 1991. *Madonna, Unauthorized.* New York: Simon
 and Schuster.

Andrews, Maxene, with Bill Gilbert. 1993. *Over Here, Over There: The Andrews Sisters and the USO Stars in World War II.* New York: Zebra
 Books.

Autry, Gene, with Mickey Herskowitz. 1978. *Back in the Saddle Again.* New
 York: Doubleday.

Barrett, Mary Ellin. 1994. *Irving Berlin.* New York: Simon and Schuster.

Bazilian, Eric. 1996. "How I Wrote That Hit Song: Joan Osborne's 'One of
 Us' by Eric Bazalian." *Musician* 210 (May):16.

Bierley, Paul E. 1973. *John Philip Sousa, American Phenomenon.* Westerville,
 Ohio: Integrity.

Bloom, Ken. 1985. *American Song—The Complete Musical Theater Companion:
 1900–1984.* New York: Facts on File Publications.

Bordman, Gerald Martin. 1992. *American Musical Theater: A Chronicle.* 2d ed.
 New York: Oxford University Press.

Boucher, Geoff. 2000. "The Other Music Stars: An Elite New Class of Producers Is Shaping the Sound of Today's Big Hits, and Reviving the
 Record Mogul Tradition." *Ottawa Citizen,* 10 June.

Boy George, and Spencer Bright. 1995. *Take It Like a Man.* New York: HarperCollins.

Bronson, Fred. 1997. *The Billboard Book of Number One Hits.* Rev. and updated, 4th ed. New York: Billboard Books.

Bruccoli, J. Matthew, and Richard Layman, eds. *American Decades Series.* 1996. Farmington Hills, Mich.: Gale Research.

Buckman, Peter. 1978. *Let's Dance: Social Ballroom and Folk Dancing.* New York: Paddington.

Business Wire. 1991. "BMI Grammy Award Winning Songwriters Talk about the Inspirations behind Their Hits." 11 December.

Cannon, Carl M. 2000. "The 80s vs. the 90s." *National Journal* 32, no. 16:1186.

Carlson, Peter. 1999. "Music Machine: 'Big Poppa' Pearlman Takes Kids and Turns Them into Stars. Then They Sue Him." *Washington Post,* 6 November, C01.

Carmichael, Hoagy, with Stephen Longstreet. 1965. *Sometimes I Wonder: The Story of Hoagy Carmichael.* New York: Farrar, Straus and Giroux.

Castle, Irene. 1980. *Castles in the Air.* New York, Da Capo.

Chaplin, Ralph. 1972. *Wobbly: The Rough and Tumble Story of an American Radical.* New York: Da Capo.

Chipman, John H. 1962. *Index to Top-Hit Tunes (1900–1950).* Boston: Bruce Humphries.

Christgau, Robert. 1988. *Grown Up All Wrong.* Cambridge: Harvard University Press.

Claghorn, Charles Eugene. 1973. *Biographical Dictionary of American Music.* West Nyack, N.Y.: Parker.

———. 1996. *Women Composers and Songwriters: A Concise Biographical Dictionary.* Lanham, Md.: Scarecrow.

Clayson, Alan. 1997. *Death Discs: An Account of Fatality in the Popular Songs.* Idyllwild, Calif.: Sanctuary.

Cohen, Norm. 1981. *Long Steel Rail: The Railroad in American Folksong.* Urbana: University of Illinois Press.

Cohen, Scott. 1984. *Boy George.* New York: Berkley Books.

Cohen-Stratyner, Barbara, ed. 1988. *Popular Music, 1900–1919.* Detroit: Gale Research.

Collier, James Lincoln. 1989. *Benny Goodman and the Swing Era.* New York: Oxford University Press.

Congressional Budget Office. 2003. *The Budget and Economic Outlook, Fiscal Years 2004–2013, Table 1.* Washington, D.C.: U.S. Government Printing Office.

Daniel, Clifton. 1999. *20th Century: Day by Day.* New York: DK.

Dixon, Robert, John Godrich, and Howard Rye. 1997. *Blues and Gospel Records: 1890–1943.* Oxford: Clarendon.

Edwards, Joe. 1985. "Nashville Sound: Hank Snow Mourns Loss of 'His' Music." *Associated Press Report,* 19 April.

Einarson, John. 1997. "For What It's Worth: Buffalo Springfield." *Goldmine,* 23 May.

Erlewine, Michael, Vladimir Bogdanov, Chris Woodstra, and Stephen Thomas Erlewine, eds. 1997. *All Music Guide: The Experts' Guide to the Best Recordings from Thousands of Artists in all Types of Music.* 3d ed. San Francisco: Miller Freeman Books.

Ewen, David. 1987. *American Songwriters: An H. W. Wilson Biographical Dictionary.* New York: Wilson.

Ferguson, Gary, and W. Lynn. 1995. *Song Finder: A Title Index to 32,000 Popular Songs in Collections, 1854–1992.* Westport, Conn.: Greenwood.

Forman, Murray. 2002. *The 'Hood Comes First: Race, Space, and Place in Rap and Hip-Hop.* Middletown, Conn.: Wesleyan University Press.

Fuld, James J. 1985. *The Book of World-Famous Music: Classical, Popular, and Folk.* 3d ed. New York: Dover.

Gaines, Steven. 1986. *Heroes and Villains: The True Story of the Beach Boys.* New York: New American Library.

Gardner, Edward F., comp. 2000. *Popular Songs of the 20th Century: Chart Detail and Encyclopedia, 1900–1949.* St. Paul, Minn.: Paragon House.

Geier, Thom. 1997. "Holy Rock-and-Roller Lording It over the Pop Charts." *U.S. News and World Report,* 7 July, p. 81.

Geller, James J. 1940. *Famous Songs and Their Stories.* New York: Garden City Publishing.

Goldberg, Isaac. 1930. *Tin Pan Alley: A Chronicle of the American Popular Music Racket.* New York, John Day.

Goodfellow, William D. 1995. *SongCite: An Index to Popular Songs (Index I, Collection/Folio Book; Index II, Title/First Line).* Hamden, Conn.: Garland Reference Library of the Humanities.

Grattan, Virginia L. 1993. *American Women Songwriters: A Biographical Dictionary.* Westport, Conn.: Greenwood.

Gray, Michael. 2000. *Song and Dance Man III: The Art of Bob Dylan.* London: Continuum.

Green, Jeff. 1995. *The Green Book of Songs by Subject: The Thematic Guide to Popular Music.* 4th ed. Nashville: Professional Desk References.

Green, Stanley. 1996. *Broadway Shows, Show by Show.* 5th ed. Milwaukee: Hal Leonard.

Greenberg, Rodney. 1998. *George Gershwin.* London: Phaidon.

Grun, Bernard. 1991. *The Timetable of History: Horizontal Linkage of People and Events.* 3d rev. ed. New York: Simon and Schuster.

Hagan, Chet. 1995. *Gospel Legends.* New York: Avon Books.

Hall, Fred. 1989. *Dialogues in Swing: Intimate Conversations with the Stars of the Big Band Era.* Ventura, Calif.: Pathfinder.

Harrison, Nigel. 1998. *Songwriters: A Biographical Dictionary with Discographies.* Jefferson, N.C.: McFarland.

Hasse, John Edward. 1993. *Beyond Category: The Life and Genius of Duke Ellington.* New York: Simon and Schuster.

Hayes, Richard K. 1995. *Kate Smith: A Biography with a Discography, Filmography, and List of Stage Appearances.* Jefferson, N.C.: McFarland.

Jacobs, Dick, and Harriet Jacobs. 1994. *Who Wrote That Song?* Cincinnati: Writer's Digest Books.

Jacques Legrand s. a. International Publishing. 1987. *Chronicle of the 20th Century.* Paris: Jacque Legrand.

Jasen, David A., and Gene Jones. 2000. *That American Rag: The Story of Ragtime from Coast to Coast.* New York: Schirmer Books.

Jennings, Peter, and Todd Brewster. 1998. *The Century.* New York: Doubleday.

Johnson, L. D., P. M. O'Malley, and J. G. Bachman. 1995. *National Survey Results on Drug Use from the Monitoring the Future Study, 1975–1993.* Washington, D.C.: National Institute on Drug Abuse.

Kahn, Ashley, Holly George-Warren, and Shawn Dahl, eds. 1998. *Rolling Stone: The Seventies.* New York: Rolling Stone Press, Little, Brown.

Kanahele, George S., Ed. *Hawaiian Music and Musicians.* Honolulu, Hawaii: University Press of Hawaii, 1979.

Kaplan, E. Ann. 1987. "On the 'Material Girl' Video." *Rocking around the Clock: Music Television, Postmodernism, and Consumer Culture.* New York: Routledge, Chapman and Hall.

Kimball, Robert, and Robert Gottlieb, eds. 2000. *Reading Lyrics.* New York: Schocken Books.

King, Norman. 1991. *Madonna: The Book.* New York: Morrow.

Kinkle, Roger D. 1974. *The Complete Encyclopedia of Popular Music and Jazz, 1900–1950.* New Rochelle, N.Y.: Arlington House.

Kornbluh, Joyce L. 1964. *Rebel Voices: An I.W.W. Anthology.* Ann Arbor: University of Michigan Press.

Kullen, Allan S. 1992. *The Peopling of America: A Timeline of Events That Helped Shape Our Nation: A Historical Perspective.* Beltsville, Md.: Americans All.

Laws, G. Malcolm. 1964. *Native American Balladry.* Austin: University of Texas Press.

Lax, Roger, and Frederick Smith. 1989. *The Great Song Thesaurus.* 2d ed. New York: Oxford University Press.

Linton, Calvin D. 1985. *American Headlines: Year by Year.* Nashville: Thomas Nelson.

Lynn, Loretta, with George Vecsey. 1976. *Loretta Lynn: Coal Miner's Daughter.* Chicago: Regnery.

Mansfield, Brian, and Gary Graff. 1997. *MusicHound Country: The Essential Album Guide.* Detroit: Visible Ink Press.

Marqolick, David. 2000. *Strange Fruit: Billie Holiday, Café Society, and an Early Cry for Civil Rights.* Philadelphia: Runnery Press.

Marshall, Richard, ed. 1977. *Great Events of the 20th Century.* Pleasantville, N.Y.: Reader's Digest.

McDonagh, Don. 1979. *Dance Fever.* New York: Random House.

McNamara, Daniel I., ed. 1948. *The ASCAP Biographical Dictionary of Composers, Authors, and Publishers.* 2d printing. New York: Crowell.

McNeil, W. K. 1988. *Southern Folk Ballads, Vol 2.* Little Rock, Ark.: August House.

Morgan, Thomas. *Shelton Brooks: A Profile.* Available: www.jass.com/shelton-brooks/brooks.html; accessed 16 September 2001. Copyright © Thomas L. Morgan, 1992–2001.

Morris, Edward. 1992. "Garth Speaks Out about Freedom." *Billboard,* 19 September.

Murray, Albert. 1986. *Good Morning Blues: The Autobiography of Count Basie.* New York: Random House.

Overy, Richard, ed. 1992. *The Hammond Atlas of the 20th Century.* Maplewood, N.J.: Hammond/Time Books.

Parrish, Michael E. 1992. *Anxious Decade: America in Prosperity and Depression, 1920–1941.* New York: Norton.

Pike, G. D. 1873. *The Jubilee Singers and Their Campaign for Twenty Thousand Dollars.* Boston: Lee and Shepard.

Pleasants, Henry. 1974. *The Great American Popular Singers.* New York: Simon and Schuster.

Porter, Thomas Henry. 1981. "Homer Alvan Rodeheaver (1880–1955): Evangelistic Musician and Publisher." Ph.D. Diss., Baptist Theological Seminary.

Raeburn, Bruce Boyd (curator, Hogan Jazz Archive, Tulane University). 2001. Interview with author, 12 October.

"Reddy, Helen." 1975. *Current Biography Yearbook, 1975.* New York: Wilson.

Rodeheaver, Homer A. 1917. *Song Stories of the Sawdust Trail.* New York: Moffat, Yard.

Romanowski, Patricia, and Holly George-Warren, eds. 2001. *The Rolling Stone Encyclopedia of Rock and Roll.* New York: Rolling Stone.

Rovner, Sandy. 1987. "Violence Hits Home." *Washington Post,* 11 August, p. Z12.

Rucker, Randy, and Linda Rucker. 1985. *Musi*Key.* Tucson, Ariz.: Musi*Key Publishing.

Safire, William. 1985. "Sex on a Platter." *New York Times,* 10 October, p. A31.

Sandford, Christopher. 1999. *Springsteen: Point Blank.* New York: Da Capo.

Sinclair, Upton. 1905. *The Jungle.* New York: Bantam Classics.

Snow, Hank. 1994. *The Hank Snow Story.* Carbondale: University of Illinois Press.

Songs of the Workers: To Fan the Flames of Discontent. 34th ed. Chicago: Industrial Workers of the World.

Sullivan, Jim. 1996. "The Ramones' Last Tour." *Boston Globe,* 11 February, Arts and Films sec., p. 53.

"Tradition in Black Art, Music Cited." *Los Angeles Times,* 19 October.

Urdang, Laurence, ed. 1996. *The Timetables of American History.* Updated ed. New York: Touchstone Books/Simon and Schuster.

U.S. Bureau of the Census. 1973. *Census of Population: 1970, Vol. II, Subject Reports, 1B: Negro Population.* Washington, D.C.: U.S. Government Printing Office.

U.S. Census Bureau. 2002. *Historical Census Statistics on Population Totals by Race, 1790 to 1990, by Hispanic Origin 1970 to 1990, for the United States.* Working Papers Series, No. 56. Washington, D.C.: U.S. Government Printing Office.

Warner Brothers. 1998. *100 Great Songs from Hollywood, Broadway, and Television.* Miami: Warner Brothers.

Washington, Booker T. 1901. *Up from Slavery.* New York: Signet Classics.

Weill, Gus. 1977. *You Are My Sunshine: The Jimmy Davis Story.* Waco, Tex.: Word.

Whitburn, Joel. 1999. *A Century of Pop Music: Year-by-Year Top 40 Rankings of the Songs and Artists That Shaped a Century.* Menomonee Falls, Wis.: Record Research.

Willen, Doris. 1988. *Lonesome Traveler: The Life of Lee Hays.* New York: Norton.

Williams, Neville. 1994. *Chronology of the Modern World, 1763 to 1992.* New York: Simon and Schuster.

Williams, William H. A. 1996. *'Twas Only an Irishman's Dream.* Urbana: University of Illinois Press.

Ziegfeld, Richard, and Paulette Ziegfeld. 1993. *The Ziegfeld Touch.* New York: Abrams.

WEB SITES

Annenberg/Center for Public Broadcasting "People's Century." http://www.learner.org/catalog/history/peseries/peprograms.html

Brief Timeline of American Literature, Music and Movies. http://www.gonzaga.edu/faculty/campbell/enl311/1900m.html

C. E. Koop Institute: Timeline of the 20th Century. http://koop.dartmouth.edu/resources/healing_timeline/testTimeline1.html

Early 1900s Popular Songs, Recording from Victrola (1920–1923). http://www.besmark.com/popular3.html

Early 20th Century American Music (1900–1922). http://pdmusic.org/1900s.html

History in Song. http://www.fortunecity.com/tinpan/parton/2/history.html

The 1900s, A Timeline by Decade and Year That Includes Audio Clips. http://members.tripod.com/archer2000/1900.html

Recording Industry Association of America. http://www.riaa.com

20th Century America. http://members.aol.com/Tchrfromoz/20thcent.html

RESEARCH CENTERS

Center for Popular Music
Middle Tennessee State University
Murfreesboro, TN 37132

This research center, funded by the state as a Center of Excellence, has a mission to document the history of the region—middle Tennessee, Memphis, and Muscle Shoals, Alabama—through its music. They have a wealth of recordings, sheet music, books, and periodicals in their holdings. Their major gift to researchers is, however, the gifted and helpful staff of archivists and reference librarians.

Country Music Foundation
Nashville

Rock and Roll Hall of Fame
Cleveland

W. C. Handy Center
Muscle Shoals, Alabama

William Ransom Hogan Jazz Archive
304 Joseph Merick Jones Hall
6801 Freret Street
Tulane University
New Orleans, LA 70118-5682

The Hogan Archive has some of the best holdings for early jazz, especially New Orleans jazz.

Williams Research Center
Historic New Orleans Collection
410 Chartres Street
New Orleans, LA 70130-2102

An excellent source of information about New Orleans, its architectural and cultural development, and its music heritage. The reference librarians are extremely knowledgeable and extremely helpful.

Song Title Index

Songwriter Index

Subject Index

About the Authors

RICHARD D. BARNET is a Professor in the Department of the Recording Industry at Middle Tennessee State University. He has worked in various positions in the music industry including artist management, booking, concert promotion, television, and live show music production, performance, and conducting. He is a former officer of the Music and Entertainment Industry Educator's Association and a gubernatorial appointee to the Tennessee Film, Entertainment, and Music Advisory Council, as well as a member of the National Academy of Recording Arts and Sciences. Professor Barnet is coauthor, with Larry L. Burriss, of *Controversies of the Music Industry* (Greenwood, 2001).

BRUCE NEMEROV is an audio specialist at the Center for Popular Music at Middle Tennessee State University. He joined the Center in 1990 after twenty years as a professional musician, producer, and audio engineer.

MAYO R. TAYLOR is a librarian at the Walker Library at Middle Tennessee State University. Prior to her current appointment, she was coordinator for Research Collections at the Center for Popular Music.